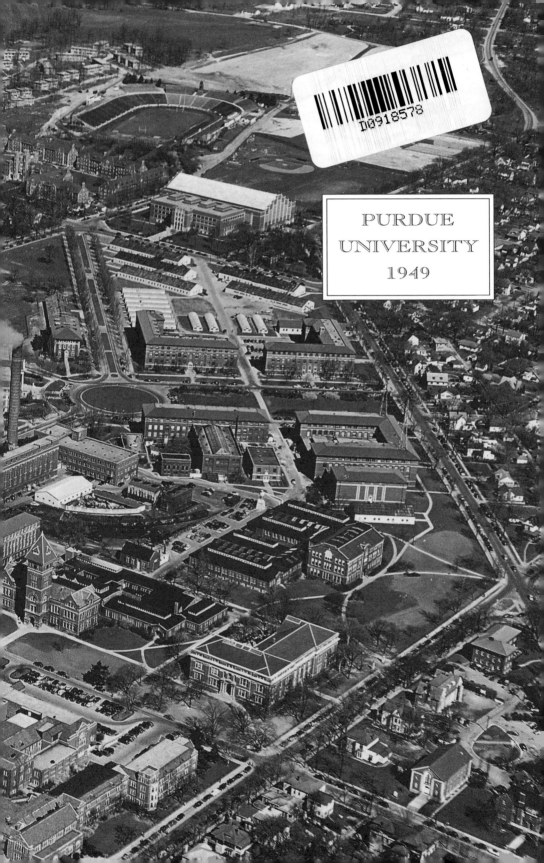

PURDUE
UNIVERSITY
1949

A FORCE
for
CHANGE

A LOT OF CLASS. Members of the Purdue University Class of 1950 never forgot where they got their start and have continued support of their alma mater through the years. Their crowning achievement, and perhaps the greatest achievement by any Purdue class, was the donation of funds for a major lecture hall equipped with the type of technological wizardry that made this generation so great. For the project, the class raised $1,050,000—the largest single class-gift in the university's history. This photo shows class members at the April 21, 1990, cornerstone ceremony. In 1995, the class added to the hall when it dedicated a statue it had commissioned that shows how students looked on campus in the late 1940s. In a further effort to show how they thought and felt and to tell the unique experiences of their lives, the class commissioned this book.

A FORCE
for
CHANGE

—— ∞ ——

the
CLASS
of
1950

John Norberg

Purdue University
West Lafayette, Indiana

Copyright © 1995 by Purdue Research Foundation, West Lafayette, IN 47907. All rights reserved. Unless permission is granted, this material may not be copied, reproduced, or coded for reproduction by any electrical, mechanical, or chemical process or combinations thereof, now known or later developed.

Grateful acknowledgment is given to the Purdue *Debris* yearbooks of 1946 through 1950 for use of photographs and illustrations.

Articles in this volume are reprinted from the *Purdue Exponent;* the *Journal and Courier,* Lafayette, Indiana; United Press International; and the Associated Press with permission.

Printed in the United States of America

Book and jacket design by Anita Noble
Designed and produced by the Office of Publication, Purdue University

Library of Congress Cataloging-in-Publication Data
Norberg, John.
    A force for change : the class of 1950 / John Norberg.
      p. cm.
    Includes index.
    ISBN 0–931682–54–1
    1. Purdue University. Class of 1950. 2. Purdue University Students—Biography. I. Purdue University. Class of 1950. II. Title.
LD4672.6.1950 N67
378.772'95–dc20   95–33507
                                                CIP

PURDUE UNIVERSITY 1949 (FRONT ENDSHEET). Bottom center, Purdue Memorial Union; above union, Heavilon Hall (with pointed tower); top right, Ross-Ade Stadium (horseshoe-shaped area); just below stadium, Lambert Field House; below field house, temporary Quonset-hut classrooms and FWA chemistry labs; upper left, Chippewa and Seneca men's temporary dorms. (Photographer unknown)

PURDUE UNIVERSITY 1995 (BACK ENDSHEET). Bottom right, Purdue Memorial Union; above union, present Heavilon Hall; left of union, Stewart Center and Hicks Undergraduate Library; left center between Stanley Coulter and Recitation halls, Class of 1950 Lecture Hall (light roof); top right, Ross-Ade Stadium; right of stadium, Mollenkopf Athletic Center and Mackey Arena (light roofs). (Photo by Vincent Walter)

*To the
Class of 1950,*

*to the spirit of
a generation that
is shining still,*

*to a devotion
that believes all things
are possible—*

*thanks for
your memories.*

CONTENTS

PREFACE

Did you ever think of our lives and history as a jigsaw puzzle?

Looked at individually, our lives are like pieces of a puzzle, scattered in confusion on a table. Each piece, while interesting in size and shape and color, has little meaning by itself. But something fascinating happens when you take an individual piece and look at it in relation to the others. The pieces begin to fit together. They form small patterns, then images. After awhile, many images come together before you. When you finally fit all the images together, you get a clear picture of the significance of the hundreds of individual pieces.

This book is a jigsaw puzzle. Almost a hundred lives are featured here. Each one taken alone is interesting. But considered individually, each life gives you no clear image. Only when all the lives are read and examined together does a true picture of history emerge.

These are the stories of the Purdue University Class of 1950. They could be stories from any American college campus that year.

These are the stories of people who grew up during the Great Depression. These are the stories of people who fought in World War II and the Korean War. These are the stories of those who stayed home and did what they could, while their sons and brothers and lovers were far away involved in the fighting. These are the stories of people who went to college during an idyllic time and who graduated into a world of promise and heartbreak.

These are stories that will never happen again. The world and its people have changed too much. Our culture is too different for these life events ever to be repeated.

These are important stories. The only way we can understand ourselves and where we are today is to look at where we have been. The only way we can see our own picture clearly is by putting together the jigsaw pieces and completing the puzzles that come before us.

The stories told here are in the words of the people who lived them. This is an oral history. It is not intended to be scholarly. It is intended to be like a fireside chat—a talk between people in a living room—such as President Franklin Delano Roosevelt delivered on radio when the Class of 1950 was young.

So imagine yourself at the end of a day, relaxing before the soft, dim embers of a warm fireplace with a person from the World War II generation, a member of the Purdue University Class of 1950. What was it like to grow up in a home without water and electricity? How did you feel when you went off to war? What was your music like? Where did you fall in love? How did you become the person that you are today?

Put together the jigsaw puzzle.

Purdue taking in record new group

The process of taking in a new class of freshmen at Purdue University, preliminary to the formal opening next week of the fall and winter semesters, continued Thursday. The campus is overrun by a record invasion of 2,863 freshmen, the largest group of first-year students ever to register at the university. The class represents less than one-third of the 10,000 to 12,000 students expected to register.

A four-day orientation program for freshmen began Wednesday. . . . A welcome reception for wives of students was held Thursday morning in the Union building, sponsored by the Undergraduate Dames Club. . . .

For Thursday evening, a smoker for all men students was scheduled in the Union building with the Student Union Board as host, also a style show at the same time for women students, also in the Union building.

JOURNAL AND COURIER, LAFAYETTE, INDIANA, SEPTEMBER 12, 1946

Introduction

They came from all over the country that September of 1946—from cities and farms, from seacoasts and mountains, from the northern steel mills and the southern cotton fields. They came from midwestern towns where people knew their names.

They came, too, from the hot far-reaches of the Pacific, from islands and beaches where their friends had bled and died. They came from the rolling fields and deep forests and blown-out cities of Europe, from sights and sounds that still flashed and rang in the dark corners of their minds. They came from foreign lands, from China and South America, from homes that no longer seemed far away in a world that had grown so small.

They came to the university that fall, as all students do, with their plans and their dreams. But they came as no group of students had ever come before or will ever come again. They came from backgrounds as varied as the gentle signs of aging on their different faces.

They were eighteen years old when they came, and they were thirty. They were fresh out of high school, and they were fresh out of war.

They were young women whose goals in life were home and family. They were young men eager for future greatness in technologies that existed only in the minds of visionaries whose dreams soared above the clouds.

They were Virgil Grissom from the tiny town of Mitchell, Indiana, who grew up there dreaming about becoming a pilot and who became the nation's second man in space.

They were Norman Coats who arrived at Purdue University that September, first, from the knobs of southern Indiana, where he had grown up near the Civil War log cabins of his ancestors and, next, from the ball turret of a B-17, where he had manned a machine gun during bombing raids in the numbing cold skies over Germany.

They were Bob Stauber, an eighteen-year-old kid fresh out of high school in Decatur, Illinois—"The Soybean Capital of the World"—so shaken by the older men around him that he called his war veteran classmates "Mister."

They were Mary Zenger from Concordia, Kansas, whose mother had not been allowed an education because she was a girl and girls had no need for such knowledge or technical training. A young woman arriving in West Lafayette by train in 1946, Zenger carried with her the dreams of her mother, seeds of hope planted in her heart where they had grown and blossomed.

They were Bill Keefe, an eighteen-year-old boy from Beverly Hills, Illinois, whose dad was a Notre Dame-educated engineer with the Pullman Company, who knew little more of the Great Depression than what he read in the newspapers.

They were Warren Eastes, a war veteran whose hometown was Mount Comfort, Indiana. During the Great Depression, his dad could not scrape up a penny to buy his young son a Butterfinger candy bar, thus creating a memory of deprivation that would last a lifetime.

As they arrived, one by one, on the Purdue University campus in West Lafayette, Indiana, that September of 1946, coming by car and by bus and by train, they were riding a wave of change. They were entering a world that already was not what it had been.

And the education they were about to receive—the beliefs and the standards they were about to establish through a four-year college education—would become forever a force for change in the country and in the world.

They brought with them depression values: waste nothing, save all you can, help your neighbor. They brought with them a lesson of war: do not put off until tomorrow because tomorrow might never come. Americans, they believed, could do anything if they put their minds and spirits to it.

They brought all of that with them when they came to Purdue in 1946. They grabbed hold of the burgeoning engineering, science, and technology that the university offered, and they rushed into the future. The war years had seen numerous technologies come into being. Peacetime uses for many of them were being developed quickly, and college students in the late 1940s were at the right place to take advantage of the new knowledge.

A TALK WITH THE PRESIDENT. Purdue President Frederick L. Hovde walks on campus with students from the late 1940s.

As they arrived on the college campus that late summer day, many felt the jolt of stepping from one life into another. A college education was an opportunity many of them had never dreamed about earlier in their lives. At the start of World War II, only two out of every five adult Americans had been educated past the eighth grade. Only 15.7 percent of Americans eighteen through twenty-one were enrolled in institutions of higher education.

Arriving on the Purdue campus that September of 1946 were men like Bogdon Mareachen, a twenty-two-year-old veteran of

3

the Pacific war, who grew up expecting to work in a factory near his Hammond, Indiana, home. After the war, he went back to his high school to get necessary credits so he could go on to college.

At the start of World War II, 31 percent of American homes did not have running water. Toilets were out back. In many rural homes on Saturday nights, family members—one after another, using the same water—took baths in metal tubs that they had carried into the kitchen and filled with water heated on a stove. In 1941, central heating did not exist in 58 percent of American homes.

Elynor Erb, from a rural Indiana town, thought she was entering a dream when she moved into her residence hall on the Purdue campus that September. She had never lived with such comforts. Also, there were lectures presented by professors. There were dances to which she wore homemade formal gowns. "This was heaven for a girl from a farming community," she says.

It was an idyllic setting as they arrived that Wednesday, September 11, 1946, for the first day of freshman orientation at Purdue. The campus was filled with open, grassy areas that in the spring would be covered by a soft yellow blanket of dandelions. The buildings were red brick, and many were covered by dark green ivy that climbed the walls with unrelenting strength and determination.

Graceful green trees provided shade from the still-warm September sun. The campus was filled with elm trees, almost seven hundred of them. They would all die from disease in the coming years. But in the fall of 1946, most were still strong and tall. Some were three feet in diameter, seventy-five to one hundred feet tall, and at least that many years old. They burst out yellow in the cool, gray afternoons of autumn. A guy and his girl could choose to sit on a concrete bench in the shade of an elm and talk an hour away.

Across fields that separated the red-brick buildings, students had walked pathways through the grass, diagonal dirt lines that

4

pointed the fastest route. Concrete walks were being poured to follow the paths.

The girls wore sweaters and skirts with bobby socks and black-and-white saddle shoes. The guys wore shirts and slacks. Many Air Force veterans wore their military pants called "pinks," which were tan in color with a pink tinge. Some wore flight jackets. Many wore military shoes or boots and peacoats. They carried slide rules attached to their belts. Senior men wore slacks and women wore skirts of yellow corduroy that were painted with symbols to reflect their interests.

Males carried their books in one hand, hanging down at their side as they walked to classes. The female students bent their arms above their waist and cradled their books in front of them.

At the center of campus life was the Purdue Memorial Union building, constructed in honor of World War I veterans. Here students lounged between classes and arranged to meet. Here young men and women sat side by side on couches and dreamed and planned a future together.

Two large connecting ballrooms in the building were decorated for an endless number of dances on weekends and some weekday evenings. The student newspaper, the *Exponent,* was dominated by news of dance bands coming to Purdue—Jimmy Dorsey, Skitch Henderson, Count Basie, all the big names of the day.

With vocalists crooning, the bands would swing their music through the ballrooms while large crowds of young men and women held one another close, lost in the innocent romantic lyrics of the day, lyrics that captured the simple pleasures of falling in love in the 1940s: "Well, what do you know, she smiled at me in my dreams last night. / My dreams are getting better all the time. . . ." The music and the lyrics captured the feeling of the long separation that these young couples had experienced during a war that took so much from their early lives.

5

The lyrics came from a war that separated newlyweds often for years with only long-saved letters to keep their love alive: "Kiss me once, and kiss me twice, and kiss me once again. / It's been a long, long time. / Haven't felt like this, my dear, since can't remember when. / It's been a long, long time. / You'll never know how many dreams I dreamed about you, / Or just how empty they all seemed without you. . . ." They were lyrics about an emptiness that Bob Peterson could understand as he returned from the South Pacific to the bride he had not seen or talked with in twenty-seven months, since the week after their wedding.

Sometimes the dances at Purdue were informal. Some were military balls with dress uniforms. Some were complete formals with the men in black tuxedos and the women in gowns. Some would start at 11 P.M. and go all night.

At the lower level of the union was the Sweet Shop where students would go for a Coke and a snack between classes. A jukebox provided music. Students relaxed in mahogany-colored booths. Or they huddled around tables meant to accommodate four but that they rearranged to seat five, six, seven, eight, nine—however many wanted to squeeze into a single area. They sipped Cokes from straws stuck in a tall glasses. Sometimes two straws in one drink served a boy and a girl.

Time on campus was kept by a clock in Heavilon Hall. In a high tower topped off by a still higher pointed roof, the Heavilon bells marked each fifteen minutes and chimed on the hour. The bells had a deep, mellow, rich sound that swept around the red-brick buildings, along the paths, and through the shading elms.

Young men and women would often walk the campus together. Cars were few. Money was scarce. A walk was a pleasant way to spend a warm evening or even a cold one. A guy who did have a car might take his girl to a parking lot built at the top of Duke's Hill. It was big enough for fifty cars. At the request of police, the lot had

6

been constructed large enough for patrol cars to roll through at night and turn around to get back out. Duke's Hill provided a panoramic view of campus for those who parked and for those who patrolled.

On campus, there were football and basketball games to attend. Programs in the Elliott Hall of Music—slightly bigger than Radio City Music Hall in New York City—offered big-name entertainment of all types. Bob Hope would perform here before the Class of 1950 graduated. So would Vladimir Horowitz.

Several off-campus bars provided further entertainment for older veterans, and locations buried in woods along quiet creeks and far removed from sight in rural fields provided safe haven for fraternity beer parties.

HEAVILON HALL. Dedicated on January 19, 1894, and destroyed by fire four days later, the hall was quickly rebuilt with its tower standing "one brick higher," at Purdue President James Smart's exhortation.

But for all the movie-perfect qualities of Purdue in September of 1946, it was a university about to burst at the seams—as were all colleges in the country that fall.

In 1940, the enrollment at Purdue was 6,966, the largest it had ever been. With the war and males leaving for the military, enrollment by the fall of 1944 dropped to 3,762. The war had ended less than a month before the start of classes in September of 1945. Enrollment jumped to 5,628.

By September 1946, enrollment was 11,462, an increase of 49 percent in one year. In 1947, it reached 14,060; and in 1948, 14,674, the immediate postwar peak. The student population had nearly tripled in three years. It had jumped almost four times in four years. This was at a university equipped with housing, classrooms, and faculty to handle 7,000 students—if that, after the wartime depletion of manpower and supplies.

7

The cause of the enrollment boom was the GI Bill, the Serviceman's Readjustment Act, signed by President Franklin D. Roosevelt on June 22, 1944. To be eligible for its educational benefits, a GI must have served more than ninety days in the military after September 16, 1940. GIs were entitled to one year of full-time training plus a period equal to their time in service, up to forty-eight months.

The bill paid up to $500 for tuition, books, and fees. Single veterans also received an allowance of up to $50 a month. It was raised to $65 in 1946 and $75 in 1948. Veterans with dependents were paid more.

With those provisions and no jobs in an economy that was converting from wartime to peacetime, millions of men leaving the military went to college. They were people like Jim Rardon, who grew up in Lafayette but never thought about going to Purdue until after he returned from the service and learned about the GI Bill. He could not think of anything better to do. So he signed up for classes in September of 1946.

THE END OF A LONG WALK. The long trail through four years of college ends at the steps of the Executive Building (now Hovde Hall) where graduates enter before moving on to Elliott Hall of Music and graduation ceremonies.

By 1947, veterans made up 49 percent of enrollment at all U.S. colleges. About 15.44 million veterans were eligible for benefits in the first GI Bill, which ended in 1956, and 7.8 million received training in various types of schools, including 5.5 million who took advantage of higher education. (The bill also provided other benefits, such as low-interest, no-money-down loans to purchase first homes.)

Introduction

Cross-country buses pulling into West Lafayette in September of 1946 were filled with young men fresh out of the service, confidently hauling their luggage and noisily making their presence known. Quietly came the young women in numbers much smaller than the men's overwhelming count. Men outnumbered women on campus by 1946 almost five to one. That would grow in several years to six to one. It was called "the ratio," and everyone knew what it meant. A social column in the *Exponent* was even titled "The Ratio."

They were young women like Kris Kreisle, a little homesick, no career goals, a little overwhelmed. But in their lifetime, they would see the role of women in society forever changed, and they would play a major part in what was about to occur. On campus that September day in 1946, Kreisle never imagined that one day she would own a successful business.

Although their numbers were small, more and more women were enrolling at Purdue by the fall semester of 1946. In 1940, there had been 1,405 women at Purdue. By 1946, there were 2,023. While small in numbers compared to males, that is an increase of 44 percent.

The majority of these women majored in home economics, worked for a year or two after graduation, and dropped out of the workforce when their first child was born. But in the 1960s when their children were older and they found themselves with time on their hands and a college degree in their résumé, they returned to work.

Purdue's huge population increase in 1946 and after caused a change in the look of the idyllic university campus. Metal military Quonset huts were put up and used as classrooms. West of the red-brick, ivy-covered buildings, inexpensive housing was quickly constructed for new faculty and staff. Because of their colors, these buildings were dubbed the "Black and Whites."

9

Military barracks from Bunker Hill Air Force Base in Peru, Indiana, were brought to the university to house students, including married couples. People called the married-student quarters "Fertility Acres," as the West Lafayette birthrate soared. They were occupied by people like John Hicks, who could sit in his living room on a windy winter day and watch the fringe at the edges of his throw rug blow upward.

A crowded trailer camp sprang up north of campus. Students lived everywhere—from the attics of classroom buildings, to the field house, to converted poultry houses, to private homes in town and country, and, in some cases, to cars parked on the street.

Along with everyone else returning to campus and adding to the crowded living conditions that September were athletes. On the football team, twenty-five-year-old war veterans who had been trained to kill faced eighteen-year-old boys right out of high school. Lou Karras remembers that war-hardened veterans had no patience with pep talks from college football coaches and that coaches did not feel right disciplining men who had fought at Normandy.

Athletes who had graduated from high school from 1942 through 1946 all found themselves in college at the same time and at the same class level, all trying out for the same teams. Bill Butterfield remembers hundreds of guys trying out for the Purdue basketball team in the fall of 1946. Dan Wawrzyniak, a star baseball player in high school, wished that just once he would have a chance to compete against guys his own age.

But for all its overcrowding, Purdue from 1946 to 1950 was a wonderful place to be. Fraternities serenaded sororities. Young people fell in love. Classes were exciting. Dances were a thrill. Worries seemed something of the past. Promise was in the future. These students had survived depression. They had won the war. They could not be stopped now.

That September of 1946 young men like Gordon Kingma were working and going to Purdue at the same time. "The group going through school at that time was a very ambitious group," Kingma says. "Everything had come to a standstill from 1941 to 1945. Our complete attention was focused on defeating our enemies. When that was done, it was 'Boy, let's get going. Let's establish some leadership in the community and the world. . . .'

"We grew up wanting to win everything. . . . We wanted families and nice homes. We wanted all the nice things that had been denied to us during the depression and the war. We wanted good, healthy lives. . . .

"We wanted to be successful."

On June 18, 1950, members of the class that came to Purdue that September day in 1946 graduated—the past now long behind them, their plans and dreams intact.

Seven days later, on June 25, half a world away, the Korean War began.

Veterans' bill signed by F.D.R.

Vast program of benefits provided
for members of American armed forces

WASHINGTON, June 22—(AP) President Roosevelt today signed the "G.I. Bill of Rights" setting up a vast government aid program for veterans of this war.

With congressional leaders and heads of veterans' organizations looking on, the chief executive put his signature to the measure authorizing federal loans, hospitalization, job insurance, schooling and other ex-service benefits estimated to cost between $8,000,000,000 and $6,500,000,000.

The president said the bill carries out most of the recommendations he has made for veterans' aid and notifies the members of the armed forces that the people at home will not let them down.

He urged additional war service legislation, however, to give veterans social security toward old age pensions for the time served in the armed forces and to provide education and unemployment compensation benefits for members of the merchant marine. What veterans want more than anything, he said, is assurance of employment after the war.

" I wish you could "
turn back the clock

Remembering how it was

Reece McGee, Sociologist

He keeps a photo reproduction in his office of a dirty World War II soldier—untrimmed beard, banged-up helmet, cigarette hanging from his lips. It is to remind Reece McGee, a professor of sociology at Purdue University, of the guys to whom so much of today's society can trace its roots—to GIs like this returning from war.

"The GI Bill democratized the whole society," McGee says.

Before the GI Bill, few people went to college, only the elite. After the GI Bill, college was opened to everyone, and their children grew up expecting to go. So did their grandchildren.

Out of the depression, the war, and programs like the GI Bill grew the technological changes, the world economy, massive suburbia, great expectations, the Baby-Boom generation, and the discontent of the 1960s.

McGee not only has studied the period. He has lived it. He received his B.A., M.S., and Ph.D. from the University of Minnesota. He has been at Purdue since 1967.

McGee knew what was happening in society during this period even as he witnessed it. In 1959 for the magazine *The Nation*, he wrote an article titled "White Collar Explosion."

"The United States is experiencing a revolution which will occasion changes as fundamental in the social, political and economic structure of life on the North American continent as did the Industrial Revolution," he said in the article. "That it is a quiet one, and that its origins and implications are not yet entirely clear, do not affect this dictum in the slightest. It is a revolution in class structure, and its roots lie in the changed composition of the American labor force."

And the reason for it, to a great extent, was the GI Bill.

"The GI Bill, in my opinion, was one of the two most far-reaching and inclusive pieces of legislation affecting education in our country," McGee says. "The other was the nineteenth-century Morrell Act, the land-grant college act that created universities like Purdue.

"The GI Bill had a tremendous social influence in the United States. It provided, all at once, from the period of about 1948 through 1952 an enormous cadre of trained people, educated people, people who were technologically expert. And these folks all graduated almost simultaneously, in a historical sense.

"The numbers are important, but the statistics vary from source to source. I recognize these numbers differ from some others, but according to Veterans of Foreign Wars researchers I've spoken with, somewhat more than 16 million people served in the American armed forces during World War II. About 5.5 million of them—one-third—took advantage of the higher education provisions of the GI Bill. There were other provisions in it. There were small-business loans, housing loans, medical care, vocational training, and so on. But about 5.5 million veterans went to college on the GI Bill, and more than 3 million of them completed degrees—all between the summer of 1945 and roughly the summer of 1950. This was an enormous body of people, most of whom would not have gone to college without the bill.

"This was occurring during a time when the American economy was changing from an industrial, smokestack economy into a service economy. We were creating a labor force for the

"I wish you could turn back the clock"

First Semester Enrollment History 1940 to 1966
Purdue University at West Lafayette

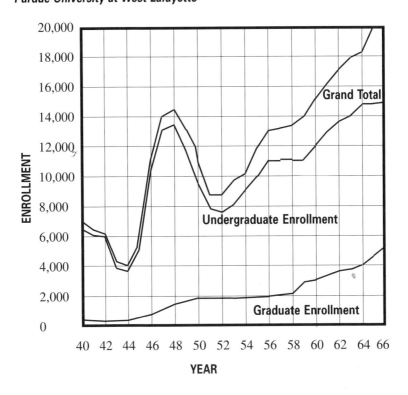

kinds of activities the economy was going to need. All these guys got work. They got married and had children. They bought houses and they had money to spend.

"All this resulted in the corporate expansion we saw between the 1950s and the 1960s. The U.S. economy went global. I doubt this could have been done without this tremendous reservoir of men and women created by the GI Bill. We wouldn't have had the people to do it.

"It was the GI Bill that opened up higher education to the masses, to the public as a whole. In 1940, 15.7 percent of Americans aged eighteen through twenty-one were enrolled in institutions of

15

Remembering how it was

Purdue University Fees
West Lafayette Campus

Fees begin with fall semester each academic year.

year	general service fee	designated fees	total resident fees	nonresident tuition	total nonresident fees
1945	$70	$38	$108	$200	$308
1946	70	40	110	200	310
1947	70	40	110	200	310
1948	70	40	110	200	310
1949	80	40	120	200	320
1950	80	40	120	200	320

Residence Hall Rates

Rate is for predominant type of double-room occupancy.

year	rate	year	rate
1945-46	$425	1948-49	$550
1946-47	550	1949-50	600
1947-48	550		

higher education. By 1991, 41.4 percent of high school graduates were enrolled. This all started with the GI Bill.

"It created suburbia as we know it. Suburbia isn't new. It goes back to the 1880s. But it happened in large scale after the war. By the 1950s, cars were being mass produced cheaply, so more people could move out of the city. And land in the city was expensive. They started putting up these subdivisions on cheap prairie, and people could afford the houses. During World War II, all kinds of new techniques for construction were created, including the modular.

"I wish you could turn back the clock"

"After the war, one of the things the GI Bill did was guarantee housing loans for veterans, no money down, 4-1/2 percent mortgages. There was this tremendous appetite to build and sell houses. All this was a tremendous boom to the housing industry.

"The classic example of the housing boom is Levittown in New York. During the war, William J. Levitt was building landing craft. After the war, he changed his assembly line to building houses, bought up essentially wasteland, and proceeded to construct a gigantic suburb. It was a unique interaction between available technology, the economy, and the tremendous need for housing.

"During the war, we had millions of people who were kept in an unmarried state for years by the Army. After the war, they were flooding back into the economy wanting to get married and start families as fast as they could. They had been putting their personal life on hold while they served their country. During World War II, it was a civilian armed force. It wasn't like the Army of today, which is made up of professionals. This was a civilian army, and very few had any thought of remaining in the service past the war. Most of them really didn't like it very much.

"To accommodate all the students enrolling in the universities, college classrooms were jammed. People were sitting on the floor, on the windowsills, standing outside the door. The food services were overwhelmed. The institutions had no idea how many were coming nor did the government. No one foresaw what was going to happen.

"I have no evidence to support this, but one of the things I can see is that this also kept a significant portion of those who would have been young workers out of the marketplace for one to four years while the labor market readjusted to the civilian economy. If all these guys had stayed out of school, if another third of the armed forces had tried to go into the workforce upon discharge, the economy couldn't have handled it. There would

17

have been enormous unemployment. The GI Bill and college kept them out of the workforce, and it trained them for the kinds of jobs the economy was going to demand.

"In 1940, about 20 percent of all employed people in the country were factory workers. They were the largest single working group in the country. By 1955, the largest single occupational grouping was what the census calls 'business managerial-technical professional.' Where did these people come from? They came from the GI Bill.

"The depression also had an effect on this generation. Most of those who served in World War II had been teenagers during the depression. When they got older and the war ended, they wanted stability. They wanted jobs, and they were willing to work to train themselves to have jobs.

"There was a kind of euphoria in the country when the war ended. By VE Day, everyone knew the Japanese would rapidly be defeated. No one was worried that Japan would win the war. It was only a matter of when it would be over. The war years had been hard years. They had been hard on the civilian population. There had been strict rationing. No one starved, but there were a lot of things you couldn't get.

"The men were all gone. The economy was healthy. The war industry put a lot of people to work and put money in pockets. But it was a hard time. Clothing was hard to get, so were heating oil, coffee, sugar, all kinds of things. And this came after the depression. When the war was over, goods started to become available, and there was a pent up demand for them. The economy was good—there were ups and downs, but essentially it was pretty good. People were very optimistic and looked forward to a better life.

"These people from the World War II era with their patriotic outlook then raised the generation that came to college in the 1960s. I wish I had an answer about the sixties. They mystify me.

18

"I wish you could turn back the clock"

But I suppose some good came out of them. It might have had to do with the affluence the World War II generation had created for their children. These kids of the sixties didn't have to worry about having enough to eat or getting a job. Since they didn't have to worry about those things, they could turn their attention to other things.

"World War II, like the Civil War, was a great turning point for the whole society. We became a different society. As a result of our participation in the war, we became a superpower.

"The war had a big effect on women. Women flocked into industry in large numbers during the war. Those working in the war industries were known as 'Rosie the Riveter.' Then when the men came back, industry kicked the women out without a thought. We also had large numbers of women serve in the armed forces. I've never been able to get an accurate figure on how many served. My estimate is somewhat less than one million. Since World War II, we've had women in the military.

"The women in college in the late 1940s were Betty Coed, and otherwise, they didn't count. They took home ec and nursing. The standard explanation for a woman taking a foreign language, sociology, or something like that was that she was looking for a husband. Nursing, home economics, and English were the most popular majors for most women. In the eyes of most men, women were in college only to find a good husband.

"When they graduated from college, these women married, and they might have worked for a short time. But when they had their first baby, they quit work and stayed home. They didn't go back to work until their kids became teenagers in high school and college.

"As the economy worsened—which it has been doing since the 1960s—many women went to work because they had to and some went to work because they wanted to. The opportunity became open to them.

"Thinking back now on the accepted roles for women forty and fifty years ago, it was unbelievably restricted—hideously sexist. It could very well be that the women who married the GIs right after the war were responsible for getting the contemporary women's movement started. During the war, they had played important roles in business and industry, and then they were pushed aside and told they couldn't participate anymore. Women remembered that. And it made them mad.

"But that all came later. In the late 1940s and early 1950s, it was a wonderfully positive time. Nobody worried about being able to get a decent job and to make a good living. The only concern was, Can I get the kind of job I really want? People weren't worried that they might be unemployed or slinging hamburgers.

"The late 1940s and the twenty years that followed were times of tremendous social and economic change—just enormous. It was a time when young people did not worry that they might not do as well as their parents. It was a time when they knew that they would."

Lew Wood

His full name is James Lewis Wood but he goes by Lew. He is director of national public relations for the American Legion, headquartered in Indianapolis, and a member of the Purdue Class of 1950.

This interview takes place in the fall of 1994, not long after nationwide publicity highlighted the fiftieth anniversary, on June 22, of the day President Franklin Delano Roosevelt signed the GI Bill into law.

"It changed America," Wood says. "No one disputes that fact.

"This legislation really has its roots in World War I. The veterans who assembled to come up with the bill—the discussion of ideas had gone on for the better part of a year—were all World

"I wish you could turn back the clock"

War I veterans. They had come back from France with nothing but the clothes on their backs, and they got maybe sixty-dollars mustering-out pay and a ticket home, where they sat without a job.

"After World War I, everyone came back to the civilian sector at the same time, and the economy wasn't good enough to put them all back to work. Veterans were selling apples on the streets. They marched on Washington, D.C., and were fired on by U.S. troops.

"It was the World War I vets who were really concerned about what would happen to the GIs after World War II. After the First World War, even before they had left France and while they were still in uniform, they met in Paris and came up with the idea of some kind of an organization that would be an advocate for veterans—looking out for veterans' rights and for what veterans deserve from a grateful nation. It would be an organization to see about jobs and education for veterans, to look after and care for the wounded, and to take care of the widows and children.

"Out of this meeting was born the American Legion. One of the prime movers in this was Theodore Roosevelt, Jr., the son of the president. His brother, Quentin, had been killed in France.

"Shortly after the meeting in Paris, another was held in the United States in St. Louis in June of 1919. Some of the men who had been in Paris also attended this meeting, and it was in St. Louis that the idea really came to full flower and the name was settled on.

"Hamilton Fish, who commanded a battalion of black soldiers and was highly decorated in France, was one of the legion's founders. He wrote the preamble to the American Legion constitution. The preamble is a wonderful document, and it has been altered only once in more than seventy-five years—'world war' was changed to 'world wars' following World War II. Fish later became a Republican congressman and was a great nemesis of FDR.

"Before World War II was over, these World War I veterans began to see what's been called 'déjà vu all over again.' But they decided that what happened to them wasn't going to happen to this next generation. They wouldn't allow it.

"At an American Legion convention in 1943, a variety of resolutions were presented and ideas began to jell. The national legion commander appointed a committee to study the situation. In 1943, John Stelle, who had been a governor of Illinois, was named to head the study committee. The committee was to go to Washington and come up with a piece of legislation that could be presented by some of our friends in Congress. The committee met right after Christmas.

"Later, after days of discussion, one committee member, Harry Colmery, a former national commander, left the meetings, walked back to his room at the Mayflower Hotel, shut the door to his room, sat down at a desk, took out some hotel stationery, and began to put the ideas into form. This became the original draft of the Serviceman's Readjustment Act of 1944. We still have part of that document preserved under glass.

"This is not to say other veterans' organizations weren't discussing the same things. But the American Legion was the biggest organization. There was some division within the legion about what this act should and should not do. Some people were afraid it might put veterans on the dole.

"The GI Bill provided for a number of things, including money for education—college or vocational training—and assistance for buying homes. Because so many GIs went to college on this bill after World War II, it prevented much of the massive unemployment that had followed World War I.

"The loan provisions of the bill gave a great spurt to the home-building industry. Levittown near New York was one of the first developments to go up. For a small amount of money and no down payment, veterans could buy homes. These were men who

"I wish you could turn back the clock"

without the bill would have had to work for a long time before even thinking about owning a home.

"Because of the GI Bill, veterans gained college educations, qualified for good jobs, bought their own homes, and started businesses with their earnings. The whole thing had a rolling effect.

"These men became the captains of industry. They became the chieftains of reindustrializing the nation. The state-of-the-art technology used in the Persian Gulf War was made possible by the knowledge and leadership of those who benefited from the GI Bill.

"The bill has paid for itself over and over. Some say twentyfold. These GIs paid higher taxes because of their ability to make more money, create more jobs, and grow the economy. The home-loan aspects of the legislation rejuvenated the housing industry and created suburbia.

"All of this was done by depression kids born in the 1920s. By the time they were five or six or seven years old, the depression was in full swing. Their families were just scraping by and could never even think of sending them to college. If it hadn't been for the GI Bill, many of them would have followed their fathers into the steel mills. Instead, those kids became engineers and executives of the steel companies."

John Hicks

He is a retired vice president of Purdue University and served for a time as acting president.

The banquet halls at the Purdue Memorial Union were filled with people the night of his retirement dinner—such is his popularity. A baseball fan, he recited his favorite poem that night, "Casey at the Bat."

John Hicks is an unforgettable personality. He can recite statistics and figures from forty years ago as easily as he can recite a poem about a baseball player who takes a mighty swing and misses.

He is quick with a joke. Older now, perhaps more sentimental, he is also quicker with a tear. Sitting, remembering, at the dining-room table in his West Lafayette home, tears well up. What makes his eyes water?

"Memories," he says. "Memories of people now gone, all deeply missed. When I start thinking about people back then, it gives me a sentimental feeling." The tone of his voice is crisp but friendly. Sometimes he leans back in his dining-room chair and places his hand to his forehead as he remembers and remembers.

"I was born in Australia in 1921. My dad was in the motion picture business. He worked for Paramount. He was in charge of film distribution for Australia, New Zealand, and the Far East from 1921 to 1932. In 1932, he was brought back to the States and made vice president for foreign distribution at Paramount. His office was in the Paramount Building in New York, and we lived in New Rochelle.

"My dad had a very good job. The motion picture industry paid very well. The depression hit him hard. In 1929, he was making $50,000 a year, which was a great deal of money in those days. Then Paramount went through bankruptcy, and in 1933, his salary went down to $12,500 a year. That was still a great salary, but it was a big cut from $50,000. I came from an upper-middle-class family. Growing up, I didn't have to work a day in my life.

"I became an idealistic sixteen-year-old. I had no idea what I wanted to do with my career. Then I read John Steinbeck's *Grapes of Wrath*, and I decided, by golly, I was going to save the tenant farmer. Massachusetts State College had a good ag school, so I went up there, majored in agriculture, and got over wanting to save the tenant farmer.

"I started college in September of 1939. Soon after Pearl Harbor, a lot us went into the Enlisted Reserve Corps. College

"I wish you could turn back the clock"

students could join the corps and continue their studies until they were needed, then they were called into service. I got called up in March of 1943.

"When you arrived at the reception center, they gave you a test to determine what branch you were going into, depending on what branch needed men and how you did on the tests. I was assigned to the Army Air Corps.

"I spent three full years in the Army Air Corps in the States and in Saipan and Guam with a B-29 outfit. I was on the ground crew. I loaded the bombs and cleaned the guns, and other guys flew the planes and dropped the bombs.

"I got out in 1946, and I only needed one semester to finish college. But at Mass State, the semester had already started. My dad had died and my mom was living north of Poughkeepsie, New York. As soon as I got home, I picked up the *New York Times* and read a story saying Vassar would admit veterans for the spring quarter. Vassar was a girls' school right in Poughkeepsie. So I went to Vassar and picked up twelve credit hours.

"There were twelve hundred women on campus—and thirty-six men. We were the first men to go to Vassar. And, boy, were we a hit with the women! They all referred to us as the *veterans*, not the *men*.

"When that semester was over, I still needed a few more credits, so I went back to Mass State in the summer of '46. That's where I met Swiftie, my wife, who had just graduated and worked at the sweet shop. She worked in New York City for a year while I finished, and we got married in June of 1947.

"In the summer of 1946, I was offered a job at Mass State for the '46–'47 school year. They were short of teachers, and they thought I was pretty good—even though I only had a bachelor's degree. I taught there for a year and decided I wanted to be a college professor.

25

"Earl Butz, who was then the head of agricultural economics at Purdue, was on campus recruiting grad students. I met him and he snowed me. Listening to Earl Butz, I thought if I didn't come to Purdue they'd close the place down. So I came to Purdue on July 1, 1947, to get my master's degree. I received my Ph.D. in 1950 and became an assistant professor of agricultural economics.

"You can't believe how difficult it was to find a place to live in Lafayette or West Lafayette in those days because of the influx of veterans. When my wife and I first got to town, we rented a room in a private home. The home owners sent their own kids to live with grandparents so they'd have the space to rent to couples like us.

Younger faces on campus. World War II veterans—older than the usual student—brought another generation to campus: their children. This group is pictured on the front steps of a married-student housing unit.

"Later Swiftie and I moved into an area that was formerly military barracks. The buildings were wooden frames covered with tar paper. They called the area 'Fertility Acres' because so many women were pregnant. You could rent an apartment for forty-two dollars a month—and that included utilities. The apartment had a little kitchen with an icebox—no refrigerator, a living room with a natural gas stove to keep the whole place warm, a small bedroom, a bathroom, and that was about it.

"We had some old throw rugs on the floor with fringe on the edges, and in the winter, the fringe on those rugs would sometimes stand straight up from the cold wind blowing in. But we were happy there. We had our first child—born October 24, 1948—while we lived out there in those barracks. We now have ten grandkids.

"I wish you could turn back the clock"

"When I showed up at Purdue in 1947, the university was nearing the peak of its post-World War II enrollment. We had over fourteen thousand students. About 85 percent were men—mostly GIs—and 15 percent women. We had five schools: engineering, agriculture, pharmacy, home economics, and science, which included studies such as English and history and chemistry and physics.

"Most of the GIs wanted to get through as quickly as they could. They came on the GI Bill, and their goals were to get an education, get married, have kids, and get a job. And a lot of them did a couple of those things all at once.

"The GI Bill had a tremendous effect on education. It increased demand. Just after World War II, some bright guy in Ohio wrote a book entitled *The Impending Tidal Wave of Students*, which was a marvelous title. He not only acknowledged the initial postwar rush of people coming to universities, but he also predicted that all their kids would come to universities. He said enrollment would tail off in the early fifties, then go up more and more as the kids of the World War II generation graduated from high school. The World War II generation did raise the birthrate a bit. They didn't all have eight kids, like I did, but they did increase the birthrate for awhile.

"Now the World War II grandchildren are coming to college. I would guess at least two-thirds to three-quarters of high school graduates today start college compared to 15 percent when I graduated high school.

"Many of the technologies we started talking about in the late forties and early fifties had not been heard of before the war. We were just beginning to get what are now called computers. They developed during the war. We bought our first big computer at Purdue sometime in the early fifties, and it was a tube thing. Some of the kids now have pocket computers that can do more than that $150,000 computer could.

27

"At that time, our view of the world was very upbeat. We had just defeated Hitler and Mussolini. We didn't see yet that Russia was a threat. We thought if enough people had a good education we could achieve a utopia. We were young and idealistic.

"Most of the guys who came to college during those years were from the middle class, the lower middle class, and some below that. They'd been through the depression, and they knew, by God, if they wanted a job and wanted to do well, they had to work hard. They'd grown up in the military during the war. They'd seen some of the world, and they'd seen some terrible things. By and large, they were highly motivated. They studied hard.

"I would have hated to have been a freshman coming right out of high school at that time—particularly a male student. At least half the male students were veterans. They were older and more experienced, and the girls dated them. If you were a kid just out of high school, you had a hard time getting a date. There was only one woman for every five or six men at Purdue.

"A lot of the men coming out of the service didn't have any civilian clothes that fit them. Many of them wore parts of their military clothing. I wore my military shoes until they wore out. They had high ankles. I loved those shoes. The GIs didn't get all dressed up to go to school, but they didn't dress like the sixties kids with the long hair.

"The sixties were different. These were the kids the World War II generation raised. I suppose in a way their outlook was our fault. We essentially had said to them, 'You kids have to decide for yourself what's right and wrong.' We didn't pound into them the kinds of stuff our parents had pounded into us. Our parents told us, 'You have to read the Bible and believe everything that's in it, or by God, you'll go to hell and burn.' We were probably a little too gentle with our kids. And we've seen a decline in the moral structure of society as a result of that.

"I wish you could turn back the clock"

"But the fifties were exciting. The economic growth of the country during the 1950s was rapid. We developed so many new things—new methods of production, new medicines. It was the greatest growth period of our country. The growth was due partly to the accessibility of education and to the scientific and technological advances made during the war.

"My grandchildren always want me to tell them about the war, to show them how a bomb worked. But what I really want them to know about that time is that the United States made a terrific effort in World War II. We essentially saved the world for democracy. I really think we did. If we hadn't gotten into it, who knows what would have happened.

"I want my grandchildren to know that World War II was a great victory. However, I want them to know also that war is terrible and that we don't want to get into war if we can avoid it. But if we're attacked, we have to put everything into it.

"I wish we could go back. It was a completely different world, and it's hard to know why it's so different today. But we have not always imparted important attitudes to our kids.

"When you think about it carefully, you realize there's a physical order of things. We've done a tremendous job of understanding the physical order. However, there's also a moral order, and over the last thirty or forty years, we've gone downhill in this area. That's where we've sloughed off—moral order. I'm not a strictly religious guy. I believe in God, but I don't go to church. Whether the moral order was passed down from God or developed by man, I don't know. But I do know we need it for stability.

"I look back and think, What did all this mean in my life? You could say it was a good time to be young. If you got out of college in 1948, '49, or '50, I don't see how you could have helped but succeed. There were so many opportunities. If you were willing to work, it was very difficult to fail. I wouldn't want to go through a depression and a war again. On the other hand, having it in my past, I can see that it certainly did a great deal to make my life fuller.

"The best years of my life were after I came back from the war. They were good years, no question about it. We had faith and such a bright outlook on the future. Maybe I glorify those years. I don't know.

"Sometimes I wish you could turn back the clock. But you can't. You can't do it."

Earl Butz

"I remember one couple who came to Purdue from New York right after the war," Earl Butz says. "He was an ex-GI, an excellent student in ag economics. The campus was so crowded at that time the only place I could find for them to live was a converted poultry house on the old poultry farm. It was better than living on the street. But this young man told me his wife was very unhappy living in a converted poultry house."

Butz smiles as he tells the story. He leans on his desk in his simple office and says he was able to find them something better than an old poultry house, eventually.

Butz was a professor at Purdue University and head of the Department of Agricultural Economics from 1946 to 1954. Now dean emeritus of agriculture at Purdue, Butz keeps his office door open while he works. His desk faces the door so he can see anyone who passes. He lectures around the country and serves as consultant to a number of business and trade organizations. A slender man, he always made certain to get home for lunch with his wife who was unable to get out. She died in July 1995.

He was U.S. assistant secretary of agriculture from 1954 to 1957 during the Eisenhower administration. He returned to Purdue in 1957 as dean of agriculture. From 1971 to 1976, during

"I wish you could turn back the clock"

the administrations of presidents Richard Nixon and Gerald Ford, he was U.S. secretary of agriculture.

The walls of his office are filled with photographs of presidents of the United States. In one photo, Butz sits on the corner of Nixon's desk in the Oval Office while the president listens.

"Not many people have sat on that desk," Butz says with a grin.

There are photos of Butz with presidents and cabinet members relaxing and talking aboard Air Force One. There are photos of Butz with heads of foreign countries, men like Soviet Premier Leonid Bresnev.

"I was the first American in Bresnev's office other than Gus Hall, the head of the American Communist Party," Butz says and explains how the meeting to discuss a grain deal came about.

Butz has a story to tell about each photo. Most stories have a humorous digression.

Butz grew up on a farm in Noble County, Indiana, and came to Purdue on a 4-H scholarship in 1928. He graduated in 1932.

"That was in the depths of the depression," he says. "Will Rogers said it was the lowest boom he had ever seen. Students at that time didn't ask prospective employers about their retirement programs. That's because there were no prospective employers. I went back to the farm after I graduated."

He returned to Purdue a year later, received his doctorate in 1937, and joined the faculty after serving briefly as a research fellow with the Brookings Institute in Washington, D.C.

He was a young man, early in his career, when the big freshman class hit Purdue in 1946.

"It was the first postwar class," he says. "A lot of those people were not too much younger than I was. They were really tremendous students. This was a time when our freshman class averaged a few months older than the senior class. They were older, they were serious, they were ready to get married. Some of the former GIs were older than some of the professors.

"They had returned from a tremendous experience in the service. They knew what they wanted to do and where they wanted to go. They could achieve. They didn't want to waste time. They were an excellent group of students, and all of us teaching at that time got our sights set on students of that ability. When they passed along and the next class came on after them, it was kind of tough for a year or two because we had our standards of performance set too high for the younger kids who didn't have the same motivation.

"I am convinced from my own teaching experience that motivation is far more important than native ability in achieving success in college or anywhere else. If you're properly motivated, you can overcome almost any difficulty. That class that came in 1946 had motivation, and it was a thrill to work with them.

"It was very crowded on campus. We had to work around the clock because when those guys came in we didn't have the classroom space. The professors had to do a lot of counseling because those fellows had just come back from a military environment and were not happy about being put in crowded temporary dorms. They were wondering, Is this the way they're going to treat us?

"Professors taught a lot more night classes. We didn't mind. We were glad to have the opportunity. I once had twenty-two class-contact hours per week. If anyone had that now, they'd put in a complaint about unfair labor practices. I told my wife at the beginning of that semester, 'Cancel everything except the absolutely necessary social engagements.' I spent my nights at my desk preparing for the next day's classes.

"Things have changed. When I was dean of agriculture, a farmer came in and said, 'What is the average teaching load of the professors here?' I told him twelve hours. He said, 'Well, that's a long day, but I

"I wish you could turn back the clock"

suppose the work is easy.' I never told him I meant twelve hours a week.

"There was a whole different attitude in society in the 1940s. We'd all put our shoulders to the war effort. Increased productivity was the cry of the day in agriculture, in industry, and everyplace else. Nobody was holding back. The attitude was, We had won the war,

POSTWAR ENROLLMENT SWELLS. New students filled more than six thousand seats at Purdue's Elliott Hall of Music during fall orientation.

we had increased output to win the war, we had worked to win the war, now let's work to win the peace. I think that attitude has departed from us today.

"All generations have an effect on society. There are great leaders in every generation. But I think there was a higher percentage of innovators in the generation that came back to school after the war. There was a higher percentage of risk-takers. There was a higher percentage of people who weren't afraid to try something new.

"They had a very positive effect on society of that day. And they are still having a positive effect on society today."

John Foley

In a small office where walls are filled with county maps and desks are crowded with green computer screens, John Foley is master of his surroundings.

He is soft-spoken and unassuming. He wears gold-rimmed glasses and an orange-brown cardigan on a cold January day, as he painstakingly goes over aerial photographs in the Tippecanoe County

33

assessor's office. He can look at these aerial shots and spot a row of corn planted forty-two inches apart instead of the standard thirty-six inches. It comes from a lifetime spent in agriculture.

His professional lifetime with Purdue University began in 1954. When he retired in 1983 from the agricultural engineering faculty, he was given the honor of professor emeritus. While with the university, he worked on Purdue projects in Brazil and Portugal.

His gray-black hair, short on the sides, is receding. His bushy eyebrows dance when he comes to a story he loves to tell.

"When was I born? Well, there's some doubt about that," he says. "I had always been told I was born on the fourth of January 1927. But when I was sixteen, I went to get my birth certificate, and it was dated the first of January. I went to my mother, and she said, 'No, that's not right.' She was sure about it. It turns out the doctor who made out the records at that time wasn't always sober. After New Year's, he probably hadn't sobered up yet and got it wrong."

Whenever he was born, Foley was eighteen years old in the spring of 1945 when he came to Purdue University for the beginning of the summer semester. He arrived from his family's farm in Spencer, Indiana, where he had grown up during the depression.

"We had corn and soybeans," he says. "In fact, it was soybeans that kept me out of the Army. We had a crop of soybeans that was rained on, and we had to leave the soybeans in the field until they dried. We turned them over two or three times, and when we got them into the barn, I put a bandanna over my face and went to work. When I went for my military physical exam, they said, 'There's something in your lungs. Come back in three months.' By then the war was over.

"All through the depression, we always had plenty to eat. We didn't have much money, but we always had plenty to eat. We didn't have to rely on the township trustee like many people did. We had gardens. My mom was good with gardens.

34

"We milked forty cows, as bad cows as you ever could see. I got up at four-thirty in the morning, and it would take us two hours to milk them.

"When I graduated from the eighth grade, my dad said, 'Well, you're going to have a girlfriend now and need more money, so I'm going to take away your twenty-five-cent allowance and give it to your sister. You decide what you want to do on the farm and we'll do it. You can make money from that.' I decided to grow popcorn. He gave me an acre. I would shell the popcorn and sell it to the movie theater and the school and the grocery store. I never did get any more allowance after that, and I bought most of my own clothes and books.

"In 1936, our barn burned down. It was a huge barn. After the fire, we had to do our milking in the orchard. We milked in that orchard all winter long. After a couple weeks, I told my dad, 'Hey, I probably should quit school until we get this straightened out.' My dad said, 'No,' so it was settled. If he hadn't said that, I might never have gotten to Purdue.

"Nobody in my family had ever gone to college before. Hardly anyone went to school much in those days. But I was making good grades.

"I couldn't stay on the farm and have a family of my own there. Our farm wasn't big enough for two families. If I had stayed, we would have had to invest quite of bit of money in more land, and we didn't have money.

"There was hope that I could do better by going to college. At first, I studied electrical engineering. But after I was at Purdue for a year, I learned what else the university offered. I found I liked ag engineering, so I switched over to that.

"I had to work part of the time I was in school, so it took me a little longer than usual to finish. I worked in the student union cafeteria. I usually worked twenty to twenty-five hours a week. I started

Remembering how it was

out getting paid forty cents an hour, which was the most money I had ever made. After a couple years, it increased to a dollar or so.

"I had never been away from home like this before. I lived in a rooming house. I owned about three pairs of pants. I hitchhiked home once a month, and my mom washed them. And, I had a laundry case you could mail home.

"That wasn't so bad. When I was younger, a kid I went to school with didn't come to class on the days his mother washed his pants. It was the only pair he had.

"I had maybe three shirts, and I washed them out. I came to Purdue with a pair of tennis shoes and a pair of regular shoes. My best clothing was my ROTC [Reserve Officers' Training Corps] uniform. We all had to take two years of ROTC.

"I ate on a dollar a day—that's it. But I liked going to the movies in Lafayette. To save bus fare, we walked from West Lafayette over the bridge to Lafayette. The GIs hadn't started coming back yet, and there were lots of girls. Sometimes I went to a movie with two girls, and they paid the way just to have a guy to go with. I sat in the middle and held hands with one on each side. It was new to me. It was kind of nice.

"I took all the math I could take in high school, but I never saw a slide rule before I got to Purdue—and they were all using those things.

"In 1945, there was a naval training school at Purdue, and the other students had to keep up with the guys in that program. They had been picked for this program from all over the country, and they had a limited amount of time to complete their studies. We were graded on a curve, and competing with those guys wasn't easy.

"In 1946 when I was a sophomore, the GIs started coming back in large numbers. I didn't spend a lot of time with them. They were older. They spent a lot of time at the bars. Many of them were eight to ten years older than I was. Some of them were really good stu-

"I wish you could turn back the clock"

dents, but some of them just goofed off. They came through on the GI Bill, and they had more money than the rest of us did.

"Before I came to Purdue, I had a bicycle, a black Monarch with yellow stripes. I thought I wouldn't need it so I sold it. But my classes were so far apart I didn't have time to walk back and forth. So I found a used bike and put it together. The tires kept leaking, and you still couldn't get new tires so soon after the war. The bike didn't need a lock. It was too old. No one would steal it.

"I had a girlfriend at home. Her name was Ruth. We got married in 1948 when I was twenty-one. We bought a trailer in Lafayette and lived in it. I graduated in the winter of 1950.

"I really didn't know how I was going to make a living with this new education. At the placement service, they said there weren't enough jobs for everyone. So I didn't even use the service. I just went out on my own, and I found people were looking for young men who had enough gumption to go out and search on their own. I found twelve jobs I could pick from.

"It was tough back then. You made it the best way you could. About the only thing we ate were hot dogs and hamburgers.

"But I appreciated going to school."

Robert Peterson

Robert Peterson's white hair is combed straight back. They used to call him "Red."

"That's the way I looked when I was twenty-two," he says, pointing to a picture on a coffee table in front of the couch where he sits in his West Lafayette home. "I had wavy hair and a cleft chin. I still have a bit of a dimple."

His fingers are twisted from arthritis, but that does not stop him from pursuing a lifelong love of photography. A retired photographer for Purdue University, he still does weddings and keeps a darkroom in his home.

While he talks, his wife of more than fifty years is in another part of the house.

Peterson talks with excitement and enthusiasm about his life. The interview is rapid and upbeat. But then the memories become too vivid. The emotions return. He takes a handkerchief and dabs his moist eyes.

Peterson was born in Frankfort, Indiana, in 1921. His dad was a carpenter who worked for the WPA [Work Projects Administration]. His mom took in washing. She traded washing for food with the grocery man.

In 1940, Peterson graduated from high school. He headed for Purdue where an older brother was already studying.

"I did this on my own," he says, puncturing the air with his index finger for emphasis. "I had always looked forward to going to Purdue. My brother had an apartment in a house at 146 Pierce Street in West Lafayette, and I split the rent with him. It was my future wife's mother's house. Dortha and I started dating in the fall of 1940. We got engaged in December of 1942.

"I took bacteriology as a major, and I figured I'd end up with Eli Lilly as a pill salesman or a lab technician. I thought I'd go to school for four years and then get a job. But after Pearl Harbor, that changed. I figured I'd get drafted.

"I waited to get drafted. I tried to get in the Navy in mid-1942 because I wanted to go into photography and the Navy had a real good photographic setup. But I was too late. The schools were closed by mid-1942. After awhile, I got a little worried because they'd call you a draft dodger pretty quickly in those days if you weren't in. I talked to my draft board and told them I was waiting. They said, 'Don't worry about it. We'll get to you.' A month and a half later I got my draft notice.

"I wasn't going to school at the time. I knew what was going to happen, so I worked full time in photography at the university while I waited.

"I wish you could turn back the clock"

"I went into the Army Air Corps. I went to Peterson Air Base in Colorado Springs. Rumors started flying we were a hot outfit and were heading overseas.

"I got an assignment in Denver packing up our supplies for overseas, and Dortha came to see me on vacation. I told her we were getting ready to be shipped overseas, so if we were going to get married, we'd better do it. We got married at a Methodist Church in Denver—no family, just the two of us. When we got to the church, they yelled out the back door to some people there, 'Hey, we got another couple here. Come on in and be the witnesses.' It was just us, the minister, his wife, and these witnesses at the ceremony.

"We were married July 17, 1943. Dortha left for home the next week. I shipped out in November of 1943. We went all through the Pacific—New Zealand, New Guinea, Philippines, Okinawa, Korea. Our photo pilots would go in before an invasion and take pictures, and we'd develop the film and make prints of the coastlines.

"I got back to the West Coast of the United States in the fall of 1945. I tried to call home, but I couldn't get through. Everybody was trying to call home. I hadn't talked to my wife since the last day I saw her a week after our marriage. For twenty-seven months, all we had were letters.

"My mother was dying of cancer. The Red Cross told my family I was coming and I'd be home right before Thanksgiving. I took a train."

Peterson stops the interview. His eyes are red and wet, and he wipes them.

"I hadn't seen my wife in twenty-seven months. The train pulled into the station in Lafayette at nine or ten at night. The station was crowded. My wife and my older sister's husband and my brothers met me."

He stops again.

"It was neat. It was emotional. We didn't say much to each other. We just hugged and kissed. We all went out and got a hamburger. It was probably the next day before things settled down. We all cried. My mom died December 5. My father lived to be 105.

"I got back in Purdue in January of 1946, and we lived in a room at my wife's parents' house. It was difficult getting back into the routine of studying. The military was an entirely different kind of life. Coming home every night to study was quite a bit different, and I had to work to make ends meet. I had to keep my nose to the grindstone. My wife worked, too.

"We took all the money we got from the GI Bill and put it in the bank. We never touched it. I got a degree in bacteriology in 1950 and went to work full time as a photographer at Purdue. In 1950, we did everything—I graduated, we bought our first car, and we had our first child.

"By the time I finished, I was tired of school. I had started in 1940—ten years earlier. I was close to thirty years old. I guess all I wanted was a nice wife and to get my family educated. My son is an engineer with General Motors. My daughter has a nice job with Ameritech. We have five grandchildren.

"I guess I've succeeded."

Bob Topping

He is not a big man, but he has a big smile to go with a ready wit.

Bob Topping, a native of West Lafayette, Indiana, was a newspaper man in Indiana and Michigan before returning to Purdue in 1962. In 1990, he retired from the university after having been director of the news service; founding editor of *Perspective*, a quarterly newspaper for Purdue alumni and friends; assistant to the vice president for development; and senior editor.

Among his books are three on the history of Purdue: *The Hovde Years; A Century and Beyond: The History of Purdue University;*

and *The Book of Trustees*. More than anyone else, Topping knows the history of Purdue.

"Before the start of World War II, it had under seven thousand students and was administered by one president, one vice president, and the board of trustees," Topping says. "Edward C. Elliott was the president, and he was a very strong one. There was no question in anyone's mind about who was in charge and what the president's duties were. There was even a short period when he served as athletic director.

"Elliott ruled. An example was an incident that occurred in 1940 when the draft came into being. A group of students wanted to have a protest rally. He said, 'No rally,' and there was none. Then these students said they'd protest by walking around the campus with black armbands. He said, 'No black armbands,' and there weren't any.

"Purdue was the main industry in West Lafayette, and engineering pretty much ruled the roost. Men outnumbered women on campus by about six to one.

"When the war started, that ratio changed quickly. Then the Navy V-12 program came along, in which young men took college courses in officers' training. A Marine program was part of that. The Army had special training programs, and the Navy had a program for training pilots. Even some Brazilian pilots were on campus getting training.

"The military was very strong at Purdue during the war. There was a Navy electronics program with four hundred men enrolled. They were enlisted men, and they took over Cary East residence hall. In fact, almost every livable fraternity was taken over by the Navy during the war. And it was a good thing. The members of the fraternities had all gone off to war. The fraternities probably would have folded if it had not been for the Navy.

"Also, one small section of the Manhattan Project on the atom bomb was done at Purdue during the war. It was very secretive.

"Black and Whites." In the mid to late 1940s, these structures—affectionately named for their colors—were built to house the increasing number of new faculty.

"So many service people were on campus that it looked like a military base. Although other universities had these military training programs, too, a lot of guys from all around the Big Ten were sent to Purdue, and some of them were excellent athletes. The Purdue football team was undefeated in 1943.

"Everything changed again after the war when the GI Bill came along. Purdue had a new president at that time. In January of 1945, Frederick L. Hovde arrived on campus to fill that office. And when he got there, the university—as he put it—was just worn out. You couldn't find anything. You couldn't get supplies. You couldn't get anything to build with. You couldn't even get telephone poles. There was no housing. And the university was about to be inundated with thirteen thousand or more students.

"The university started immediately to build some structures, like housing for faculty. The buildings stood where the Married Student Courts stand now. They called them the 'Black and Whites' because the frames were covered with black tar paper and they were trimmed in white. These structures were built for four thousand to five thousand dollars a piece. National Homes [a manufacturer of prefabricated structures] worked on them in the Armory.

"They were crude, but the university rented them because there wasn't any housing in town. At that time, West Lafayette was a town of six thousand people. It was like a lot of sleepy little towns. Students overflowed from the dorms and lived in attics of campus buildings, at the airport, and in a vacant factory building

"I wish you could turn back the clock"

in Lafayette. The field house was used for temporary housing. Then they started bringing in military barracks from bases in the area and building some Quonset houses.

"The university had a rule that prospective students had to have a local address in order to enroll—to make sure they had a place to stay. Actually, some guys who couldn't find a place parked their cars in front of a house and used that address. They slept in their cars, studied in the library, and took showers in the gymnasium until they found a place.

"I lived at home while I went to school, so I didn't have housing problems like other guys did. My dad, A. N. Topping, was an electrical engineering professor who had come to Purdue in 1903. In 1941, he retired, but they called him back to teach during the war years. After the war, he retired again, and they called him back again because of the influx of students under the GI Bill.

"After the war, they had to recruit everyone they could find to teach. I remember I had an algebra course at Purdue from a guy who had taught me math at West Lafayette High School. They called all kinds of professors out of retirement. In fact, if a faculty member's wife had any kind of credentials at all, she was brought in to teach.

"The last year my dad taught was in 1949, and that's when they named him Best Teacher. He had contracted Parkinson's disease. He became so debilitated he couldn't even hold a piece of chalk, so he said, 'That's it.' He was born in 1871, so he was seventy-eight years old when he was finally able to retire.

"In my home, it was always just assumed that I'd go to Purdue. It was taken for granted. There were a few West Lafayette High School students who didn't go on to Purdue, but not many.

"When the war broke out, I was sixteen years old. When I was seventeen years old, I joined the Air Corps Reserve so I could become a cadet when I graduated from high school. I finished

43

high school at an accelerated rate in 1943. I wasn't eighteen yet, which was the required age to go into the military. So I went to Purdue that fall. Purdue was also on a program of accelerated semesters because of the war. I finished one semester. Three weeks after I turned eighteen, I got called.

"I was in the Air Force for two and a half years. I did all my duty in the United States. I was an airplane mechanic. I worked on B-29s.

"I got out in April of 1946, and I worked for a while delivering milk to all the Purdue facilities involved with food. In the fall of 1946, I enrolled in the university, and I finished in February of 1950.

"As far as dating in those days, you'd hope to get one, but you usually didn't. I didn't date much in those years. I guess I had a few dates, but I never went steady or anything.

"I majored in English and I was editor of the *Rivet*, a campus humor publication. The *Rivet* had started in 1947. A buddy and I thought we were funny, so we wrote some stuff and gave it to them. That's how I got started.

"After I graduated, I had a hard time finding a job. I wanted to work for a newspaper, but no one was looking for a newspaperman from Purdue where there weren't many courses in journalism. My first job offer was in the little town of Oxford, Indiana, in Benton County—the *Oxford Gazette*, a weekly.

"Then, the Korean War started in June of 1950, and I was back in the service. I had joined the reserves when I left the Air Force in 1946. I don't know why I decided to join the reserves. I thought it was a good decision at the time. I figured at least if another war broke out I'd be in the Air Force and not an infantryman slogging through the mud. As soon as Korea got going, they were looking for guys who could work on B-29s, so I got called.

"I was sent to a base in California. But I didn't work on B-29s. When they found out I had newspaper experience, they immediately put me to work editing the base newspaper. That was good.

44

"I wish you could turn back the clock"

I got to know a lot of newspaper people in California, and I even had some job offers there when I got out. But I wanted to go back to Indiana.

"The people who went through college at this particular time had some unusual qualities. They were more mature, and by and large, they were people who would not have had a chance to get a college education if it had not been for the GI Bill. This was their chance to make it or break it. Dad said that in all the years he taught his best students were those who came after the war. They did their work and they were serious about it.

"Our class was the largest class that had ever graduated from Purdue. This class came to Purdue when Hovde was just starting his presidency. He liked those students, and they liked him. I'm not sure he knew how to handle the things that happened in the 1960s, when the children of the postwar group came to campus. He was bewildered about why anyone would want to tear the place down.

"I don't know how it was that this group of people who came through the depression and the war had children who made up the 1960s generation. I guess all those people who went to college on the GI Bill and became the first in their family to have a degree then thought all their kids should go to college—without considering that maybe not all the kids belonged there.

"When I think back on those days in the 1940s and early 1950s, I find something interesting. I served in the military during two wars, and I always figured the United States was serious about winning them both. Do you know why?

"Because they didn't let *me* go overseas."

Ode to the Quonsets

By Bette Arkin

A picturesque little village of Quonset huts strange
Takes up most of Stewart Field and the rifle range.

The roofs slope and the windows are set low,
But they're illuminated from within by a florescent glow.
In each petite hut the classrooms two
Resemble the monkey house at the Columbian Park Zoo.
The acoustics are fine so a word is not missed.
The professor is protected from a secret hiss.
The classrooms were crowded and grades start to fall
So the midget village answered the call.
Wading to the knees in clayish mud
Off to class we eagerly trudge.
Classes in the Quonset huts are open to all.
Providing you are not over five feet tall.

PURDUE EXPONENT, OCTOBER 12, 1946

Tom Wilhite

In 1950, the *Debris*, Purdue's student yearbook, was dedicated to the Purdue Man—and "The 1,755 Who Added the Feminine Touch." The editor of that book, which won an All-American award, was Tom Wilhite, a twenty-three-year-old man from suburban St. Louis.

The 1950 *Debris* was a fun book with touches of humor throughout and featured the Purdue Man in classic poses amid pursuit of the classics. The Purdue woman was featured in a supporting secondary role. The concept originated with the book designer that year, and everyone liked the idea.

There was even an all-campus contest to see which male student most resembled the drawn character of the Purdue Man. A junior, Mort Palmer, won. Some people thought he had been the model. He had not.

"I liked the idea," Wilhite, says. "It was different and humorous, instead of being so serious like the books had been before. It really helped publicize the book."

46

"I wish you could turn back the clock"

That year's *Debris* was a great success. But a concept that worked in 1950 with the emphasis on the Purdue Man would cause a furor on modern campuses.

Those were different times.

"In 1950, coeds were a real, real minority on campus," Wilhite says. "Some of them even thought of themselves as fluff—neat to have around but not to be taken seriously. There was only one coed that I knew of in civil engineering, which I studied. She was very attractive but very aloof. I think she was trying to prove she was a serious student. She wore white gloves and a hat to class every day."

Wilhite still lives in the St. Louis area. Married to his high school sweetheart, he has a company that manages condominium and home-owner associations.

Born in 1927, he graduated high school in 1945 and was anxious to get into the war.

"In those days, the whole country was very, very excited with patriotism," he says. "Some of my high school classmates left school early—some of them before their eighteenth birthday if their parents would sign for them. They came back later after the war and finished high school.

"I enlisted in the Air Corps Reserve and went immediately to Purdue. The university was on a three-semester year at that time, so I could start right in. I was going into the Air Corps in the fall, and I wanted to go to Purdue because I thought a semester of college would help me qualify to go into pilot training.

"I got called in at the end of that semester, but the war had ended. The Army didn't have much to offer us, so I ended up in cryptography and got moved around about every two months for a year. I never left the States. I thought I was going to be in for two or three years. But they only needed me for one.

"That summer of 1945 when I was at Purdue was the best time to start college. Because it was summer, the regular students

Remembering how it was

weren't on campus. I think there were only fifteen hundred students on campus.

"It was a small campus. It reminded me of colleges I had read about as a youngster in Tom Swift books—beautiful vine-covered buildings. That's how Purdue struck me. A friend and I boarded a Wabash train in St. Louis, and when we got off in Lafayette, several upperclassmen were waiting to pick us up in a big, black four-door Packard.

"Kappa Sigma fraternity had invited me to stay with them for a week. I pledged and lived there for the summer.

The Whoopurdoo   By Sandy

"WELL, GEORGE, OLD BOY! IT'S SURE GREAT TO HAVE YOU BACK IN THE HOUSE."
(*From the September 1946* Purdue Exponent)

"When I came back in the winter of 1947, it was completely different. There were thousands of people on campus. The fraternity house was so crowded I had to live in a rooming house down the block. The next year the chapter room in the basement was converted to accommodate nine or ten people, and I moved there.

"I was coming back from the military, but I didn't feel like a veteran. As a high school boy, I had wanted to be in the war and fly and be like John Wayne in the movies. But by the time I got in the service, they had shut everything down. I was really disappointed I didn't get into the war and didn't get to fly. I saw all those vets walking around wearing their flight jackets. The whole campus was khaki and olive. I felt kind of embarrassed, so I didn't talk much about my experience. There were guys who had real

"I wish you could turn back the clock"

stories to tell. They were real heroes. I wished I had had the chance.

"It was a wonderful time. We'd gone through the war, and life had been tough even at home with rationing. Then the war was over, and we were very, very excited. There were parades and heroes—times were good.

"You couldn't beat it."

chapter 2

"The loneliness" is disappearing

Some who added the feminine touch

Elynor Erb Richeson

From the mementos on the table, black-and-white snapshots of youth pulled from the long-unopened pages of a photo album, Elynor Richeson picks up a dance card from the Purdue University Junior Prom, 1950.

There are ten lines on the card, ten places to write the names of young men with whom a pretty young woman could dance away the night. But all ten lines have the same name written in: "Gordie," the man she would marry.

Richeson's early life was closer to a nineteenth-century rural lifestyle than to the space age of her later years. She grew up on a farm without electricity and without running water. Baths were taken on Saturday nights when water was warmed on a stove and poured into a metal tub placed in the kitchen. She went to Purdue University at a time when women from rural Indiana did not often do such things.

"I never had a woman in one of my classes."

—GEORGE KOVATCH, PURDUE, 1950

Richeson laughs as she pages through a 1950 *Debris*, Purdue's yearbook. "The Life of the Purdue Man," it says on a title page, picturing a proud-looking young man with pipe and slide rule.

50

The subtitle, "And the 1,775 Who Added the Feminine Touch," depicts a young woman in an apron.

The text reads: "The Purdue Man ignores the weather as he whirls in the college maze. He enrolls for classes and scratches for knowledge. Academics are a necessary evil in a Purdue Man's life. His tensions mount during hardwood and pigskin seasons. . . . Golden silence and noisy fun fill his odd moments."

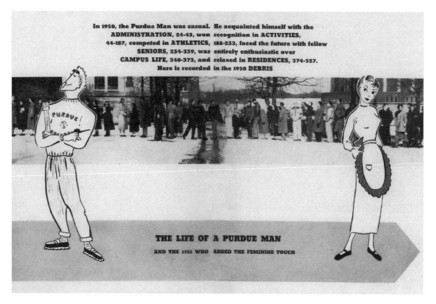

In 1950, the Purdue Man was casual. He acquainted himself with the ADMINISTRATION, 24-43, won recognition in ACTIVITIES, 44-187, competed in ATHLETICS, 188-233, faced the future with fellow SENIORS, 234-339, was entirely enthusiastic over CAMPUS LIFE, 340-373, and relaxed in RESIDENCES, 374-527. Here is recorded in the 1950 DEBRIS

THE LIFE OF A PURDUE MAN
AND THE 1755 WHO ADDED THE FEMININE TOUCH

MAN, OH, MAN. The 1950 yearbook, the Debris, *was dedicated to "The Life of a Purdue Man." Women, added almost as an afterthought, provided "The Feminine Touch."*

In a drawing on one page of the yearbook, the Purdue Man reads a volume titled *How to Stay Single in One Lesson.* On the next page, the apron-wearing young woman reads *How to Catch a Man in Five Lessons.*

"It's interesting. I never paid much attention to this before," Richeson says, paging through the yearbook. "At that time, we

51

girls didn't think there was anything strange about this. Of course, it certainly looks strange today."

She laughs.

Richeson came to Purdue in 1946 to pursue a degree in liberal science. No liberal arts degree was offered at the university. Liberal science was a special program designed for young women of that day who were entering a postwar era of social change. Forty young women were accepted into the program each year.

Richeson, a quiet, delicate-speaking woman, worked after she graduated from Purdue in 1950. She quit when her first child was born. By the 1960s, she was back in the workforce full time as a teacher. She would probably consider herself more a person who took the opportunities offered by a changing time than a social reformer. But she did, indeed, participate in a changing era for women.

"When I went to high school, I didn't take home economics any more than I had to," she says. "It wasn't that I hated it. I just wanted to learn other things. I grew up with two younger brothers and two older brothers, and I think I was a little boyish when I went to Purdue. Most of the girls at Purdue majored in home ec. I thought, 'How much can you learn cooking?' I had been cooking since I was eleven years old—cooking and ironing and doing domestic chores for my brothers. I was interested in studying other things.

"But, you know, back then we didn't have this man-woman thing—this tension that exists today. In school, however, they were trying to encourage us to be something more than housewives. We had a class called "Women in Women's Work."

"You know, there are women in this yearbook who accomplished more than being 'sweethearts' of organizations. We prided ourselves on learning. I took Russian for two semesters way back then just because it was different. I didn't think about how I would

52

"The loneliness is disappearing"

use it. Gordie and I traveled to Russia in 1993, and I was surprised that I remembered enough of the language to be able to read signs and parts of the newspapers."

Richeson was born in 1928 in the small farming community of Francesville. The depression was hard on this area. Her father lost everything in farming and became a hired hand.

"I think of my childhood as happy, but when I look back, we were really quite poor," Richeson says. "We lived off the land—gardens and things like that. I think we moved five times while I was growing up. We'd live in one place until Dad got another job, then we'd move again.

"The first school I went to was a little country school called Fairview. It was a one-room schoolhouse. A big tree grew in front of the school. The tree had a big limb, and there was a gunnysack filled with stuffing hanging from it. We'd climb that tree and swing during recess.

"At the back of the classroom was a stove. I remember there was a family down the road that had many children, which was common in those days. Those children walked to school. I remember this so well—the oldest daughter brought a kettle of soup and set it on the stove in the morning, and it bubbled away. At lunchtime, she got out bowls and served her brothers and sisters.

"During the depression, we ate a lot of vegetables. My mother would can beef. I don't know where she got the beef. It would be cooked, put in jars with the grease poured on top, and sealed—and it would keep.

"We ate chicken. I had to pluck them. One of my brothers or my dad would hold the chicken over a stump, chop its head off, and let it run. It sounds bad when you think about it now, but that's what we did. We let it run so the blood wouldn't splatter. Then we'd dip the chicken in boiling water to loosen the feathers. They came out easily after that.

Some who added the feminine touch

"My mother did a lot of sewing. She'd make things over. If we had an old coat, she would wash the wool, press it, and recut it to make a coat for a younger child. I had four brothers and two sisters.

"We had very little money. Even in college, there was no extra money to do things.

"We had one or two cows. When the pasture land was overeaten, we would take the cows along Indiana 43 and let them eat there. We always had milk and cream and butter.

"I don't remember much about Pearl Harbor. But I remember hearing the song 'Let's Remember Pearl Harbor' on the radio. People used to sing it all the time.

"When the war started, my dad got a job at Kingsbury Ordnance Plant up north. We had more money then.

"I didn't date much in high school. Gas was rationed. I'd go to basketball games and a movie now and then. That's about all we did.

"I had two brothers in the service during World War II. One was never in active combat. The other was in the Pacific, but he was in an evacuation hospital, so we always knew he was farther back from the fighting.

"While I was in high school, our lives were just on hold until this whole thing was over. We thought, Okay, we'll live through this and then the war will end. We just lived one day, then another, and then another.

"We heard about people getting those dreaded telegrams that said a son had died. They put small gold stars in their windows. I heard a story about a man putting money in the bank one day and saying, 'If this war goes on a little longer, I'll be rich.' Another man whose family was affected by the war—so the story goes—socked him in the jaw.

"One thing I always wanted to do was go to school. I knew I wanted to go to college. I loved to learn. I wasn't career oriented.

54

"The loneliness is disappearing"

I didn't think about what I would do with a degree. I just wanted to go to college. I always thought I'd have a husband and a family, and my husband would support the family.

"No one else in my family had been to college. My brothers attended later under the GI Bill. If I hadn't pursued college on my own, I wouldn't have gone. My parents were busy trying to make a living. I said, 'This is what I want to do.' They said, 'That's nice.' It was my principal's interest that helped me get to college. But my parents really sacrificed to keep me there. My mother began working outside the home then.

"My high school class had fewer than thirty students. I think I was the only one in my class who went to college, which wasn't too unusual for a community like ours. There was a competition in our county. I took a test and was awarded one of two scholarships. I came down to Purdue with my principal and met the head of the School of Liberal Science. It was wonderful. It was amazing to me that I was going to be there.

"In the fall of 1946, my parents drove me down to West Lafayette and helped me move into my dorm room in Cary East. That was a men's quad, but they put freshman girls in Cary East. I remember being so excited carrying things to the room. I had one roommate. At home I had always shared an upstairs bedroom, which had very meager furniture.

"There were quite a few boys on campus, and many girls dated older boys. Their mothers warned them to be careful about dating older men, but the girls were very excited. The guys were very serious about school and walked around with their slide rules on their hips. They wore old GI clothes. Many were more interested in finishing their education than in having fun. They were more sophisticated than we were.

"I was a very innocent young girl, and I was serious about my education. I met my future husband within the first year. He

55

was a senior at Jeff High School in Lafayette at that time. I dated him all through school.

"Everything we did for fun, with the exception of an occasional movie, was on campus. There were only a few cars. We walked everyplace. I didn't have any spending money. For fun, Gordie and I used to walk to the Village area. We'd buy some popcorn at a stand called Dad's—and walk.

DAD'S PLACE. *Dad's popcorn stand, where students could also get apples and a smile, was a popular and inexpensive stop on a walking-date.*

"When I was a freshman, for the first six weeks or so, the freshman girls had a 7 P.M. curfew during the week. We could go to the library to study, but if we did, we had to be in by ten. Most of us were in our rooms by seven. After those hours were lifted, curfew was 10 P.M. during the week, 1 A.M. on Friday and Saturday, and 11 P.M. on Sunday. We had to sign out and sign in.

"We had a housemother. And if we had a guest over, she'd walk around and say, 'Remember, girls, keep your feet on the floor.' If you sat on your legs, she'd come back and say, 'Feet on the floor, ladies. Feet on the floor.'

"We used to go to the Sweet Shop and get hamburgers and a Coke. Gordie and I always liked grilled ham-salad sandwiches. He always paid. I don't know where he got his money but he had it.

"On Thursday afternoons, we went to the Hall of Music where they had movie convos. They showed short travelogues, cartoons—little short films. The cost was all included in our fees.

"There were dances. We saw Lawrence Welk, Eddie Howard, Tommy Dorsey, Skitch Henderson, Jimmy Dorsey, and Duke Ellington. This was heaven for a girl from a farming community.

56

"The loneliness is disappearing"

"My mom made my dresses for formal dances: a pink satin brocade—a long gown with a modest neckline and a black velvet ribbon around the waist; a taffeta; and a white organdy with a modest collar.

"Many kids were doing the jitterbug. Gordie and I liked slow dancing. When they played jitterbug music, you could just hold onto each other and sway.

"The junior prom went from eleven o'clock in the evening until four in the morning. Some people went out for dinner beforehand. I don't think we ever did. It was very exciting in the dorm before a dance. The boys would send us corsages. Everyone would be getting ready—pressing and seeing each other's dresses until it was time to go. At four in the morning, we'd come back to the hall for breakfast. You don't get tired when you're that age.

"We invited President Truman to the junior prom. He didn't come.

"We were married in 1950. Gordie had left Purdue and was working at National Homes in Lafayette. We bought a little National Home with all the things I wasn't used to in the home where I grew up. I was excited to be able to go into the kitchen, turn on the faucet, and have running water.

"I went to work for National Homes Acceptance Corporation in the bookkeeping department. After the war, women worked until they got pregnant. I worked until 1952 when we started our family. We had five children, all sons. I wanted to take care of my own children. I didn't want anyone else to do it.

"I didn't go back to work as a teacher until 1966. It just sort of happened. It wasn't something I planned. This year [1995] I am retiring after nearly thirty years of teaching at Saint James Lutheran School in Lafayette.

"Much that is happening today bothers me, such as the lack of respect for institutions. I see things that aren't being taught in

Some who added the feminine touch

the homes—simple customs like table manners and common courtesy. And language—the use of vulgarity troubles me. I'm very concerned about the moral values in this country—the lack of personal responsibility, the idea if you do something bad it's someone else's fault.

"We've seen so much change. Sometimes I wonder where we're going."

Transfer, please!
Liberal science school opens its doors to men

By Pat Mertz

How many of the approximately 10,000 Purdue eds who last spring were weeping many a sad tear into their coffee cups when they considered the disgraceful ratio of 5.43 realized that there were many classes where a ratio of 40 to 0 existed—40 women to 0 men, that is! While the discouraged ed was frantically scanning the schedule of classes for one class which might include one or two of those scarce Purdue coeds, there were many classes just out of his reach labeled "Liberal Science Only."

Men Welcome

Yes, unbelievable as it may seem, right here among the mighty engineers for the past year, Dr. Dorothy Bovee, director of the Liberal Science program, has administered the affairs of the baby of the School of Science, populated by women only. Now that the Liberal Science program has made its place on campus and has received recognition on other campuses, it is being opened to men students this fall.

These men will, of course, be subjected to the same admission requirements as the girls. . . .

Men, as well as women, may now enter the Liberal Science program providing they are interested in a curriculum similar to that of traditional liberal arts, but

58

"The loneliness is disappearing"

one which puts more stress on science. The L.S. student's program is flexible, and he or she need not choose a major until the end of the sophomore year. Then the last two years are spent in more concentrated study of a major field which may be chemistry, statistics, physics, high school teaching, bacteriology, psychology or one of many others. . . .

First called Experimental Science, it became Liberal Science for Women and now it is officially called Liberal Science for Men and Women.

PURDUE EXPONENT, SEPTEMBER 24, 1949

Sarah Margaret Claypool Willoughby

Born in 1917 toward the end of the First World War, Sarah Margaret Willoughby grew up in a time that was only slowly changing from the customs of the nineteenth century to today's fast-paced society. She has lived to see the world change again and again.

Brunette, attractive—a striking beauty in her earlier photographs—she received her Ph.D. from Purdue in chemical engineering in 1950, giving her the distinction of being the first woman to earn a doctorate from Purdue in an engineering discipline.

Willoughby had a career in industry before joining the chemistry faculty at the University of Texas at Arlington in 1954. She retired from teaching there in 1983 and was designated an emeritus professor of chemistry.

She has many stories to relate about her early experiences in a man's world, and she attempts to make humorous those incidents that would greatly incense younger women now. For example, she enrolled at Speed Scientific School, a division of the University of Louisville. The dean of the engineering school called her out of class and told her that her enrollment would have to be canceled because the school "had no facilities to accommodate women." She told him she would do without the bathroom and was not leaving. And she stayed.

Her mail often came to her under the title "Mr." This caused her problems when she was the only woman at conferences where rooms were assigned by pairs. Her confirmations arrived addressed "Mr." and included the name of her male roommate. She would write back saying if she was going to have to room with a man, she would at least like to be allowed to review the applicants.

Born in Bowling Green, Kentucky, Willoughby has a charming quality in her voice that reflects her southern background. This charming quality has not been diminished by the frustrations of being a woman earning her way in a world so dominated by men.

"Bowling Green was a college town," she says. "No industry. Growing up, we went to formal dances arranged by our Cotillion Club. Young ladies wore white kid gloves, took dancing lessons, and belonged to the Junior Music Club. We had teas, played golf and tennis, and swam in the river that bordered the country club. I started piano lessons at age five and golf lessons at age seven. There were lots of wonderful things to do, and there was no worry of drive-by shootings.

"My father was city tax assessor/collector during most of my growing up years, so I was one of those brats that had the run of the city hall offices.

"The stock market crashed in 1929 when I was twelve years old, and the central Kentucky oil boom collapsed about the same time. My father's investments in both were wiped out. He never discussed his troubles, and I never knew how worried he was. Afterwards, we lived pretty much the same—except that the country club membership was forfeited and later I went to a state college rather than a private college as had been planned.

"I had an excellent high school chemistry teacher who was really inspirational, and I decided as a senior in high school that I

"The loneliness is disappearing"

wanted to major in chemistry in college. Whether or not this was showing off, I'm not sure. I enrolled at Western Kentucky University, where I don't ever remember being harassed as the only girl in class. I was very young, and they just sort of babied me.

"I graduated in 1938 at the age of twenty, married almost immediately, and went to Louisville with my husband, John Richard Evans II. The following year we had a child, a boy. After Pearl Harbor and the beginning of World War II, my husband enlisted in the U.S. Army Air Corps as an aviation cadet. In December of 1942, he was killed in an airplane crash during his training. He was within six weeks of getting his officer's commission.

"During 1942, I had been working for the Curtiss-Wright Corporation as a junior engineer, but after my husband's death, I decided to return to school. Among other possibilities, I was offered a technical assistant position—essentially a fellowship—at Purdue in 1944, which I accepted.

"I thought the Purdue campus was beautiful. The Navy V-12 program was in progress, and it was wonderful to see the men in uniform marching to class every morning.

"In 1948, I remarried, and in 1950, I graduated from Purdue with a Ph.D. In the years that followed, I had two more children.

"I worked for Monsanto Chemical Company in Boston for several years and then in 1954 came to the University of Texas in Arlington, where I taught and did some engineering consultant work for a Dallas firm, continuing this work after retirement. I have only been idle a few years.

"I was inducted into the Hall of Distinguished Alumni at Western Kentucky University in 1994. I was appointed a Kentucky Colonel in 1989 and a Distinguished Citizen of the State of Texas in 1973.

"It didn't occur to me while I was doing all this that it was unusual for a woman. But as I look back on it, I realize I was a real trailblazer. Very few other women had professional careers at that

Some who added the feminine touch

time. When I went to Louisville to look for work in 1939, the first question they always asked was 'Are you married?' When I said, 'Yes,' they said, 'Sorry, we don't hire married women. We have to keep the available jobs for men supporting families.'

"Even after the end of the war, I was never paid as much as a man, and this was a real concern. My husband had died and I had a small child. I can assure you, had I spoken out about the injustices, they would have told me to just go out and find another job.

"Of all the difficulties that career women had in the forties and fifties, though, the worst was the lack of female role models and female peers. These days there are many women who give moral support and encouragement to each other in their attempts to advance intellectually and professionally. And I've tried to provide that to the young women in my classes and to others of my acquaintance.

"The loneliness is disappearing."

Kris Kreisle Harder

In the fall of 1946 when she came to Purdue from Tell City in southern Indiana, her name was Kris Kreisle, and she knew what she wanted to find at college.

"I went to Purdue because my brother was studying engineering there," she says. "But I really came to get my 'Mrs.' degree. Which I did."

It really wasn't as obvious as she says. But it was on her mind.

Her mother had graduated in 1918 from Indiana University at a time when women didn't often go to college. Her mother had taught before becoming a wife and mother.

Harder's father had studied at Michigan. He ran the family lumberyard through the hard years of the depression. By 1946, those hard financial times were long gone—but not forgotten.

"I was the youngest of four children, and my mother always said she wanted all of us to get a college education," Harder says.

"The loneliness is disappearing"

"She said you can lose your money, but they can't take your education away from you. But I also hoped to find a husband at Purdue. We all did. We thought that was important, and most of us were married at twenty-one. I was."

Harder lives in Garden City, New York—a state she never expected to make home when she was growing up in Indiana near the Ohio River. She owns a business, The Pear Tree Shoppe, a fine-gift store. Before she started that, she raised her children. When she was going to Purdue, she had no thought of someday owning her own store. She really gave little thought to a career.

"I had no career plans at all," Harder says. "My brother's college had been interrupted by the war. He had been in the Marines and was a junior at Purdue when I was a freshman.

"When I started college, I was really homesick. I was homesick until the spring of my freshman year. But college was great. We lived in Cary Hall, only one dorm for girls surrounded by boys' dorms. I had come from a small high school, and this big university overwhelmed me at first. But now when I look back on it, my four years at Purdue were among the best years of my life.

"We were young and carefree. The war was over. I remember spring and spring evenings at Purdue. We were on campus until the beginning of June. May was a neat time to be on campus—the honeysuckle was in bloom and it smelled so good. The fraternities and the sororities had parties, and we'd go to the Tippecanoe River and swim.

"Purdue was in its heyday. All the boys had come back on the GI Bill. We had all these wonderful formal dances—about six a year—with big-name bands. We got all dressed up in formals and tuxedos.

"I met my husband, Frank, at Purdue during my sophomore year at a broom dance in the student union. The guys took brooms to the dance. When a guy cut in on a couple, he handed the broom to the guy he was cutting in on. Then that guy had to dance with the broom until he cut in on someone else.

Some who added the feminine touch

"I was dancing with one of Frank's fraternity brothers. Frank wanted to meet me, so they had set it up. Frank cut in and handed his friend the broom. Frank and I started dating. Because he was on the track team, he was away a lot on weekends, so I didn't want to commit to only dating him. I wouldn't have been able to go out on weekends. So we dated on and off. We got pinned, then depinned, and then engaged in June of my senior year. In September of 1950, we got married.

"Frank was my age, but I thought he was older and had been in the Navy because he wore a Navy jacket around campus with his last name on it. It was his dad's.

"The ratio of boys to girls was great. It was something like five to one. The only problem with Purdue then was, unless you were bright enough to be in engineering, which I was not, the curriculum was very limited for women. We had home ec and the School of Science.

"I majored in home ec. I wasn't science oriented. I have to admit home ec was not the greatest thing. We studied foods and nutrition, and I took a lot of psychology courses because I was going to be a nursery school teacher. I had to take sewing courses and cooking courses.

"Our program had a practice house. Six women would live in the practice house for six weeks. We had to take care of it— keep it clean, cook our own meals, and do everything we would do in our own house. It really was a fun experience.

"I joined a sorority, Pi Phi. We had hours in the sorority houses and in the dorms. We had to be in at 11 P.M. on weekdays and 1 A.M. on weekends. I was president of the sorority, so my job was to shove all the men out the front door at eleven or one. When I was in the dorms, the housemothers made sure you were in. Now girls going to college can stay out all night, and who knows where they are.

"Having hours was a great excuse to go home if you had a dull date. Oh, once in awhile, we'd sneak in late through the back

"The loneliness is disappearing"

door. But not too often. We respected authority. We did what we were supposed to do.

"There were pinning serenades after hours. It was so much fun. We would be getting ready for bed. The fraternity would come to the house, and we'd all go out on the porch. The girl who had just been pinned and was being serenaded would stand together with her pin man while the fraternity guys sang to them. Then the sorority would sing. I was just telling my children how wonderful it was.

"On Thursday night and Sunday night, we dressed up for dinner. We wore heels and hose. We always had a hostess at the table, and you couldn't eat until she ate. We learned all the social graces. Living with that many other women, you learned how to cope with a lot of things. I always had roommates, and we had to squeeze our clothes into tiny closets.

"After I finished at Purdue, I raised my children. We had five. When my youngest child was four years old, three of my friends and I decided the town we lived in needed a needlepoint shop. We started with our own needlepoint and craft items, and we took everything else on consignment. It was a lark, we thought. But it grew and it grew, and we moved from one location to a better location to an even better location. When needlepoint died out in popularity, we dropped it, and we sold very fine gifts and accessories. Of the original four girls who were partners, I'm the only one still in it. There are five of us partners now. It has really meant a lot to me. It was my idea and I developed it.

"There's been a lot change since I graduated from Purdue— the whole social thing in women's lives. I have to admit I'm not a women's liberationist. I am glad I stayed home with my children before I went to work. I have two married daughters who went to college, and they're staying home with their children, so is my daughter-in-law. They're all mothers like I was. They'll work when their children are older. But now, they're home and I'm glad. Staying home with my children was a fun part of my life.

65

Some who added the feminine touch

"Now, working is great. I love it. It's a challenge and a great experience to develop something from nothing.

"A lot of women my age wish they had done something like this."

Junior prom at Memorial Union from 11 p.m. to 4 a.m.

Coed hours 5 a.m.; 6 a.m. if residence serves breakfast

Skitch Henderson and Russ Morgan will provide the music for the Junior Prom in the Union Ballrooms and the Faculty Lounges tonight. Dancing will begin at 11 p.m. and end at 4 a.m. . . .

Every fifth couple will be given a stub on entering the dance which will entitle them to participate in the Grand March at midnight. . . .

Prom night will be one long evening of entertainment from the time dancers enter the Union into a land of fairy people and Mother Goose nursery stories. Many of the well known characters from Mother Goose will be on display throughout the building.

PURDUE EXPONENT, APRIL 23, 1948

Dancers outwit Morpheus at prom with caffeine, bottles

By Norma Knaub

Are you one of the lucky students who will attend the prom this year? That blissful night and morning of music, dancing, strapless gowns and rented tuxedos! Don't let the late hours disturb you. There are numerous ways to get yourself through the entire evening so you won't have to miss one precious minute.

Cat bad business

Of course, it is a pity that you must idle away so much of the evening before you get started. A rough and tough

"The loneliness is disappearing"

bridge game should help you pass away the time till zero hour. Only a sucker will take a cat nap. . . . Nappers may sleep through and miss the big moment. Yes sir, the best policy is to stay awake. Anyone who can't stay awake 24 hours without sleeping is either a freshman or a sissy.

Eyelid propping scoop

Several cups of black coffee taken at 15 minute intervals will help. . . . Some people advocate the deft placing of toothpicks between the eyelids to disguise that languid look. . . .

Do you wear glasses? If not, you would be very wise to rush right down to Kresge's and purchase some becoming spectacles. By neatly embellishing the lenses with painted wide-awake eyes, you will create a big impression. . . .

Out of bounds for kids

Another method for creating the life of the party appearance is available to those students considered adults by the State of Indiana. Less merit is attributed to this method than any of the others. It has been tested on several occasions and found to have definite disadvantages. The expense is one factor to be considered. Depending on the capacity of the individual the cost will vary, but it can consume most of a month's allowance if not watched carefully. The effects of the above-mentioned method have also been investigated and the results are appalling.

Purdue Exponent, April 22, 1948

Sally Papenguth Bell

Sally Bell lives in Corvallis, Oregon, the wife of a university professor. She studied psychology at Purdue University and at one

Some who added the feminine touch

point had it in her mind to become a counselor. She became a secretary, then a wife, and then a mother.

She is the daughter of "Pappy" Papenguth, the swimming coach at Purdue for thirty years, including the time she was at the university. He was the swimming and diving coach of the 1952 U.S. Olympic team.

"We moved from Indianapolis to West Lafayette in 1939," Bell says. "My father had been the coach of the Indianapolis Athletic Club for thirteen years, and he took the swimming coach job at Purdue in part to help my brother and me get an education. Money was tight.

"On Pearl Harbor Day, I was reading the Sunday funnies, lying on the living room floor. We were all quite shocked, but I don't recall that we did anything special.

"We listened to the radio a lot. I had a habit of listening to the radio. I had a table-model radio of my own, and I can remember listening to the fireside chats of Franklin Delano Roosevelt. I remember I was in Chicago with the girls' swimming team when FDR died, and that was a shock to me. I was walking along and I heard people say Roosevelt had died. I couldn't believe it. A chill went down my spine when I realized what had happened.

"I loved to listen to the radio. I liked those fifteen-minute daytime programs. They were like soap operas. I guess I listened to anything that was on. When my folks wanted to know what was on the radio, they'd ask me because I always knew the schedule. I can remember lying awake at night and listening to 'I Love a Mystery,' 'The Shadow,' and 'The Green Hornet.' It was more fun than television, which came later. You created pictures in your mind of what was happening.

"The war years in West Lafayette were odd, really. A lot of military people were around. The Navy V-12 program and other military programs were on campus. We had ROTC students living in our house.

"The loneliness is disappearing"

"Many of the young men who swam for my dad either enlisted or were drafted. My brother was in the service, but he was never sent overseas to fight. He was sent to Okinawa after the war.

"I graduated from high school in 1946 and started at Purdue that fall. It cost my father only twenty-five dollars a semester. Since he worked at the university, all I had to pay were student fees. I pledged Kappa, but I lived in at home.

"I majored in psychology. I always intended to go into counseling, but I never went to graduate school.

"I was active in theater groups but very rarely on stage. I did a lot of backstage work, such as carpentry. That's how I met my husband, Dick. We both worked at play shop. We did carpentry work and built sets, and then a big group of us went out together. Dick had an old car, a broken-down old coupe. A coat hanger held up its exhaust pipe. He had torn the back out and put in a seat. Sometimes when we all went out together, I'd wind up in his car, and sometimes he'd take me home.

"I was on a private swimming team coached by my dad. It was a Lafayette team with a lot of kids from the country club. Purdue did have a girls' swimming team, but they didn't travel. They'd stay in their pool and do times, then compare their times with other schools' times.

"I did some on-air work at the campus radio station, WBAA. I read character parts from scripts for 'School of the Air.' They were simple sketches. Sometimes I did the sound effects for these programs. For sound, we actually slammed little doors and did other easy effects. But city noises, trains, planes, cars, or crowds were generally recorded on devices called transcriptions and played on turntables.

"One summer I went to business school and took secretarial training, typing, and shorthand. So after I graduated from college, I went to work at the radio station as secretary to the manager. As people left, I handled their jobs and wound up also being the

Some who added the feminine touch

receptionist. In addition, I did 'Lady Storyteller' on the radio, reading children's stories. It was fun.

"Dick graduated in 1952. He graduated one day, and the next day we got married and left for California in his car. He had bought a new car from his dad. Just before we got married, we packed everything we had in that car and hid it in a garage so it wouldn't get filled with rice.

"My husband had a job in San Francisco with Bechtel. He was at his new job only two months when the Korean War started and his draft came up. So we drove back to Lafayette where he dropped me off, and he went into the Army.

"While he was gone, I worked in Lafayette as a secretary at Ross Gear. When I was able to go to the base where he was stationed, I got a job as a secretary at the hospital. After I was there for a year, we were sent to California. The Army was going to send him overseas, but the Korean War ended.

"Dick decided to go back to college because he wanted to teach. We returned to Purdue where he got a master's degree on the GI Bill. We had a baby, so I raised the baby while he went to school. Eventually, we had another child when he went back to Purdue for a Ph.D.

"Both of our children are girls. One works for the state police in Salem, Oregon. The other is an assistant professor and researcher at the University of Southern California.

"I never actually worked in psychology. I was mostly a secretary. My mother told me while I was still in school, 'You ought to get some secretarial training because you can always get a job as a secretary. If there's another depression, they always need secretaries.' It was nice to have those skills to fall back on.

"In my life, I never had the feeling I wasn't doing what I wanted to do. My mother always told me I could do whatever I wanted. After we had children, what I wanted to do was stay home and take care of the family."

70

"The loneliness is disappearing"

Coed swim squad schedules intercollegiate aquatic meets

By Merlita Forsythe

An eager bunch of University Coeds met to discuss plans for forming a women's swimming squad. The plans were just in their infant stage and needed some maturing.

The formation of this squad seemed to be a natural trend because there was a growing interest in swimming activities for women on campus. In the past, there had not been much competition or incentive to improve swimming skill for those girls who were top quality. . . .

Only three practices a week are the amount required to keep in training. . . .

It is interesting to see how this "baby" matured through the enthusiasm of a few girls.

Purdue Exponent, January 16, 1948

Mary Zenger Byers

When Mary Zenger Byers ("Tootie") came to Purdue University from Concordia, Kansas, in the fall of 1946, she was following in the footsteps of Doris, her older sister. Doris Zenger had been one of the first women to enroll in the university's aeronautical engineering program. Those were the days when women prepared for teaching careers in home economics.

Byers thinks, however, that the beginnings of the women's movement predate both her and her sister.

"We often consider our daughters as the leaders in the feminist movement," Byers says. "Not so in my thinking. I think of my mother, Vera Zenger. Back in Kansas, she was widowed when she was thirty-seven years old, but she was a real motivator. She brought my sister Doris up on Amelia Earhart and me up on Jane Addams of Hull House fame. She always pushed college as necessary for her daughters. Even when we were in grade school in

71

Some who added the feminine touch

our rural Kansas community, she'd say, 'My daughters will go to college.'"

Byers talks quickly. You feel that she has so much to say she's hurrying to get it all in. She was very busy with activities in college, such as being associate editor of the *Debris* yearbook and a member of Pi Beta Phi sorority. She has been that way her entire life.

"As children of a farmer, my sister and I never went without food during the depression era," she says. "My mother was a tremendous seamstress and made our clothes. I got my first store-bought dress when I was a sophomore at Purdue. We didn't have electricity in our house until I was eight years old. I was ten when we had our first house with an indoor toilet.

"I was ten and my sister was thirteen years old when our father was killed in a train accident in 1939. After that, my mother started working two jobs. She was in charge of yard goods at a department store, and she worked at a grocery store at night. She also sewed. She had dreams that we were going to college and were going to finish.

"My mother's father made her quit school after her junior year of high school to take care of the other children in the family. Her mother had been killed in a train accident. My grandfather didn't believe in education for girls. He certainly would not let any daughter of his graduate from high school ahead of his only son.

"My mother was a marvelous basketball player. She loved Latin and geometry. She had dreams. But her daddy didn't have those dreams for her.

"My sister went to Purdue to study aeronautical engineering, and when my time came, my mother felt comfortable sending me where my sister was. I majored in sociology and psychology.

"I remember the hardest part of going to Purdue that first year was getting there. I had to go by train through Chicago. My mother told me there would be bad people in Chicago. I had to

"The loneliness is disappearing"

change train stations there, and I carried my own bags so I wouldn't have to talk with anyone.

"At Purdue, I lived in Cary Hall East on the third floor, and I liked the people. Everything looked great to me. I was ready for a new experience and never even stopped to think that I would be in a class with so many GIs.

"There were so many more guys than girls! I kept a date book, and I still have it. The other day I counted. In all of my high school years, I had twelve dates. When I met my husband during my senior year at Purdue, he was my ninety-ninth date. I didn't get to a hundred.

"I was a teetotaler my entire experience at Purdue. Kansas was a dry state. As a teenager, I was not surrounded by beer parties or any alcoholic drinking. Some of the drinking I saw at Purdue bothered me. There were too many coeds that I had to help put to bed.

"I went back to Kansas after I graduated, and I taught in a rural school. I got married in the Presbyterian Church in Lafayette in May of 1951.

"From 1952 to 1960, I was the first paid youth worker for the Methodist Church in Whitefish Bay, Wisconsin, in suburban Milwaukee. I got paid sixty dollars a month for ten hours per week.

"From 1952 to 1959, I helped my husband, Morgan, an All-American swimmer at Purdue, start the first co-ed swim club in Wisconsin. No salary for seven years. Just love.

"I had three children, and I did what most mothers of our era did—PTA, Boy Scout leader, Girl Scout leader, Sunday school teacher.

"When the kids were off to college, Mom went back to work. However, my earlier education was now obsolete. I joined the staff at Cardinal Stritch College. I had to compete for a job against kids coming out of college who had many skills I didn't have. If a woman drops out of the workforce for any length of time, she'll

Some who added the feminine touch

have a difficult time getting work in her own field again because too much will have happened and changed. She has to be retrained.

"In 1978, I started race-walk competition for women. My son had been an all-America race walker in college, and he thought it would help my leg strength. So Mom became one of the first women competitive race walkers in the country and garnered eleven age-group records along the way from 1978 to 1983. At that point, my left knee said, 'No more.' Then I found out I had lupus and fibromyalgia.

"So, I became one of the first nationally certified USA track-and-field women's race-walk judges. If you can't compete, judge.

"When I think about it, I put my life on hold all those years to be a housewife and mother. Daughter Robin has a bachelor's degree, an M.B.A., and a law degree. My son, Jay, a geophysicist, has a master's degree. Daughter Polly, a costume designer, received an M.F.A. from Purdue in 1994. None of my children had to take out loans for their education. I put my life in a secondary position for them and for my husband, who has three degrees, two from Purdue and one from Notre Dame.

"I get asked the question, Why did I do that? Why did I do all those menial jobs so all these other people wouldn't have to take out loans? My actions were very typical of women who grew up in my era. We were brought up in puritanical times. Our job as women was to see to it that family life ran smoothly.

"And we put our own lives second to that."

74

"The loneliness is disappearing"

chapter 3

"Times were very tough"

The Great Depression's lifelong effects

Kenneth Johnson

Kenneth Johnson ("K. O.") was born in 1922. He grew up on farms in Missouri and Arkansas in the days when homes had no electricity, when light came from lanterns, when baths were Saturday-night rituals in metal tubs placed in the kitchen. He grew up with wood-burning stoves, cold bedrooms, and horse-drawn equipment in the fields. He grew up looking at the sky and watching planes fly overhead, wondering what flying would be like.

When he was a boy going to a one-room schoolhouse during the hungry depression years, Johnson knew what he wanted to do. He did not yet know the name for that kind of work. But he knew what he wanted to do.

He grew up to design and build airplane engines for General Motors and General Electric. He came up with twenty-five to thirty patents. He now lives in Cincinnati.

Johnson is a very mild-mannered man. His hair is combed forward. Sitting in the lobby of the Purdue University lecture hall built by donations from the Class of 1950, he never stops smiling as he remembers. Even hard times can be pleasant when you remember them fifty years later. You were young then.

"My father died when I was a year and a half old," Johnson says. "My mother remarried. There were five children in our family and five children in my stepfather's family. We had a forty-acre farm in Missouri and then moved to an eighty-acre farm in Arkansas.

"I remember during the depression I had no idea what money really was. There was no money for children. I had two toys—a little truck and a little car my aunt had given me. I still have them.

"We mostly had enough to eat, but we ate an awful lot of beans. During the winter, food wasn't so plentiful.

"I went to a one-room school surrounded by mud. I'm proud of my education there. I was at the top of my class. Of course, I was also at the bottom because it was a class of one. When we started, there was one other boy in the class, but by the fourth or fifth grade, his family decided it was time for him to go to work. There had been a girl in the class, too, but she got sick.

"In the one-room school, it was all reciting. The teacher would bring each class to the front of the room, and the pupils in that class would recite. My problem was that I listened so much to the classes ahead of me I didn't do my own studying. I had only two teachers who had some college training. The rest were all high school graduates.

"We didn't have any electricity until I was in high school. We had gas lanterns and you went to bed when it got dark. There wasn't much to do after dark anyway. We got up pretty early, too.

"I remember our first refrigerator. It operated on kerosene because we didn't have electricity. Before that, we had a box for cooling, and when we watered the cattle, we pumped the water through it. The water cooled the box a little. We kept milk in the box. It was better than leaving the milk sit outside.

"The outhouse was out back, and we took baths in a number three washtub. The cookstove heated the kitchen, and a wood-burning stove heated the living room. The rest of the house wasn't heated. We all slept in unheated bedrooms.

"We considered ourselves much better off than a lot of people in the depression because we had food. Many people didn't.

"Times were very tough"

"In Arkansas, where we lived, to attend high school, pupils had to pay tuition and provide their own transportation and books. Going to high school was actually more difficult than going to college. I wanted to go to high school.

"I always knew what I wanted to do. Back then I didn't know what it was called, but I knew what I wanted to do. We grew cotton on the farm, and when an airplane flew overhead, I paid more attention to it than to my work in the fields.

"Many kids dropped out of school before the eighth grade. My stepfather supported my continuing in school. He had to drop out when he was eight or nine years old. My mother had been to high school.

"I graduated from high school in 1941. I signed up to go to a Baptist liberal arts college in Arkadelphia, Arkansas, and it didn't offer what I was looking for. So I went to St. Louis and stayed with a stepbrother and took a class in aircraft riveting. When I finished, I became a short-order cook at a White Tower restaurant, which competed with White Castle. I was told if I didn't work more than two weeks, I wouldn't get paid. I got a job at Curtiss-Wright, so I didn't get paid at White Tower.

"I was trained as a riveter, but I was hired at Curtiss-Wright as a short-order cook. I got a riveting job with them later.

"Even before Pearl Harbor, I had decided I wanted to be a pilot, so I signed up for a cadet program. But they had so many people signed up, I kept working until I got called. I signed up with the Army Air Corps and the Navy Cadet programs. I also tried to sign up with the Marines, but I was too short.

"I didn't get called until January of 1943. By that time, the Army Air Corps had so many people signed up for their cadet program that they had to either call us or turn us loose to the draft. So they called me—along with several thousand others.

"I remember at a flight training school in Kansas in late 1943 or early 1944 an instructor named Valish was flying with a student

The Great Depression's lifelong effects

who wasn't doing well with his aerobatic flying. The instructor told the student to turn the plane upside down and hold it there until he told him to go on over. Well, the student turned the plane upside down and waited for Valish to tell him to go on over. But the instructor didn't say anything. So the student turned around and looked at the seat behind him.

"Valish wasn't there. He had fallen out. He had opened the canopy partially because the sun was hot even in the winter, and he had fallen out. One of his boots was hanging on the canopy. The student called the tower, and he was so panicked they had to calm him down. They told him to go look for the instructor. He finally saw Valish in his parachute dropping through the clouds. We all had parachutes.

"I trained in a P-47. It was fall of 1944 before I went to Europe. The crossing by boat took fifteen days. I was seasick the first four or five. They had a movie on board called *The Male Animal*. They showed it over and over. The theater was right outside my door. By the time we reached England, I knew every line.

"In England, I had a date with a girl from Stratford, and she was going to take me to meet her parents. But I was moved to Paris and missed our date. In Paris, they assigned us to the Forty-eighth Fighter Group, which was somewhere in the vicinity of Castle, Germany, but they weren't sure exactly where. It took us two weeks to find our group.

"The barracks there were great. It was an old German training field, but the runway was short. It was too short for us to take off with our bombs. So we went on strafing missions. We flew two hundred feet above the ground and hit anything that moved.

"I never really saw anything move. The first time I saw a German airplane was at the end of the war. The Germans were trying to get to Switzerland. We forced one plane down, and the pilot, his wife, a boy, and a dog all got out of this two-seat plane.

"Times were very tough"

"When the war in Europe was over, I stayed in Germany to train for the Pacific. We had just shipped out from France when the Japanese surrendered. They heard I was coming and gave up.

"When I got out, I was looking for an engineering school, and a friend recommended Purdue. I had the GI Bill and that was helpful. I had also saved thirty-five hundred dollars, which was some great pile of money in those days.

"I came to Purdue in January of 1946, and everything was in order except I didn't have a place to live. A good friend of mine, John Leamon—we wound up marrying sisters—found me a place to stay in Stockwell, a half-hour drive out in the country.

"I stayed there two or three weeks. The university was building temporary dorms, and I wanted to get in those. To do that, however, I had to move to the field house first. The field house was nice—it had a pool—but it was challenging. Weight-lifting equipment was hanging over my bunk. I lived there for two months, and then I got into the temporary dorms.

"The temporary dorms were better than the field house. Of course, they didn't have a swimming pool. They were wood. They didn't seem cold or too bad to me, but all my life I had never been accustomed to much.

THE RITZ THEY WEREN'T. But for the single male student occupants, these and similar structures were a step up from a factory, basement, or attic.

"School was fun. I did a little golfing. I had a car and I was always busy keeping it running. Girls were scarce. I spent a lot of time in Lafayette getting acquainted with girls. When I met my wife, she had already graduated and was teaching in town. She graduated in 1948. I always say she's older because she graduated first. Of course, she didn't go to war.

79

"Purdue and the Class of 1950 were fantastic. They gave me a new world, and they allowed me to do things I always wanted to do. I never have been able to understand people who don't know what they want to do, because all my life I've known—all my life, since I stood in those cotton fields and watched a plane flying up above.

"I studied aeronautical engineering in school. I finally found out that's what they called the thing I wanted to do."

Gordon Kingma

Wearing a hunter-green sweater on a warm Saturday afternoon in February, Gordon Kingma sits at his kitchen table drinking coffee. There are bird feeders outside the window. His refrigerator door is covered with pictures of his ten grandchildren.

His wife, Barb, is in another room in their new ranch home outside of Lafayette, Indiana. Whenever Kingma cannot remember a fact or date, he calls to her for help.

He is the retired president of the Greater Lafayette Chamber of Commerce. Before that, he retired from Lafayette National Bank. He now writes business news for the *Journal and Courier*, Lafayette's daily newspaper. He just does not like staying home with little to do.

Kingma is a friendly man who likes to smile. But when the conversation turns serious, he lowers his brow and speaks with emphasis and determination.

He was born in Lafayette in 1925, shortly before the start of the depression. His dad worked all those years. During part of the depression, his grandfather and an uncle who lived nearby came for evening meals.

"I remember at dinner my mom always said, 'Save the meat for the men. They've been working hard,'" Kingma says.

"Times were very tough"

"We always had food and clothes, but there was a great deal of unemployment in Lafayette. At Saint Lawrence School, where I went, they asked us to turn in our hand-me-down clothes, and they were given to the poor kids. It was kind of embarrassing. Sometimes you'd see a kid wearing a sweater you had turned in two days ago.

"After eighth grade, I went to Saint Francis Seminary in Cincinnati. I was going to become a priest. I suppose that was because of the influence of the sisters and priests at school. They were always pushing the youngsters they thought could handle the academics.

"Early in my second year at seminary, I couldn't get out of bed one morning. They didn't know what the devil it was. They blamed it on muscle cramps. Whatever hit me hit me in September. I stayed in school until Christmas, and when I got home, the family doctor told me what I had.

"Polio.

"He suggested I stay home and go to Saint Elizabeth Hospital for so-called therapy. They strapped my feet on a stationary bike and I pumped around. They used an electric machine on me. They put a pad on my foot and another on my back and shot an electrical shock through to revive those nerves. It didn't hurt anything. It didn't help anything either. There was a lot of polio in those days. Everybody thought it was the result of going to swimming pools. I didn't even know that President Roosevelt had suffered from polio. They sheltered people from that information.

"I stayed home that semester, but I was mobile. I worked at the soda fountain in Hooks Drugstore downtown. I didn't have any pain at all. But my left leg is a little smaller than my right. I got through it somehow. I'm really very lucky. The following September I went back to school.

"After the first semester of my senior year, I decided I didn't want to become a priest. I came home and finished at Jefferson High School in Lafayette.

The Great Depression's lifelong effects

"I graduated in 1944 on a Friday night. On Monday morning, I walked into the *Journal and Courier* newspaper office, asked for a job, and was hired.

"I was eighteen years old, and that was right about the time of D-Day. Many guys I knew were in the service, and there I was 4-F because of the polio. A lot of my friends were flying airplanes and I wanted to go. It was the thing to do. Patriotism was just enormous in the country.

"Although I'd had polio, I looked good. I'm sure people looked at me and said, 'What's he doing here when my son has to go.' There were times it was embarrassing. But in retrospect, I was pretty darn lucky. One of my classmates was a prisoner of war in Germany. Another guy—he just got shot to pieces. A couple of guys didn't come back at all.

"I played sax and clarinet in a dance band at the USO [United Service Organizations]. I got to see the guys in service, and I felt a little more a part of it. There was some great music then—'People Will Say We're in Love,' 'Twilight Time,' 'I Don't Get Around Much Anymore,' 'In a Sentimental Mood,' 'Stormy Weather,' 'Smoke Gets in Your Eyes.'

"I had a job at the paper, but I was confused. I really didn't know what I wanted to do. I was the only reporter on the street until the end of the war. I did everything. We worked seven days a week.

"You can't believe what downtown Lafayette was like on the dates of the surrender of the Germans and Japanese. It was wall-to-wall people. It was just like the picture you see from New York with that sailor kissing that girl. People were running in and out of the *Journal and Courier* newsroom getting last-minute bulletins. The church bells were ringing. I don't remember if I wrote a story about it or not, but I sure remember being out there and having fun.

"I started at Purdue in 1946 taking night classes. I'd go to work from 7:30 A.M. until 4:30 P.M., then I'd go to class. It sounds hard, but I was young, and I don't remember its being hard. Purdue

"Times were very tough"

was a great experience for me. It was neat to be around other people pursuing education. There was not much fooling around. Classes were dead quiet, serious. People really worked.

"My family had a big house, and we took in a student. He was a young guy from Pittsburgh who was majoring in poultry management. He had a Model A Ford in perfect condition, except the radiator leaked. One day he put in a quart of stuff they give hens to harden eggshells, and that ruined the radiator.

"I did work at the Purdue radio station, too. That was a nice time of my life.

"One of the big pressures coming out of the depression was being financially solvent. You got a job and you saved money. My mother and father did not encourage me to quit work and go to school full time. They said, 'You've got a good, steady job, one of the best in town. Be satisfied.'

"I never did finish at Purdue. I didn't get a degree. At the rate I was going, it would have taken me a long time.

"I got married in 1952.

"The group going through school at that time was a very ambitious group. Everything had come to a standstill from 1941 to 1945. Our complete attention was focused on defeating our enemies. When that was done, it was 'Boy, let's get going. Let's establish some leadership in the community and the world.'

"After winning the war, we all were exhilarated. Our emphasis had been on winning. We grew up wanting to win everything. It's questionable if we did win, but we felt we'd won because the other guys put up the white flag.

"We wanted families and nice homes. We wanted all the nice things that had been denied to us during the depression and the war. We wanted good, healthy lives. A lot of my friends had six to nine children—the Baby-Boom generation. That wasn't unusual then. It would be today.

"We wanted to be successful."

83

The Great Depression's lifelong effects

Norman Coats

In the knob country of southern Indiana, Norman Coats grew up near the log cabins where his grandfather and his great grandfather had settled. He might be there himself today, he says—along with his children and grandchildren—but for the extraordinary events of his generation.

Coats, of St. Louis, is a retired vice president of Ralston Purina. He talks with enthusiasm and self confidence. He knows what he thinks about his generation. He has been considering the subject all his life.

His hair is graying now and receding a bit. He has some lines of experience on his face. But in 1944 when he graduated from high school, he was a smooth-faced, dark-haired youth with a look about him that the world was his.

"It's interesting," he says. "I was thinking about this just the other day. From the grade school I went to, not one other boy among my schooolmates even graduated from high school. You can see what the educational opportunities were."

He was born in 1925, dirt poor, before the depression began. His father was a berry grower and truck farmer, taking produce to a market in Louisville.

His family had no radio in their home when he was a boy. The first radio arrived in 1940. It was battery operated, and it didn't work much of the time. To keep butter from melting, the family had to take it down to a little hollow and put it in the spring where the water was fresh and cool. There was no electricity. Toilets were out back. Baths were taken in a big tub hauled into the kitchen for the occasion. Water was carried inside, heated on the woodstove, and one after the other, the children bathed, the eldest first.

"I was second," Coats says.

It was a humble beginning. When Coats talks about this time, you get the feeling he'd like to go back and live it again.

"Times were very tough"

"I came out of the knob country of southern Indiana," he says of those wooded hills. "My people had been in that country since before the state came into the Union. My people had never been to college.

"I was born up in the hills from Borden, which is about twenty-five miles from Louisville on the Indiana side. My dad was a farmer. The land was poor. We farmed the hills and ridges, and it wasn't easy. My grandfather and great grandfather lived in log houses. My great-grandfather built his after the Civil War—a half mile from where I was born and raised.

"Times were very tough. People didn't have any money. When we got a few dollars, my mom always said it wasn't for spending, it was for saving for a bad time—for a rainy day. We were already deep in the depression. It was a time when people lived off the land to a great extent.

"As a kid I recall occasionally getting a job with the neighbor. He'd pay me seventy-five cents a day for working from seven in the morning until six at night. The men got a dollar. I hoed strawberries. There were a lot of strawberries there.

"Every day we ate the same—beans and potatoes and biscuits and pork. We always killed hogs in the fall.

"Clothes were hand-me-downs, and we went to one-room schools. There were about fifteen of us in the whole grade school. I was the janitor. I started out in the fifth grade sweeping the floor and building the fire. I got a nickel each day for building the fire and a nickel for sweeping the floor, so I made fifty cents a week. I saved up my money and bought myself a shotgun. My old dog, Rover, went with me every day to school, and some teachers would even let him lie by my desk.

"I remember Pearl Harbor Day. We were having a family gathering on that Sunday. All of the family and my cousins were there. About the only recreation we had in those days was the

The Great Depression's lifelong effects

family all getting together. We didn't have a radio. But my dad and uncle had gone to town, and when they came back, they mentioned that Pearl Harbor had been bombed. I remember thinking, What in the world is Pearl Harbor? I had never heard of it before. I didn't know what it meant. I didn't realize what was going on.

"But all of us boys who were gathered there that day—and there were about a dozen—every one of us ended up in the service. We all came back but one. He was killed leading an infantry attack in the Philippines. After the war when we had family meals, my aunt who had lost her son would get up and leave the table. The pain of seeing everyone there but her son was too much for her.

"During the war, there was a cohesive spirit that I have not seen in this country before or since. Everybody helped in whatever way they could. To save gas, the speed limit where I lived was thirty-five miles an hour. If anyone passed you, you would give them a 'V for Victory' toot with your horn. It was like Morse code—dit, dit, dit, dash. That would slow them down more times than not because nobody wanted to be accused of being unpatriotic.

"In 1943 when I was a senior in high school, I went to Purdue to compete in a 4-H Club judging contest, and I visited the university's Hall of Music. I had never been that far away from home. I went in that Hall of Music, which was bigger than Radio City Music Hall in New York, and I had two thoughts. My first was that somehow I would graduate from Purdue. My second was that this hall sure could hold a lot of hay.

"Immediately after graduation from high school in early May of '44, I went into the Army Air Corps. I enlisted while I was still in school and they let me finish. I became a machine gunner on B-17s. I was in the ball turret under the plane. When I got in there, they closed the door behind me, and I couldn't wear a parachute. The space was too small for me and the parachute.

"Times were very tough"

"It was very high risk. Nobody wanted to fly in the ball turret. But I volunteered to do it. I was just eighteen years old. That's the reason eighteen-year-old kids fight wars.

"One time when we came back from a mission, there was a hole in the plane beside my turret, but I never got injured or shot down.

"We flew missions out of England over Germany. We hit all the big targets—Hamburg, Berlin, Hanover. We flew in big formations—several hundred planes. Once I flew on a thousand-plane bombing raid. Nothing like that had ever happened before, and it will never happen again.

"I can remember it was cold. In the turret, it was sixty degrees below zero. We were flying at twenty-five thousand to thirty thousand feet—more than five miles high. I was in a fetal position in there for eight hours straight.

"Sometimes you had to hold your urine because the relief tube from the turret froze up. You couldn't go when the tubes were frozen because it would spill in your suit and short out the heating wires you needed to keep warm. You always had that problem of holding your urine while you were in combat.

"I remember once the plane on our left got hit and started to go down. The guys in it were trying to jump out. I watched them and thought, Here I am sitting here with no parachute. I thought, If I ever get back home, everything else in my life is going to be easy. I guess that's been true.

"I flew eighteen missions. We lost a lot of planes and a lot of comrades. Near the end of the war, they loaded us up with food, and we dropped it over Holland. People on the ground spelled out 'thank you' with rocks. We were getting ready to be sent to the Pacific, but the war there ended, too.

"I came home and started Purdue in the fall of 1946. I had the GI Bill. Without that, I suppose I would have found some way to go to college, but it would have been much different and taken me longer.

87

The Great Depression's lifelong effects

"There was no place to live on campus. I stayed in a private home for awhile, and then I stayed in an old house where the Purdue farm manager lived. It was a big two-story house, and a bunch of guys and I stayed there with the farm manager and his wife.

"I studied agriculture. We were serious students. Of course, we hadn't been in school for awhile and getting back into the routine of studying was difficult. We didn't have time for a lot of fooling around. We knuckled down and we worked hard.

"One amusing thing occurred, however. The cost of haircuts on campus was raised from seventy-five cents to a dollar, so we all boycotted the barbershops in the union building. I think there were four of them. I can remember walking by and seeing all the barbers sitting there with nothing to do. We just let our hair grow. We'd get it cut once in awhile when we went home. But eventually we came around. That was the only protest movement I ever took part in at school.

"I went to class in my GI clothes—my flight jacket and my khakis. However, in our senior year, we all wore cords with words and dates written on them. Some of the guys liked to play tricks and write things on other guys' pants. We were always playing tricks on each other.

"I married Phyllis in the fall of 1950. She was a Lafayette girl. I met her at the Purdue Memorial Union. We have three children—one daughter and two sons. They all went to college.

"After we were married, I stayed at Purdue to work on my master's degree in agricultural economics. I went to work with Ralston Purina in St. Louis right after leaving Purdue, and I stayed there until I retired in 1986. When I retired, I was vice president of Purina Mills with responsibility for economic and market research. I still do some consulting for them.

"You know, after the war we felt our nation could accomplish anything. And that spirit carried over into each person. Individually we felt we could do anything, too.

"Times were very tough"

"And we did do quite a bit. We had a common purpose of doing something with our lives. We wanted to make something out of ourselves.

"And we did. Yes, we did."

$1 clips spur eds to action; boycott of barbers begins

By E. P. Kundmuller

Posters and petitions from one corner of the campus to the other yesterday proclaimed the start of the latest campaign to stop the "boom town" inflation of over-crowded Lafayette and vicinity.

Efforts at present are being directed against the local barber shops and their one dollar "clipping" which has been in effect for the past few months. The push to reduce haircuts was started by a letter which was published in Saturday's *Exponent*. It was signed by Eugene P. Van Arsdel and other students. . . .

Van Arsdel said he was gratified by the way student support sprang up overnight. He cited an example by mentioning the scores of postcards and letters he had received and the unpredicted appearance of a number of posters. A few of their slogans read as follows:

At a buck a throw, let it grow.

Don't get clipped.

Student Senate officials said the matter would be given due consideration.

The barbers maintained that one dollar is a just price for a haircut.

PURDUE EXPONENT, OCTOBER 1, 1946

Mauri Williamson

Mauri Williamson was born in 1925 in the little town of Economy, Indiana. And it is a good thing it happened that way.

The Great Depression's lifelong effects

Economy has given him a lifetime supply of jokes for his endless speeches as head of the Purdue University Agricultural Alumni Association. There were about eight thousand members when he started the job in 1953 and nearly thirty thousand when he retired in 1990. Although the organization became big, his hometown of Economy remained small.

"There were 251 people in 1925 and there are still 251 people there today," he says. "Every time someone is born, someone leaves town."

When he had an office at Purdue, his closet was designed like an outhouse. "Put your coat in the toilet," he would tell visitors.

Williamson is retired. He lives outside West Lafayette in the country, or what was the country before the city started spreading. He likes the feel of being among the farms. He helps his son farm some of the same land his father and his grandfather worked.

"Really, I was the first one in my family to leave the farm," Williamson says. "And I didn't go very far.

"There were three boys in the family and I was the oldest. I had always planned to be a farmer. My dad was a big farmer. He had 320 acres. The neighbors called it the plantation because it was so much bigger than their farms. My dad would go to the sand hills of Nebraska to buy feeder cattle. Mom had three hundred chickens, and we had some sheep.

"When my granddad died in 1944, he had one thousand acres. That was a lot of land in those days. His three sons split it up. My granddad was real progressive. He bought tractors back in the teens. Old-timers talk about how they thrashed and shucked corn—a lot of that is lies, you know. I never did much thrashing and shucking. My granddad bought a combine in 1936 to do the thrashing. Then he bought a corn picker, and we didn't have to shuck corn by hand. I was lucky.

"We had a terrible time in the depression, but we made out a lot better than most. I remember my mom telling me—with a great

90

deal of guilt—how she had to borrow money from Granddad to get through a year or two. We were never in danger of losing the farm. Granddad owned it. But there was absolutely no money. We put out a garden and grew our own food. Today, my son the farmer—he'd starve to death. He doesn't know anything about gardening.

"My two granddads are good examples of what happened during those times. Both were fine men and one was as good a farmer as the other. The 1920s were a lot like the 1970s—all optimism, everything was wonderful. Everyone was talking about how we were going to feed the world. My mother's father borrowed some money and bought a farm. My dad's father farmed what he had and saved every penny. In the 1930s, my granddad on my mother's side went broke. He had no money to pay back what he owed. But my granddad on my father's side bought land in the thirties—cheap. That's when he accumulated all his land.

"I remember Pearl Harbor Day. We had just returned from church and were sitting in our new house. Our old house had burned and we had built a new one. I can even remember having my leg draped over the arm of the chair I was sitting in. It's funny how you remember these things. When we heard the news, it was like someone had died. My mother was sort of crying. Here I was fifteen years old, and in no time at all, I'd be in it. And I wanted to be in it.

"As soon as we declared war, it tore things up. Some of the teachers in my high school marched off to war. The coach, who also taught math, went. Others went and never came back to that little school after the war.

"I remember what one teacher, who was also the high school principal, said in 1941—and no one really believed him—he said, 'Before this is over, we'll all be in it.' I remember thinking, How awful. But he was right.

"When I graduated from Economy High School in 1943, the war was pretty well along, and I had a farm deferment until 1945.

The Great Depression's lifelong effects

A few of the farm kids volunteered and went earlier, but I waited to get drafted. I wanted to go. I served in a hospital corps in California, and my conscience has always bothered me because I wasn't over there with the other guys. Mom didn't want me to go to war. She didn't want me to get shot up.

"I was in the Navy and, as I said, I ended up working in a psychiatric hospital in California. We saw the war secondhand, through the guys who came back and were treated there. A lot of the men suffered from combat fatigue. More than once we spent our duty time holding a guy all night—just sitting on his bed and listening to him swear at the captain who wasn't around when the shooting started. The guys really relived it. Working in the hospital, we didn't see the shooting, but we saw the results. We saw a lot of massive injuries. We saw how combat destroyed guys' minds. You never heard much about that.

"I remember one guy in our ward whose face didn't look like a face. It had been blown away. I don't know, it might have been merciful if he hadn't lived. We got a lot of Marines and, boy, you talk about war stories! They came back with one leg, no legs. They talked about the heat of battle. I remember this one guy who had been on a battleship and who had slammed the captain for staying in a safe place while the rest of them were out there dying. Guys just screamed. It was terrible.

"I got out in July of 1946 and went back to the farm. I had intended to stay there but the GI Bill came along, so I went to Purdue.

"Registration for classes at that time was in the Armory—and there were no computers. They had this great big board at one end of the Armory with all the classes listed on it. Maybe Animal Science 111 would have five sections. You'd get your schedule all figured out and stand in line. Just as you were about to hand in your schedule, you'd look up, and they would have taken

"Times were very tough"

down the section you had signed up for. That section was full, and it messed up the rest of your schedule, so you had to start all over again. You talk about chaos! It was kind of fun when you think back on it. It took all day to get that done.

POSTWAR REGISTRATION. Class registration went on for three days at the Armory. Most students were from Indiana and surrounding states, but in the late 1940s, nearly 250 came from other countries.

"You just parked wherever you wanted to on campus. There weren't any parking permits or meters. Not many people had cars. During the war, you couldn't buy a car. I had a '41 Chevy. My dad had more money than the average guy. The shortages lasted quite a while. In 1948, we bought a pickup truck with no bed because they weren't making beds yet.

"I was planning to go back to the farm when I graduated. Dad never said anything about it, but Mom never could understand why I wanted to go to college to be a farmer. A lot of guys did go back to the farm from college, but also a lot of guys went to college to get away from the farm. There were still a lot of memories of how bad it had been during the depression.

"The economy was getting better, however. From about 1946 to 1948 were good years for farmers. There had been price controls on hogs during the war, and when they took the controls off,

93

hogs went from sixteen dollars a hundred to thirty-eight dollars a hundred in one day. Of course, most people didn't have any hogs to sell, so it didn't matter much.

"I majored in animal husbandry, and I got involved in a lot of things. You know, I've always thought the main advantage of going to college is that you're four years older when you finish. I see these young guys at Purdue today, and I don't ever remember being that dumb when I was in school. Of course, I was.

"I liked college. A lot of the older guys just wanted to learn how to get a job. They didn't want to be part of the cultural activities. But I enjoyed it all. I was in the Glee Club, the University Choir, and the Concert Choir.

"I always thought if I had been rich I would have followed Thomas Jefferson's lifestyle. I would have gone to Earlham College, which was only fifteen miles from home, and I would have studied the liberal arts—history and philosophy. Then like Jefferson, I would have gone back to farming. But that isn't the way it works anymore.

"Don't let anyone kid you about what students were like back then. They weren't a bunch of angels in those days. They drank hard, they fought hard, and they studied hard. When the football team didn't play a good game, the guys threw whiskey bottles on the field. They didn't drink beer. They drank the real stuff.

"You didn't drink in the living units. There was Harry's, the campus bar. If you were white and male, you could go there. A girl? No way could she have gotten into Harry's. Now you go there on a Friday night and you might find a whole sorority. There were some bars in Lafayette, too, but the only place around campus was Harry's. If Smitty's grocery in West Lafayette tried to get a license, the university was right there to kill it.

"During your senior year, you wore cords—yellow corduroys—and you decorated them. Seniors in animal husbandry would

"Times were very tough"

draw a cow on their cords. The guys in engineering put the gas law or a chemical formula on the back of theirs. You could hire people to paint your cords. Some decorations were very elaborate.

"When you were a senior, you wore a derby and carried a cane to a football game, and you marched around the field. At the first touchdown, you threw your derby up in the air. If you pledged a fraternity or a sorority, you wore a little green beanie. Guys back then were older, but they enjoyed all this. Those were good and simple times. Nowadays, kids consider such customs childish.

"In the summer of 1948, I got married. We lived in a twenty-six-foot trailer parked near a main house. The trailer had no bathroom. You had to run to the main house. We lived in that trailer for two years on campus, and we thought it was pretty nice. The RV camper we have now is thirty-five feet long.

"We graduated in June of 1950, and I went with the Glee Club to Europe. We

SENIOR CORDS. What marked you as senior in the late 1940s were corduroy pants, decorated with your graduation year, your major, and other funny and personal symbols, such as fraternity affiliation. Women seniors wore cord skirts.

sang in Berlin, and you never heard such an ovation as we received. There was still a lot of rubble from the war—it had only been five years—but there was no hostility.

"After I graduated, I went back to the farm with my dad. I wasn't the best farmer in the world. I was too social. One day I was cleaning out the barn, pushing a big shovel of cow manure, when I slipped and broke my kneecap. I usually say it was my leg because it sounds better, but it was my kneecap.

"I wanted to go to grad school, but I was married and had two kids. I needed a job. When this position with the Ag Alumni

The Great Depression's lifelong effects

Association opened up, I took it. I told them I'd try it for a year. That was 1953.

"Maybe I should have gone to grad school. I'd have made more money. I might have been a dean. But I wouldn't have been nearly as good at that. I was lucky. At least I didn't have to worry about slipping in cow manure anymore.

"I've been lucky all through my life. I have a good wife and family—my son's the best farmer in Indiana.

"But farming has changed. The GI Bill changed farming. Way back we had subsistence farmers who had small farms and raised what they could. They did things by hand. But when the boys all went off to war, farmers had to become more efficient. They had to get milking machines. When the boys came back and went off to college, farming became even more technical. The small-town schools consolidated. The small grain elevators went bankrupt. The little towns died. It's really not as much fun out there now as it used to be.

"You know, there's no place to loaf anymore. You used to loaf at the elevator or the blacksmith shop. Or there would be a bench in town where you could sit and whittle. I don't know where I would go to loaf around here now. The K-Mart restaurant, I guess.

"There just aren't many places anymore where you can loaf."

Jim Rardon

Jim Rardon lives in a Lafayette neighborhood where people work hard for a living and know the value of their work.

He has six children and seventeen grandchildren, and on this cold February day while he watches a Purdue University basketball game on television, several of the children and many grandchildren are with him.

The grandchildren are playing and making noise, like grandkids do. Rardon enjoys it. This is a house where the family enjoys gathering and making noise and being together.

96

"Times were very tough"

"Which one's you, Dad?" a daughter asks, looking over Rardon's shoulder as he pages through a Purdue yearbook.

"That one," he says, pointing to a young man with smooth features and deep, dark eyes. "I had hair then, wavy hair."

She makes a face. She prefers the way he looks now. His face has deep character lines, and his hair is not so dark and wavy anymore.

He was born in Lafayette in 1926 into a working-class north-end neighborhood, really not too far from where he lives today. His dad worked fifty-one years on the Monon Railroad as head storekeeper. This is a family of people who stick with jobs.

Rardon worked thirty-four and a half years at University Bookstore in West Lafayette before he retired. He now works in insurance.

He never planned to go to college. No one in his family had ever gone to college. They did not have money for it. Rardon thought he might become a printer.

"One time during the depression, my dad got down to working half a day—that's half a day a week," Rardon says. "Then it got down to none, and he went with the WPA as a timekeeper.

"We survived the depression, like everyone else. It was tough, but it was the same for everybody. You didn't feel like you were picked on. It was no fun, but as kids we didn't realize how serious it was because everybody else had it the same. It was just the way it was.

"In some respects, the depression kept families closer because they had to do things together more. We didn't have a lot of stuff. We had a garden. We ate a lot of gravy and beans. Looking back, the depression would have scared the dickens out of me if I had been older and known more—if I had been the age I am now. But when the depression came, I was young and naïve and I didn't worry much.

97

The Great Depression's lifelong effects

"When I think back on those times, I don't think of all the bad times. I think of all the good times—the closeness of our family and friends and how everyone helped out.

"When I was in grade school, my dad got very ill. He had mastoid surgery. That was very serious at the time, and he was in the hospital for a while. My mother would go there to be with him. We kids would walk home at lunch, and the neighbors would feed us. After school, the neighbors would take care of us until my mother got home.

"We had an old box-radio and I used to love listening to it. I liked the mysteries, 'Jack Armstrong,' and comedy shows like Fibber McGee and Molly and Jack Benny. We had regular shows we listened to, just like people have regular TV shows today. And we read more in those days. I read a lot and played outside. We made up games, and we played games like 'Duck on a Rock.' You put a little rock on top of a big rock and tried to knock it off. There was a duck pond nearby and we were always playing out there.

"Pearl Harbor happened when I was fourteen years old and a sophomore at Jefferson High School. The next day was a Monday, and it was very serious at school. I played the clarinet in the band, and the band teacher brought a radio so we could hear the declaration of war. We all knew what we were going to be doing. We knew sooner or later we were going to end up in it.

"I graduated high school in 1944 when I was seventeen years old. I enlisted. Everybody else was going in, so I didn't want to stick around. Something had to be done and you wanted to be a part of it. It wasn't like the Vietnam situation. They didn't let the rich kids off. It wasn't discriminatory at all. Everybody wanted in on it.

"My dad had to sign for me. He thought I was crazy. He didn't want me to get involved. I look at my kids and grandkids now, and I'd feel the same way he did. But he signed.

"Times were very tough"

"I went to Great Lakes naval boot camp and signal school and then was selected for Compool—men who sailed on merchant ships as gunners' mates and signalmen. I got to the Ulithi Atoll and the Leyte Gulf, and after the war ended, I made two trips to Japan. They kept me in the service for what was called 'magic carpet duty'— bringing guys home. I saw Hiroshima and Nagasaki. They were blown out from the center like a saucer. I have some tiles and a radio I picked up there, but I don't know where they are.

"In Japan everything was destroyed. It was a whipped nation. I felt sorry for some of those people even if I didn't condone what they had done. I lost a lot of friends and a lot of people suffered. I guess we really didn't know how to feel. But that's part of living.

"I was in for two years, and I was nineteen years old when I got out of the service.

"I was home on leave in January of 1946, and John McGonigal, a friend of mine from high school, and I were out running around spending all our money. The war had just ended. We went to the bars. We wore our uniforms, and some of the bars would serve us even though we weren't old enough.

"One night we were having a few libations, and it was still early when McGonigal got up to go. I said, 'Where the heck are you going?' He said he had to leave. I said, 'We've been home two weeks, and we haven't gotten home before three or four in the morning yet. Where are you going?' He said he wanted to get up early in the morning to go over and enroll at Purdue. He wanted to start school in the fall. He asked me what I was going to do. I told him I didn't know. I hadn't even thought about it. He said, 'Why don't you come with me in the morning?' I told him that would be okay, come by and pick me up.

"I didn't even find out about the GI Bill until that next morning. I had been out all night. The counselor looked at me and laughed. He said, 'What do you want to be?' I said I didn't know but I knew I didn't want to be in an office. It was more fun being out in the weather. I thought being out in the woods would be fun, so I decided to go into forestry.

"I started in the fall. I lived at home for awhile. Then in July of 1949, before my senior year, I got married, and we lived in an apartment. She was a Lafayette girl I met after coming home. We had a little girl born in April of 1950.

"We didn't have enough money to party much. Believe it or not, I worked a lot. I studied a lot. I never really had much preparation for college, so I had to take make-up courses. My first year was a lot of work. We were serious students. We wanted to get in and get out. We wanted to get started on our lives. When my wife and I were dating, we'd go out on Wednesday and Saturday nights. The rest of the time I studied. I just didn't have time or money for much else.

"In our senior year, we all had cords. Only the seniors could wear them, no one else. If you wore them before you were a senior, they ripped them off you. Sometimes they ripped them off you even if you were a senior. They were regular yellow corduroys with a slide rule pocket. We painted school dates and I can't even remember what all we put on them. Some guys hired professionals to paint them. Most of us just screwed them up ourselves. I can't remember what I had written on mine. You couldn't wash them. They got so stiff they stood up in the corner by themselves.

"It was tough getting a job after graduation. The Korean War was about to break out and nobody would hire you. I had to do anything to make a buck. So finally, Bob Mitchell, a fellow graduate, and I went to southern Indiana for a job in a veneer plant, and we worked in a log yard—a big stack of logs and a big crane. It was very dangerous. We worked there through the summer. Along toward August, Bob came in one day and said he was

"Times were very tough"

leaving to go back to the Marines. I tried to find him for years after that but couldn't. I finally figured he'd been killed in Korea.

"I thought I'd have to go back in the service, too, but they never called me.

"If it hadn't been for the GI Bill, I probably would have been a printer. I would have liked that, too. Sometimes what you do is not what you plan to do. It's just how your life works out.

"But I wouldn't change anything. I just wanted to live and be happy. And I am happy. I have a good family. I always wanted kids and I had them. What more is there to life than that? Not many people have six kids anymore.

"Six kids. That's also why I keep working.

"You know, the first house I grew up in here in town didn't have a toilet. The outhouse was out back. Our class of 1950 has lived through the depression, when many of us had nothing, to witnessing our nation put a man on the moon. It's mind-boggling. And do you know what else?

"It's not over yet."

Freshmen take heed; cord tradition violated

Time changes all things, it is said, and time has left a jagged dent in Purdue's Senior Cord Tradition.

Perhaps the Class of '50 doesn't realize that it's breaking the rules. But, erring seniors who are now violating some of the regulations of this time-honored tradition may find themselves in a rather embarrassing situation if the most eager freshman class to hit this campus in many a year gets wise to the Senior Cord Tradition as it really is.

The reference is, of course, to seniors who are wearing their cords on campus before Senior Day.

In the past, no senior was foolish enough to admit that he even owned a pair of cords before the first home

101

The Great Depression's lifelong effects

football game. And if some unfortunate, uninformed upper classman ever strolled onto campus prematurely donned in his new, yellow cords, he was promptly relieved of them by an only too obliging band of freshmen.

There is reason for the Senior Cord Tradition as it was. When started in 1906, it was hoped if the entire senior class appeared in their cords on the same day, that it might boost class spirit. . . .

And it worked. On the first home football game of each season, the graduating class put on their cords for the first time and paraded to the stadium en masse. . . .

At the present time, senior cords are being worn on campus with casual abandon—ten days before they are supposed to appear. . . .

Perhaps the freshmen can revive the old tradition of removing forcibly these cords from the tradition-breaking seniors, no matter where, when or under what conditions.

PURDUE EXPONENT EDITORIAL, SEPTEMBER 22, 1949

Duane Williams

They call him "Bus"—everyone does and he's not really sure why.

"It's always been a joke that I got the name in the hospital when I was born," he says with a laugh. "They told me I was named after a dog. I guess it's short for Buster. My aunt always called me Buster."

He has a full, round face and white hair. Sitting in the Purdue Memorial Union during an Acacia fraternity reunion, he has no trouble remembering the days when he was a young kid at school, thinking he knew a lot more than he did, like all young kids in school.

Those were happy times, and he smiles and laughs as he tells the stories. The depression times were happy too, he says, in their own way, in a different way—a way of good family values

"Times were very tough"

and good times, doing simple things, people being with people, friends with close friends.

Williams tells war stories, too. He describes the times in general terms. "It was bad," he says. "It was no fun. It was rough."

Like a lot of veterans talking about the war, Williams's eyes become moist.

"I was involved in a lot of fighting with the Japanese," he says. "Tree to tree fighting, bush to bush. It was a rough time. I was a pretty lucky guy. I got the Purple Heart. I wasn't hurt bad. Lots of people were killed and a lot of bad things . . . you know. Tough time, all the way through."

These words aren't coming easily.

"I've seen a lot of dead people and that's not pleasant. It's hard to talk about. You have to think about the good things. There are so many bad things I don't want to talk about. I do think about those things from time to time. But it's not very much fun."

Williams, of Indianapolis, would rather talk about his family—five children, all married, and seven and a half grandchildren. "My youngest daughter's due this spring."

Born in the small town of Kendallville, Indiana, to a father who sold wholesale to little grocery stores, Williams grew up an only child. His sister died before he was born.

"We got through the depression," he says. "The fact that my dad was in grocery sales I'm sure helped us, but it was a pretty good struggle. We grew a lot of our own food, and we'd buy wholesale from the farmers or they'd give food to us. We ate a lot of potatoes.

"Our family had a funny experience when you look at it today. My dad came home one night with two cases of pink salmon. He couldn't sell them. No one would buy pink salmon. Today people'd kill for them but back then no one wanted that salmon. Mom served us salmon for weeks—salmon patties, dishes like that. Here we were

The Great Depression's lifelong effects

in the middle of the depression on a steady diet of salmon. My kids all laugh when I tell this story. But I remember salmon.

"The town I lived in had only six thousand people, so you knew everyone. It was quite wonderful looking back because everyone helped one another. We had—I wouldn't call them tramps—transients who came to the door and my mother fed them. They got off the railroad cars hungry.

"We didn't worry about crime. The house was always unlocked. People who didn't have a job would mow the lawn or do anything around the house to help, and all they wanted was something to eat.

"We didn't need a lot of clothing. We had old clothes—overalls and blue jeans. The only time we dressed up was to go to church. We weren't overly religious, but we went to church almost every Sunday. That was enjoyable.

"We had a lot of good times on the weekends. Family and friends had pitch-in dinners and picnics. We could have ten, twelve, sixteen people at get-togethers with kids and grown-ups, and everyone ate food like fried chicken.

"It was a great time to grow up with the values we had then that we don't seem to have now—loyalty, integrity, and everyone pitching in. If someone had a problem, we would mow that person's lawn, or if someone was sick, the women would nurse that person night and day. Friends do things like that.

"On Pearl Harbor Day, I was on my way to Fort Wayne in an old Model A Ford. We were all high school juniors going to a movie. We heard about the attack on the radio. It affected us because we were going to graduate in May of 1943. We knew right away we wanted to get into the war.

"I graduated in May of 1943, and a lot of my friends had already gone the previous November and December. I had bad eyes so I didn't get in right away. I didn't know if they were going to take me, so I came to Purdue in September of 1943. I was on campus only thirty days before I was drafted. To tell you the truth, I don't even remember if I got my tuition money back.

"I was ready to go in the military. Most of my friends had already gone and I felt somewhat guilty about that. I was drafted into the military police in October of 1943. I went to basic training in Michigan and then to officers' candidate school. I stayed on at a prisoner-of-war camp between Kalamazoo and Battle Creek.

"In the spring of '44, they needed us overseas. We ended up in New Guinea. We fought our way through New Guinea, then we headed north for the invasion of the Philippines. I was in the landings at Luzon.

"My company was responsible for all the USO people who came in to entertain. I met Bob Hope, Bing Crosby, and Dinah Shore. They were nice people. They were there for a purpose—to entertain—and they were first class. We put them under tight security because the troops were a little wild. They had a lot of young girls with them—headliners. They would come in for two or three days and then be gone. The original cast from *Oklahoma* came. Because I played the piano, Les Brown would let me sit in sometimes. It was a different world, a different time.

"My company was also MacArthur's personal bodyguard. That was very interesting. I personally was involved with MacArthur and Paul McNutt, who was commissioner of the Philippines and a former governor of Indiana. I was MacArthur's driver and personal assistant. He was pretty tough, but he had the world beat at that time.

"I was commissioned a second lieutenant. During the war, we had temporary commissions. After the war, I was offered a permanent commission as a captain if I would go to Japan with MacArthur as part of the occupation. I said, 'No, I'm not going to do that.' I had had enough of war.

The Great Depression's lifelong effects

"You earned points by how long you'd been in the service and the battles you'd fought, and I had enough points to go home. So I got on the first troop ship home. I've always wondered if that was a good decision.

"Woody Herman was on board the troop ship coming back. He had been entertaining in the Pacific, and he and his band played for forty-five days on that ship. It was unbelievable. I don't think anybody slept. And I don't think anybody was tired.

"I got back home in February of 1946. I found out Purdue was starting classes in February. In less than a week, I was on a bus headed back to school. Half of us who entered Purdue that February had been to college before the war, then had gone through the war. On the bus that I took, there must have been fifteen or twenty of us vets who got off together. Young kids right out of high school made up the rest of the class. I felt sorry for them.

"Those kids took a beating from us because we knew what we wanted and worked hard. We'd work our tails off until ten o'clock at night when someone would blow the whistle, then we'd go out, get snockered, and play cards all night. We all made good grades. It's just that after the war we had different hours and the high school kids couldn't keep up with us. They didn't want to and we didn't want them to.

"My folks didn't have a lot of money. I had the GI Bill and played jazz piano in a big band. I played for a living here on campus for four years. I also had a five-piece group on my own. And I waited tables. I cooked breakfast at the Acacia house for two years to pay my dues. I waited tables at Lincoln Lodge on weekends for three and a half years. I was busy, but I enjoyed it. I made my own way. I had a good life.

"I was married the last two years at Purdue. I met her on campus. Her name was Henry—Henry Burns. There was a lot of kidding about her name. But it was fun.

"Times were very tough"

"I majored in mechanical engineering and graduated in February of 1950. I had several different job offers.

"After I left the Army, I stayed in the reserves. I don't know why, but I did. After I graduated, I almost got caught in the Korean War. My outfit was training. Two companies were called, and mine was one of them. I had to resign from my business, write my will, and take care of everything. We went down, packed, and went to the assembly point. At midnight, we had a call that said they were taking only the other company. We were out of there. In two weeks, I resigned my commission and got out. That was the end of my military career.

CHRISTMAS CORDS. *In this cartoon from a December 1949* Purdue Exponent, *an electrical engineer hopes Santa will fill his corduroy "stocking" with a good job after graduation.*

"Air-conditioning was my avocation. I got into residential air-conditioning early in its development. It came along big in the midfifties, about the same time as television. I designed and developed units. I loved working with air-conditioning. It's what I wanted to do most of my life.

"I've been a design engineer, a vice president of a Westinghouse division, and a corporate president. Now I'm a marketing vice president for an air-conditioning company in Indianapolis.

"The war affected me. I was a snot-nosed kid when I first came to Purdue, and I was a smart-ass when I went to war. But war turns you around pretty fast. I became very fatalistic because of my experiences. My wife, Carol, gets on me about it to this day. In war, however, you can't procrastinate. You do it right now because you could be gone in ten minutes. It's probably wrong to think that way, but it's easy to get that mental state.

"Hank, my first wife, and I were divorced years ago. Carol and I were married in 1962 and have been very happy. We've been very

The Great Depression's lifelong effects

successful and raised a big family. All five kids are married, they have good jobs, and they are all contributing something to society. I'm very proud of that. Now we have started on the grandkids.

"The war and my childhood had a good impact on me. When I came back to Purdue, I knew what I wanted and what I was going to do. Nothing was going to keep me from getting a good education, making a decent life, and having a family. I felt I had a mission and I have accomplished it.

"To some it may sound foolish, but when fate says there is a chance you may die before you get your life going, your outlook changes forever."

Gene Egler

He has seen a lot of change in his life, and change just seems to keep coming faster. Maybe some people have trouble coping with it. Change does not bother Gene Egler. He seems intrigued by it, like a man trying to peek around the corner to see what is ahead.

Sitting in the Purdue Memorial Union on a spring Saturday, Egler is near a group of students who are watching professional basketball on television instead of studying for finals. He recalls the events of his life matter-of-factly.

He has returned this weekend from his home in Statesville, North Carolina, for a reunion of Acacia fraternity brothers, men he has not seen in forty-four years. Friendships are renewed quickly. Years fall away at times like this. They melt. You can almost feel young again.

His work as a field engineer and later as vice president of international marketing at the Hazeltine Corporation took him all over the world before he retired in 1986. He lived in Europe for fifteen years.

"I left Purdue as soon as I was finished in 1950," he says. "I didn't even stay for graduation. I was ready to get out in the world.

"Times were very tough"

I went to work for Allison Engines in Indianapolis testing jet engines but only stayed there a few months before I followed a girl to Texas. I didn't marry her. I went to California and held many minor jobs—practically starving. While bumming around the country, I worked for Hughes Aircraft among others.

"By 1952, I was ready to settle down. I met my wife, a stewardess, in Norfolk, Virginia. We met on a plane, a DC-3. I asked her for a date, and in three or four months, we got married. Our four children were born in Maryland, Alaska, Norway, and England. All are successful—one will become a Ph.D. in 1996.

"I was born in 1926 and my dad was a farmer. We had a medium-size farm, about eighty acres. We had our own beef, pork, vegetables that we canned, butter, milk, eggs, chickens—everything we needed. We didn't suffer as far as food was concerned. Sometimes we'd run short of meat and have to live on corn and beans for awhile until the chickens came on in the summer or until the next butchering time.

"Our house had no electricity and no plumbing. There was a hand pump outside. We used kerosene lamps. I bought a radio in 1936 when I was a kid. I paid thirty-six dollars for it along with a wind-charger generator on a pole with a propeller. But there wasn't enough wind to keep the battery up. That was our first radio. We had only that radio and a Victrola record player.

"A lot of our social life involved the church—Sunday mornings, Sunday nights, sometimes Wednesday nights. There were church suppers—bountiful, lots and lots of food even in those times.

"I had two brothers. I was the middle son. A little sister born in 1931 died at the age of five from pneumonia. Her death was the greatest tragedy of our lives.

"We worked hard. We worked from daylight to nightfall. We had to milk the cows, clean out the stables, pull milkweeds out of the soybeans—anything. For needed cash, we sold sweet corn and tomatoes to canners and milk to a factory.

The Great Depression's lifelong effects

"We didn't know as children how bad the depression was. We had an annual mortgage payment of, I think, four hundred dollars, and sometimes that was tough. My mother made some of our clothes from seed sacks. That's right. They designed seed sacks and flour sacks so they could be made into shirts and dresses.

"Even during the war when there was rationing, we had meat and butter and milk. And we had gas. Gasoline wasn't a problem for farmers.

"I remember on Pearl Harbor Day my uncle and aunt had taken us to an ice show in Indianapolis. The news was on the street when we came out. My aunt and uncle said they hoped the war wouldn't last long enough for us to get in.

"I graduated high school in 1944 and went immediately into the Navy. I got the shock of my life when I learned I was partially color-blind and couldn't qualify for flying. Coming out of that failure, I met another boy who hadn't passed the pilot's test. He said he was going to take the Eddy test for radio technicians, so I thought I'd try that too. Electronics became my lifetime career track.

"I was on a troop ship headed to Hawaii and the Pacific when they dropped that first A-bomb. You can't imagine what a relief that was. We were headed for the Pacific where we'd get shot at, and here comes the A-bomb before we even got to Hawaii. What a relief! They announced it on the ship's loudspeaker. I went on to China.

"I got home in June of 1946 and was accepted to Purdue on the GI Bill. Even without the war and the GI Bill, I would have gone to college. My mother was a schoolteacher. She had gone to a two-year school. It was always agreed in my family that I'd go to college. I made straight A's through grade and high school.

"My first year of college was at the Purdue extension in Indianapolis. I held two part-time jobs, one as a carhop and the other as a radio technician for Red Cab.

"Times were very tough"

"When I first arrived at Purdue's main campus in West Lafayette, it was confusing. All I knew was where my classes were. I joined Acacia fraternity and lived in the house. I cooked breakfast to cover the meal fees. The fraternity house was a very orderly place. We had strict rules, such as for dining—you passed all the food to the right, and you never left the table except when it was necessary. There was never any drinking in the house.

"We had a hell of a lot of fun. It was serious work, but there was a lot of carousing and drinking too—outside the fraternity. We had all seen a little of the world for a couple years or more. We were more attuned to what it was all about.

"I was one of the lucky ones. I had a new car—a 1949 Ford club coupe. It was black and a handsome vehicle. A friend and I often went to Indianapolis to date some nurses. He courted his future wife in the back seat of that Ford. I met them again forty years later, and they remembered the back seat of that Ford very well. Me, they remembered kind of secondarily.

"It wasn't until I got to college that I realized how hard the depression had been. I learned we had been poor. But life was good. We weren't unhappy at all. It was a good childhood. The experience of the depression molded responsible individuals. I think the children of the depression became very good citizens.

"I've seen a lot of different places in my life. I've seen a lot of changes—from horse-drawn and man-powered equipment on farms to where today my nephew runs a couple thousand acres with huge machinery. He took over the family farm—and more.

"I think maybe the changes are still accelerating. No generation has seen as much change as ours.

"And it's still coming—exponentially. We must hope that positive progress comes with recovering social and cultural conditions."

The Great Depression's lifelong effects

chapter 4

" We had a ton of "
guys playing

On the gridiron and the court

John DeCamp

John DeCamp was at Purdue University before the war and after the war. For many, he became the voice of Purdue.

His is a rich voice—even long after his retirement as play-by-play announcer for university football and basketball. His last football broadcast was at the end of the 1973 season. His last basketball broadcast came at the end of the 1982 season.

DeCamp lives part of the year in Phoenix, Arizona, and the other part in West Lafayette. On football Saturdays in the fall, he can be seen hiking up the steps of Ross-Ade Stadium where his long-ago descriptions of the day still echo in the memories of alumni.

"I'm a native of Kendallville, Indiana" DeCamp says. "I started at Purdue in the fall of 1938. In those days, they gave all starting students a routine tuberculosis test. My test was positive, so I was sent to a sanitorium outside Fort Wayne for four months. In the fall of 1939, I started all over and graduated in April of 1943.

"I had a degree in electrical engineering, and I went to work for U.S. Rubber in Mishawaka, Indiana. After working there for two months, a chest X ray found TB again. I went into the same sanitorium in December of 1943 and got out March 1 of 1945.

"I applied for a job at WBAA radio station at Purdue because it was half time, and I hoped it would get me ready to return to full time at U.S. Rubber. But I stayed on at Purdue because I came to realize I liked radio better than engineering.

"Before the war, Purdue was a technical school and it was smaller. After the war, it got bigger quickly. Those GIs who came back were serious people. They worked hard. The university was a very intense place.

"I became production manager of the radio station in the summer of 1946, and I had quite a few veterans of the Marines and Navy and even some in the Navy training program who worked as student announcers. They were good kids."

Bob DeMoss

He was seventeen years old, a college freshman right out of high school, and the starting quarterback for Purdue University, when he walked into the stadium at Ohio State University in 1945.

The war had just ended. His team was a combination of wounded veterans who had come back early, military men who were stationed on the Purdue campus, and few ragtag freshmen who looked like kids and were kids compared to the older guys around them.

Ohio State was the number one ranked team in the nation that day and had just been featured on the

"Bob DeMoss was a freshman quarterback in the fall of 1945. One of my most vivid memories is of listening to the broadcast at a friend's house that year when DeMoss was quarterback and Purdue went to Ohio State and won 35–13. That's the first time I had heard of Bob DeMoss. He was a nice young man. I don't know any other way to describe him except to say he was a nice young kid from Dayton, Kentucky."

—JOHN DECAMP

113

cover of *Life* magazine. The game was being carried all over the world on the Armed Forces Radio Network.

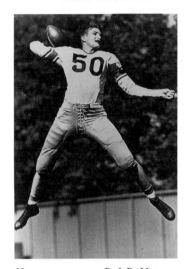

NO PASSING FANCY. Bob DeMoss began a lifetime with Purdue when he hit campus in the fall of 1945 and quickly became a quarterback sensation. He went on to coach a string of great quarterbacks at Purdue.

These were football players DeMoss had idolized for years. And there he was opposing them—a kid out of a little river town in Kentucky, across the Ohio from Cincinnati, a kid who thought his real sport was basketball, anyway.

He threw three touchdown passes that day. Purdue won. DeMoss's life has never been the same.

He was Purdue's starting quarterback for four years, played a few games in the pros, and then returned to the university as an assistant coach until he became head coach from 1970 through 1972. In 1993, he retired as assistant athletic director.

He was with Purdue for forty-eight years from that first day he walked on campus as a freshmen to his retirement. "It's been a good place to work," he says. "It's been a good life. Nice people. Nice kids to coach. Nice town."

In the lower level of his West Lafayette home are mementos of his days—photos, awards. There are pictures of Purdue friends like Neil Armstrong. There's a photo of his kindergarten class in Dayton, Kentucky. He's in the back row. And in front there, that pretty little girl became his lifetime sweetheart.

At Purdue, he was a Big Man on Campus, although he does not think so. He could have dated lots of girls. But it was the girl from back home he invited up for dances. It was the girl from back home he married in 1949. She is the one who has shared his life.

114

"We had a ton of guys playing"

He was the first of the great quarterbacks at Purdue, and he came from another era, from a time when athletes had to work for their room and board, when recruiting was a rather simple affair. He played his college ball at a time when all the great athletes from 1942, 1943, 1944 were returning to campus after the war to finish their eligibility and get their degrees.

One year, Purdue's fullback was thirty-one years old. And DeMoss, the quarterback, as he puts it, "was just a kid."

Born in 1927 in Dayton, Kentucky, his father was an accountant who lost his job in the depression and went to work on the loading dock of a department store in Cincinnati.

"I remember we had to move out of our house and in with a relative who had a job," DeMoss says. "That house was right next to a high school, but I still went to the old one twenty blocks away. I went back and forth on roller skates.

"I can remember we wore our shoes as long as we could. We put baseball cards in the bottoms over the holes to keep the water out. I wish I still had some of those cards.

"We played ball in the street and in the school yard. Twelve months of the year we played something. We went to school, we went home, and we played ball. We found tree limbs that were shaped right, put on roller skates, and played hockey. I started playing basketball in the sixth grade, and I played football in high school. There were only forty-five people in our graduating class, but we had good athletic teams.

"We didn't have a position called quarterback on my high school football team. First, I was a wingback, a blocking back. My senior year I played tailback. He was the guy who did most of the passing, running, and kicking. Only twenty-one kids went out for football. When we scrimmaged, the coach had to play safety. Everybody wanted to block the coach. We played both offense and defense in those days.

On the gridiron and the court

"In basketball, I was a forward. We had a good basketball team. I made all-state two years in a row. I never made all-state in football. My best sport was basketball.

"In Dayton, our school superintendent was a friend of Red Mackey, Purdue's athletic director. In my junior year, we had a good team, and Red Mackey was the speaker at our banquet. That year, all three good senior players went to Purdue. The next year, I visited both Purdue and Indiana. Cincinnati was also calling me to come play.

"At that time, recruiting was not like it is today. It was done by word-of-mouth, and to be honest, you didn't have any idea what you were doing.

"I still remember my visit to Purdue. I can remember standing at the top of the stadium at the southeast end. Looking down, I watched a baseball game, and then looking back, I watched a track meet in Ross-Ade Stadium.

"We didn't graduate from high school until the middle of June in 1945. As soon as we graduated, we started getting ready for the Indiana-Kentucky high school all-star basketball game. We became the first Kentucky team ever to beat Indiana.

"I had decided to go to Purdue, but we were being recruited every day. When the all-star game was over, I remember Adolph Rupp, the University of Kentucky basketball coach, coming over to me. He said, 'Bob, I want to talk to you. You're coming down to Kentucky, aren't you?' I said, 'Yes sir.' I went downstairs and standing outside the dressing-room door was Cecil Isbell, the Purdue football coach, in a suit and tie. 'Son, nice game,' he said. 'You're still coming to Purdue, aren't you?' I said, 'Yes sir.' I don't know what I would have done if Cecil hadn't been standing there. In my mind, I was really a basketball player.

"I came to Purdue in July. In those days, they had three semesters a year, and I came right up after graduation. I remember

"We had a ton of guys playing"

standing in line in the Armory to register for classes. Then I went to the athletic department, and they took me to the Delta Upsilon fraternity house and said, 'Son, this is where you're going to live.'

"At that time for your scholarship, they paid your tuition and found a fraternity where you could work in the kitchen to earn your room and board. At first, there weren't any fraternity kitchen jobs open, so I went to work in a little restaurant. I served breakfast and ate breakfast there, I served lunch and ate lunch there, I served dinner and ate dinner there. I finally got a job in the Sigma Chi house.

"Three fraternities asked me to join. I thought they were clubs. I took pins from all of them. At one time, I had pledge pins from Delta Upsilon, Sigma Chi, and Phi Delta. I was going to see how many I could get until they told me it didn't work that way. I finally joined Sigma Chi.

"I started in engineering. I came here right out of high school. I was working in the kitchen, I was practicing every day, and I was studying engineering. I got good grades in high school, but I wasn't meant to be an engineer. The next semester, I went into physical education, and then I went into forestry.

"When I got to campus in 1945, anyone who could walk could play football. On the team were freshmen, 4-Fs, guys who had been wounded and had come back early, and guys from the military training programs on campus.

"I was the starting quarterback right off the bat, and I was surprised. We won seven games and lost three that year. It was the best season I had at Purdue. We threw the ball a lot. Cecil Isbell was way ahead of his time. We had a guy in motion and guys going out for passes almost every play. That was unheard of in those times. We wore leather helmets without face masks.

"In my freshman year, we had a great game against Ohio State. It was broadcast all over the world on the Armed Services Radio Network. We beat Ohio 35–13. The next year I met guys on campus

On the gridiron and the court

who had been in the service in 1945 and listened to that game on the radio. They'd say to me, 'Are you the one who was quarterback for that game?' I'd say, 'Yes, I was.' They'd say, 'You can't be.'

"On the Purdue team in 1946 was Andy Berkeley. He was the first guy from Dayton, Kentucky, ever to come to Purdue on a football scholarship—that was in 1941. He went in the service, got wounded, and had a plate in his head, but he was back playing again in 1946. We had a thirty-one-year-old fullback in 1946. Our center in 1945 had been discharged from the Army because he had been shot up. Our right guard was a Marine who had been shot up. Our two ends were also from the Marines.

"I made the basketball team my freshman year. Twenty-three guys tried for five starting spots on the team. When you passed the ball to someone on the team, you never got it back. I had high expectations for basketball, but I couldn't get it done. I didn't go out for basketball my sophomore year. They told me to concentrate on football.

"That 1946 team would have been a tough one to coach. At halfback were eight guys who had started at Purdue at one time or another, left for the war, and come back. We had halfbacks coming out of our ears. We had guys coming back who, before the war, had started at tackle and at end. We had guys who, the year before, had started for the team that went 7–3. Some of the older guys hadn't played much, but they didn't need a scholarship because they came back on the GI Bill. They were allowed four years of eligibility, so if they played one year before they went to the war, they could play three more when they came back.

"We had a ton of guys playing football. And those were all tough guys. They'd been through a war. I just listened a lot. I learned to do a lot of listening around these guys.

"Ironically, there wasn't a single quarterback who came back from the war. Most of those guys played in a system that didn't

"We had a ton of guys playing"

have a quarterback. They had played the single-wing offense. Purdue didn't run the T-formation until 1943, so it was a different ball game for a lot of those guys.

"We traveled to the games by train. We'd take off on Thursday night on a sleeper, get to our destination Friday for a practice, and catch a train back on Saturday after the game. In 1947, we played Boston in Fenway Park. We left on Wednesday night right after practice. Four of us played bridge all the way out there and back. Boston was undefeated and we were a little worried, but we beat them. The first time we flew to a game was in 1948. We flew in a DC-3 to Iowa— ten thousand nuts and bolts flying in formation.

"We had some good teams, and we played good teams. Remember, all the schools were loaded up with guys coming back from the war. Michigan and Notre Dame were national champs. Things haven't changed much.

"My girlfriend, who became my wife, came up here for the games and for big dances, and she stayed at the Kappa sorority house. We got married in 1949. I was in forestry and I was three hours short of graduating.

"I hadn't thought much about what I was going to do when I graduated. Some people know exactly what they want to do after they graduate. Other people are in school three or four years before they know what they want to do. They are just trying to find their way. I was one of those people. I never thought about being a professional football player. Really, being in the pros wasn't as big a deal then as it is now.

"But in 1949, I got drafted by the New York Bulldogs who were in the NFL. I signed with them. I got a bonus of one thousand dollars, and I signed for seven thousand dollars, which wasn't bad in those days. My wife and I went out to New York, and I had a four-game pro career. The team wasn't very good. But you know, it's funny. For some reason there's a run on autographs of guys from the Bulldogs. Right now upstairs I have a stack of letters from people.

"Really, although it was an NFL team, it was a fly-by-night deal. We had better organization at Purdue, better equipment, everything. When I went to pro camp, we had thirteen quarterbacks. However, I do have a lot of good memories. Bobby Layne used to pick me up every day for practice. He was a good guy. Bobby was probably making twenty-three or twenty-four thousand dollars.

"After I got cut, I went back home to Dayton and worked in the Cincinnati department store where my father had worked. That same fall, I came to the Purdue-Marquette game in West Lafayette. I walked into the locker room after the game, and Stu Holcomb, my former head football coach in '47 and '48, said, 'Are you going to be with us next year?' I asked him what he meant. He said, 'I want you to coach quarterbacks. We have four young quarterbacks coming in and I want you to be their coach.'

"I started on the payroll in January of 1950. I coached spring practice and worked that summer on the golf courses. I was still short those three hours to get my degree, so I took them and graduated in the spring of 1950.

"The game of football is a lot different today than it was then. The guys are all faster and bigger. But I think we had more fun. There weren't so many rules. We took the game seriously, but we could still have fun. Some guys had too much fun, but that happens.

"I played with a lot of great guys, a lot of good people. When we get together now, we talk about those days. You wouldn't believe the lies. We never missed a block or a tackle—or dropped a pass. Then we get out the films and look at them. We were awful.

"Many of my teammates have had successful careers. When we graduated, the opportunities were there, and those guys were all sharp people. They had been in the war and they weren't afraid to work. That's the key. They weren't afraid to work because they had to work. Everybody worked.

"We had a ton of guys playing"

"Going to college at that time with all the veterans coming back—it was a great experience. Nothing like that had ever happened before.

"I hope we don't ever have a time like that again."

Triumph probably greatest in Purdue's history

By Gordon Graham

COLUMBUS, Ohio, Oct. 21 —The proud Buckeyes of Ohio State "got the buck" before a fierce charging and perfectly prepared football team here yesterday as 73,585 shocked spectators saw Coach Cecil Isbell's Boilermakers roll over Carroll Widdoes' heralded eleven 35-13, grinding into submission a team which had won 12 straight games and had not given up a single point this season. . . .

In many ways the spectacular triumph goes down as the most important in Purdue football history. . . .

DeMoss "automatic"

Bob DeMoss continued his storybook rise among the nation's leading passers. Columbus fans were still shaking their heads today about DeMoss completing his first six passes when the checks were really down. Two of them were touchdown affairs to the clever Billy Canfield.

JOURNAL AND COURIER, 1945

Angelo Carnaghi

Although he was born in Detroit in 1926, Angelo Carnaghi's parents were both born in Italy. A handsome man, he came from a family of Old-World values that ran into fast-changing times.

"Even my sister was born in Italy," he says. "I was the first one in my family born in the States. When I was growing up, I had no idea what college even was. My dad was a foreman for the city water company.

"I started playing football in my junior year of high school, and in my senior year, my coach asked me if I was interested in going to college. He knew one of the Purdue assistant coaches.

"They offered me a scholarship. This was a big decision in my family because back then the males would all go to work to help support the family. I had to get permission from my dad. This was an Old-World Italian family. My dad said he'd worked all his life, so four more years without my help wouldn't make any difference.

"I went down to Purdue in the summer of 1944 and started to play football. My scholarship paid for books and tuition, and I worked in the kitchen at Delta Upsilon fraternity, which I joined.

"Freshmen could play on the varsity. I started off as a running back and ended up a center and defensive linebacker. I weighed about 185 pounds. That year some older guys from the Navy V-12 program as well as some seventeen-year-olds right out of high school, like myself, played for Purdue. We had about an even record.

"Angelo Carnaghi— you know, there used to be a cartoon strip called 'Ally Oop.' Ally Oop, had muscles in his gut and so did Carnaghi—and this was before the days when a lot of guys used weights to bulk up."

—John DeCamp

"I played football that fall of '44, then in November when I turned eighteen, I got drafted. That's not the way I had planned things, but that's how it worked out. I was in the Army. I was sent to the Philippines, but the fighting was over when I got there. I came back to Purdue in the spring semester of 1947.

"Football then wasn't like it is now. We didn't have a weight room. I majored in pharmacy, so I had labs until 4 P.M. After lab, I practiced until six, went to dinner, and then watched football films.

122

"We had a ton of guys playing"

"We had a lot of fun. Abe Gibron was on the team. He ended up coaching the Chicago Bears for awhile. Gibron and an assistant coach used to go around and around. At practice, the coach would shout, 'Hey, Gibron, you're lining up offside.' Gibron would shout back, 'I am not.' So the coach said, 'If you don't believe me, come over here and look for yourself.'

"When I first went to Purdue in 1944, I really had no idea what I was going to do. No one in my family had any idea what college was all about. We lived in a blue-collar neighborhood. No one went to work in a coat and tie. I started in aeronautical engineering but switched to civil engineering. Finally I got into pharmacy, and that was good.

"In 1947, I met my wife, Jeannine, at Purdue. We were married right after I graduated. I went right to work for Eli Lilly in Indianapolis on July 3. I got paid on the fifteenth and we got married on the twenty-ninth. That's all the money we had. My wife was in the class of 1951, but she didn't finish. She stopped when we got married.

ANGELO CARNAGHI. Unanimously chosen by his teammates as captain in the fall of 1949, Carnaghi played center for Purdue and was selected for the Blue-Gray and North-South post-college-season games.

"We thought we'd live in Indianapolis a couple years and then move. We didn't have any family there. But I stayed with Lilly for forty years. When I retired, I was vice president of pharmaceutical production and distribution. I received an honorary doctorate from Purdue in 1993.

"I was captain of the football team my senior year, and I had a chance to try out for professional football. But linemen were only making about five thousand dollars a year then, so I didn't try.

123

"Those were good years at Purdue. I had an academic scholarship, an athletic scholarship, and the GI Bill. Also, in the summers, I made good money working construction. I had more money than I'd ever had.

"It's funny when you stop to think of how one person can change your life. If my high school football coach hadn't mentioned going to college to me, what would have happened to me? My parents had aspirations for me to be a finish carpenter or a policeman.

"If I hadn't gone to college, what would have happened to my four children? Three graduated from Purdue and one graduated from Miami of Ohio. My children, when they were growing up, automatically thought about going to college. There had never been any mention of that in my house when I was growing up.

"As a matter of fact, the first day I went to work at Lilly, I didn't wear a necktie. I had never worn a necktie, but I looked around and everyone there had a necktie.

"The next day, I wore one, too."

William Butterfield

In the 1950 Purdue University yearbook, other senior class officers standing beside William Butterfield look to be the same size as he. You have to look closely to see that they are all standing on steps and that Butterfield is on a lower step than the others. He was a basketball player.

He was elected senior class president in 1949–50. He says his opponent, Billy Christensen, deserved to win it more. Only a man confident of his own worth could make that kind of statement.

At six feet six inches, Butterfield was a big man for his day. He played center for his high school and Purdue teams.

Born in 1928 in Evansville, Indiana, where he still lives, Butterfield's father owned an office furniture and supply business. Butterfield ran it when his turn came, and one of his sons runs it

"We had a ton of guys playing"

today. Butterfield is off pursuing other interests, other companies he owns in Evansville.

"I graduated high school in 1946," he says. "I don't know that we had that much knowledge of the war while I was in high school. Of course, we read about it in the papers and our parents talked about it. But we weren't that aware of what was going on.

"What I wanted to do was play basketball. I went to Bosse High School. We won the state championship my sophomore and junior years and were picked to win it my senior year. But we lost the first game of the tournament. I absolutely lived for basketball.

"My dad said I could pick where I'd do my undergraduate work if he could pick my grad school. I wanted to go to Purdue. Five or six of the players who graduated the year before I did all went to Purdue.

THE LETTERMEN. *Purdue basketball coach Mel Taube (right) goes over plans for an upcoming game in December of 1948. The team—undefeated at this point in the season—had seven lettermen. Standing are (left to right) Norris Caudell, forward; Bill Butterfield, center; and Andy Butchko, forward. Kneeling are (left to right) Bill Berberian, guard; Howard Williams, guard; Dick Axness, center; and R. Scotty Theissen, guard.*

"We didn't think about getting into the pros like kids do today. The pro salaries weren't that good. You could make more if you went into business. So, in college, I just wanted to play basketball and get an education.

"I was recruited by Purdue, but I wasn't offered a scholarship. My dad could afford to pay.

"I arrived on campus in the fall of 1946 with all the returning GIs. It was the biggest freshman class Purdue had ever had.

When it came time for basketball, 350 guys showed up for the first practice. Everyone got a pretty good shot to make the team, but I think the coach knew what players he wanted.

"I started one game my freshman year, and I started off and on for the next three years. I earned three letters.

"In my freshman year, we had great potential. We had several potential All-American players, but the team didn't play together away from home.

"I had held offices in high school, so when someone asked me if I wanted to run for senior class president, I said, 'Yeah.' I was in a fraternity and the guy I ran against was independent. He was more capable, but being in a fraternity I had more organization. And being a basketball player helped me.

"The guy I ran against was Billy Christensen. He ended up with a 6.0 grade average in engineering and became a vice president of IBM International. He's an unbelievable individual.

"At Purdue, I majored in liberal science. When I graduated, I went to Harvard Business School for my M.B.A. Then I went back to work with my dad.

"A son of mine runs the office furniture and supply business now. I spend about half my time in the Right to Life movement. Morals are completely decaying in our society today. People don't believe there are absolute rights and wrongs, but there are. We have eight children and twenty-three grandchildren.

"I'm also involved in two or three other businesses. I own an athletic club, a tourist agency, and a satellite business.

"I'll never retire. I wouldn't know what to do with myself if I did."

"We had a ton of guys playing"

chapter 5

"I told her
I'd give her a call"

Boy meets girl

Billy Christensen

In the 1950 Purdue University yearbook pictures, he is a mild-mannered-looking young man with glasses and a friendly smile. He looks like a guy you would like to sit and talk with.

Retired in New Canaan, Connecticut, he is busy in his garden most summer days. He has to schedule you in between his yard work. A busy career has left him with little patience for idle time.

"I had always been a good student," Christensen says. "When I was in high school, in today's terminology, I would have been called a 'math freak' or a 'science freak.' However, my experiences at Purdue and in the military had opened me up a bit to working with people, and I decided I didn't want to spend my life slaving over a lab bench. I wanted to do something involved with other people. I had job offers from Boeing, Douglas, and Proctor and Gamble. I almost took the Boeing job. If I had, I probably would have ended up a laid-off aerospace engineer.

He likes to tell how he found his first job after graduation from Purdue. It was in 1949 during his last semester there.

"On Friday night after that Thanksgiving, I went to a local haunt near my home in south Chicago to see which of my friends from high school I might run into. I met an old friend, and we chatted over a couple of beers. I asked him what he was doing,

127

and he said he was working for IBM. The more I talked to him, the more I liked how the company sounded. He said he'd set up an interview for me. The next week he called and I went to IBM for the interview. I graduated from Purdue, stayed a week to help with the freshman orientation, went home on Friday, and started work at IBM on Monday during a sleet storm. Everyone was late."

Christensen retired as vice president and general manager of IBM World Trade Corporation, the international arm of IBM.

"If I hadn't gone out for a few beers that Friday night, none of this would have happened," Christensen says. "It's funny how your life works out."

When he started with IBM in 1950, the company was heavily into punch cards. Christensen had no insight then about what lay ahead. Within a few years, the company introduced its first generation of computers.

"For a poor kid off the streets of the south side of Chicago, I can't complain," he says.

Born in 1926, there were four children in the family. Christensen's father, the son of a Norwegian immigrant, was a blue-collar worker who had to quit school and go to work after the eighth grade.

"My father kept working through the depression," Christensen says. "But he wasn't bringing home very much money—maybe five or ten dollars a week. My older brother worked after school, and when my older sister and I got old enough, we worked.

"When I was eight years old, I had a magazine route, selling and delivering. I handled the *Saturday Evening Post, Cosmopolitan, Liberty,* and *Colliers.* I also had newspaper routes, and my sister and I developed an egg business. A guy from nearby brought in eggs every week and we delivered them. When I got older, I got a job in a drugstore as a soda jerk, so I did about every kid-job you could think of. So I've been working ever since I was eight years old.

"I told her I'd give her a call"

"In the summer of 1943, I worked for R. R. Donnelly and Sons on the south side. They printed the Sears catalog. We worked ten hours a day because of the manpower shortage—made good money: sixty-four cents an hour.

"My mother insisted we weren't poor. She said times were just hard. We never went on relief. In those days, going on relief was an admission of failure.

"I graduated from Hyde Park High School in February of 1944. I skipped half a grade.

"I wanted to get into the war while I was in high school. I remember Pearl Harbor Day. I was fifteen. My first reaction was, Oh damn, it's going to be over before I get into it. I wanted to get into that war.

"I was seventeen when I graduated. I tried to enlist and I had my dad's permission. But my eyes weren't good. I had 20/200 vision. The military in 1944 still had prewar standards for people who wanted to enlist, if you can believe that. They said I couldn't enlist. I'd have to wait to be drafted when I turned eighteen.

"At that time, there was a citywide competitive scholastic exam. My high school math teacher had gotten three of us to take tutoring after class. Three scholarships were awarded, and two of them went to our school. I got one of them.

"The scholarship was to Illinois Tech, a very fine engineering school on the south side. My parents encouraged me. Like any family of European stock of that time, education was very important. I can't remember a day in my life when I didn't assume I would go to college.

"My older brother had been to a junior college and then went into a program as a government-trained civilian pilot. People often say Pearl Harbor caught us by surprise, that we weren't ready, which is not true. Roosevelt did a lot of things to get us ready. One of those things was this civilian aviation program that he started in the

1930s where you could learn to fly at government expense. My brother was good enough when the war came that the Army used him to train pilots, although he was still a civilian. He was killed in August of 1942 in a training accident. It was very hard on us.

"Since I couldn't get into the military immediately after high school, I took my scholarship. Universities were operating on an accelerated wartime program then. You worked at a fast pace. I turned eighteen in July, registered for the draft, and asked to be taken at the first opening. I went in the service in October of 1944. I hadn't taken my finals yet, but they excused me. I had completed one year of college.

"I went into the infantry and shipped out in early 1945 for the Philippines. I saw the last six months of the war. The Army discovered I had a year of college engineering under my belt and decided I couldn't be wasted, so they put me in a regimental combat team as a forward artillery observer. If there's anything more dangerous than being an infantryman in the jungle, it's being a forward artillery observer.

"It's hard to describe what it's like. You learn to keep your head down as much as possible and to keep all your senses alert. The United States was winning the war. We were on the offensive and on the move most of the time. That's the dangerous part. When you're a forward artillery observer, each time you move, you have to find a new spot out in front—sometimes way out in front—of the infantry. You learn not to show any sign of what you are doing in case the enemy sees you. You don't carry your binoculars over your shoulder. You stick them under your shirt. Officers don't wear any insignias.

"We finished up on July 4, 1945. MacArthur declared the Philippines secure. All that remained was mopping up. That was the most dangerous part of the war for me. When you mop up, you don't know where the enemy is. We had some pretty hairy experiences.

"I told her I'd give her a call"

"At the end of July, they pulled us down to a beach for amphibious training. They told us we would be involved in an amphibious operation, it would be major, and it would be the end of the war. They didn't tell us where we were going. But we knew.

"Then they dropped the bombs and the Japanese surrendered. We sailed to Japan. We sailed into Tokyo Bay before dawn on the morning of September 2. The ship where they signed the peace that day was only a quarter-mile away. We watched the whole thing. It was very exciting. Planes were flying overhead. It was an awesome display of force—just in case. When we landed at a Japanese naval air station, we made a full combat landing. We didn't take anything for granted, but there was no resistance. We felt great joy that it was over and pride that we had won.

"Later we found out how lucky we were that the United States dropped the bombs. The whole Japanese coastline was full of caves and artillery. We found out our mission was to be a D-minus-1 diversionary landing—one day before the planned major invasion—in southern Japan, which would have been really something. Later a guy wrote a fictional account of what might have happened, based on the plans. We got decimated.

"They were sending guys home, but I didn't have enough points to go back yet. I got promoted to supply sergeant. I wanted to get home and start at Purdue in the fall of 1946, but the military declared my skill to be essential. All of our officers were being sent home so I was doing the supply officer's job. They held me over until October of 1946, so I missed the fall term.

"I arrived at Purdue in February of 1947 for the second semester. I lived on campus in converted bachelor officer's quarters that the university had gotten from some military base. The accommodations were luxurious by my standards. In Japan, we had been sleeping in tents. There were barracks in some places in Japan, but they were full of fleas, so we slept in our tents.

Boy meets girl

"On campus after the war, everyone had a very positive feeling. We had won the war and survived the war, and we all felt good about that accomplishment. We were proud and we were grateful that our lives were getting back on track.

"You never heard anyone complain about the years they had lost. You didn't even hear a lot of war stories from the guys. Mostly, you had to draw people out to talk about the war. Because there were so many veterans, the telling of war stories was looked down upon.

"On the GI Bill, I got tuition and books and seventy-five dollars a month. In those days, that meant I wasn't starving, but I wasn't living in luxury either. I think I had to pay seventeen dollars a month for living quarters, which left just fifty-eight dollars for food and everything else. So I worked about twenty hours a week, mostly slinging hash, to make some more money.

"I had a 5.84 average on a 6-point scale, and I was very involved in campus activities. I was vice president of the senior class. I had run for president. It wasn't my idea. Some of my friends talked me into it. I lost to Bill Butterfield, who was a basketball player and belonged to a social fraternity. He was well known on campus. I was also president of the mechanical engineering fraternity and vice president of the Reamer Club.

"I guess the reason I got involved in so many activities was to meet girls. In engineering, 99 percent of my classmates were males.

"In my senior year, I bought a car. When I was in the service, my top pay was 120 bucks a month. Because I was never in a position to spend much, I had it sent home, so I had saved two thousand dollars. At Purdue, I lived on my GI Bill money and what I could make working. When I needed a new suit or a pair of shoes, I bought it with my service money. By my senior year, I had about six hundred bucks left, and I thought, By George, I'm going to enjoy my last semester. So I bought a 1938 Buick Special

"I told her I'd give her a call"

coupe. It had a long hood and a little bubble of a canopy. It had two seats with a jump seat in the back.

"By having the car, I met my wife, Ros. We were at a picnic and I needed to get back early to study. I asked if anyone needed a ride. She said she did. I dropped her off and I told her I'd give her a call—and I did.

"Actually, the spring before that I had gone through a broken romance. So I came back to campus in the fall of 1949 with the mission to see how many girls I could date in one semester— my last semester. Ros was number eight and that's as far as I got. But on a campus with a male-female ratio of five to one, and later six to one, eight isn't bad.

"I didn't know what was going to happen with IBM when I went with the company. It was really a matter of destiny the way things worked out. My career spanned the entire computer age. It was very exciting.

"Growing up in the depression and living through the war stamped our generation with a certain attitude. When I was working so hard for such long hours and I'd get called back to work while we were on vacation, I used to say to the kids, 'You have to learn something. In this life, you do what you have to do and you don't complain about it. When you complain, you just waste energy.'

"That kind of thinking came from the depression and from the war. The world doesn't owe you a living. It's a shame the younger generations today don't understand that.

"I think my generation is clearly marked by the times in which we lived. A depression and a war made the way hard for us to get where we were going."

Honoraries hold picnic tomorrow

The Reamers and Gimlets, athletic boosting organizations on campus, are collaborating on a picnic to be

Boy meets girl

given this Sunday at Monitor Springs. Guests of the afternoon will be the Gold Peppers. . . .

This will be the first get together of the organizations this year and is designed to further cordial relations. . . .

PURDUE EXPONENT, NOVEMBER 12, 1949

Ros Grindy Christensen

"Most of the men I met on campus ," she says, "were older than I was and former GIs, including the one I married.

"He was vice president of the Reamers, and I was president of Gold Peppers, a women's honorary. In the fall of 1949, my senior year, the Gimlet Club and the Reamers and the Gold Peppers had a picnic.

"I had a big test the next day and I didn't really want to go. But I was president and I felt I had to put in an appearance. I was hoping for a ride back early. This fellow at the picnic asked if anyone needed a ride back to the campus, and I said yes.

"We were married the next June—June of 1950—in the University Church the day before I graduated. There were probably fifteen to twenty other couples married in that chapel on the same day."

The four years Ros Grindy Christensen spent at Purdue University were among the happiest days of her life. It is difficult now, so many years later, to say why. Maybe it was because that is when she met her husband. Maybe it was because the war was over and her brother and so many others were home safe and well from overseas. Maybe it was because she was young and her life was opening opportunities before her. Maybe it was all of that.

She grew up in North Adams, Massachusetts.

"In 1946, I graduated from the Emma Willard School in Troy, New York," Christensen says. "It's the oldest girls' prep school in the United States.

134

"I told her I'd give her a call"

"At Purdue, I pledged Delta Gamma sorority and went to live in the sorority house my sophomore year. My freshman year I lived in a dorm, Cary East. The other sections of Cary were all for men. It was great being a female on campus because there were so few of us compared to the men.

"I didn't go out most weeknights. I had my nose in the books. But on the weekends, there was always something happening. At the student union, they had dances, and many of the big bands came in. We went to fraternity and sorority parties, and sometimes we just went to the movies.

"I loved Purdue. I would say my four years there were probably among the best I've known. I liked the girls in the sorority. I

DANCING IN THE DARK. *Junior Prom Committee chairman Bill Keefe and Katie Dittrich McMillin led the grand march in 1949.*

liked the classes. I liked the activities I was involved in. It was a good, full, rich life and I enjoyed it. I was fortunate. The war was over, and the only place to go was up. Everyone looked to the future with optimism. But by the same token, people were willing to work. It wasn't a free ride.

"Women had hours. That didn't bother me. Occasionally I used to say, 'What a drag. I'm having a good time and I have to get back.' Then, too, if you were at the library doing something, you had to close up the books and dash back.

"In a way, I think having hours was probably very good. Young people today could use a little more discipline. They're given too much leeway. Even today some young women would probably be just as glad if they did have hours.

"When we were seniors, we got to wear gold corduroy skirts. Men wore gold cord pants, some decorated in wild colors. In general, women didn't paint their cords like the men did. Almost all the women had a black sweater to go with their skirt. We wore bobby socks and saddle shoes—preferably black and white shoes to carry on the color scheme. In addition to my sorority pin, the only jewelry I can remember wearing was a watch and maybe pearls. Jewelry wasn't around as much as it is today.

"I recall wearing the gold cord skirt to events like football games and to special meetings of organizations I belonged to. If you look up the Gold Peppers in the 1950 yearbook, I think you'll see every single one of us had on a gold corduroy skirt, bobby socks, and a black sweater—and we had our little beanies on our heads. [She's right.]

"There was a lot of prefab housing on campus. Student enrollment grew because of the returning GIs and the increase in women coming to school. The sororities couldn't house all the women. In my sorority, it was so crowded that every member for one semester in her junior year had to live in temporary university housing. The housing unit was far from the center of campus, and it was cold out there on the plains. The wind and the cold came right through the walls.

"If someone arrived with a flashlight, you could see light through the cracks between these parallel pieces of wood—or whatever they used for siding. The walls were flimsy and it was cold inside. Living there was like being sent to Siberia for a semester. You just hoped you'd survive and get back to the sorority.

"After graduation, I moved to Chicago with my husband, who had a job with IBM. I worked in Chicago for two reasons. First, money—we didn't have two nickels to rub together. Second, I would have been bored silly sitting alone in an apartment even in those days before women's lib.

136

"I told her I'd give her a call"

"It wasn't unusual for women to work before they had children. But they weren't paid on the same wage-scale as men.

"We had to do a lot of moving around. They used to say IBM stood for 'I've Been Moved.' The husbands would say it meant 'I Bring Money.' Anyway, I didn't work after we left Chicago and moved east. Our two children were born in 1956 and 1960.

"In about 1978, I did go back to work as an international travel consultant. We lived overseas just outside of Paris from 1963 to 1971 and we took a lot of trips. We really covered Europe. I began to know more than the average person about travel in Europe and I enjoyed it. That's why I got into that field.

"I stopped working in about 1988, but I hope to keep traveling the world for many more years, even though I've already been to all the continents, including Antarctica."

George Benko

He and his wife live part of the year in Indianapolis and part of the year in Florida. The fall evening of this interview he is in his southern home getting it ready for their winter stay.

It is a good retirement for George Benko, who left the Diamond Chain Company in 1986 after thirty-six years. He was director of material control when he left.

It was a good career. But it was not what he had planned for himself when he was growing up in Lakewood, Ohio, just outside of Cleveland. What he wanted to do then was fly.

"I was born in 1925," he says. "My folks were both immigrants from Slovakia. It was part of the Austria-Hungary empire then. Dad came to the United States in 1910 and Mom in 1919.

"Dad was a laborer. He came here because of the situation they were living under in the Austria-Hungary empire. He wanted to come here, save a lot of money, go back there, and live like a king. But

World War I started and that squelched that. He also became more accustomed to the culture and got married, so he stayed.

"There were seven of us kids, one died at the age of five. Dad worked for the Cleveland Welding Company. During the depression, he might work only one or two days a week, whenever an order came in that required the machine he ran. My mother was an excellent economist. She scrimped and saved, and we were able to pay off the mortgage on our house during the war years.

"My parents were Lutheran and my father was very religious. The first thing he would take out of his paycheck was a tithe for the church. My mother got mad when he did that. She was religious, too, but when the choice was between feeding the family or giving money to the church, what came first? If God can't be forgiving about something like that, what kind of a God have we? But, we were charter members of a new church and it had bills, too.

"We had chicken soup every Sunday with only two legs to go around. And we all loved the legs.

"I graduated from high school in 1943 and I enlisted in the Army Air Corps. I was a great aviation enthusiast. I used to walk to the Cleveland Airport on Sundays—and it was ten miles one way. I'd sit there for hours and watch the planes come in and go out. There were all kinds of planes—top-wing, bi-plane, low-wing, transports.

"I entered the service in September of '43 after I graduated from high school. Before I went in, I worked during the summer for NACA—the National Advisory Committee for Aeronautics. It later became NASA. They were doing engine research at the Cleveland airport, and I went to work as an apprentice.

"I learned to fly in the Air Corps, but I never did go overseas. By the time I finished my training in B-17s, it was March of 1945 and they weren't sending new pilots to Europe anymore.

"I told her I'd give her a call"

They didn't fly B-17s in the Pacific so I was assigned to B-29s. Then, the Pacific war ended.

"While I was in military training, I subscribed to *Flying and Aviation Magazine,* and there was an article in it about the Purdue School of Aeronautical Engineering. I made up my mind at that point that I was going to school at Purdue.

"But I had an interesting tug of war with myself when it came time to decide whether to stay in the service or be discharged and go to school. I had always wanted to fly. It had been my number one ambition. By the time I was nineteen years old, I had reached my number-one ambition in life.

"I decided I wanted to keep flying, so on the day I had to sign up again, I started walking toward the hut to do it. I got halfway there and said to myself, You can do better. I turned around and headed for Purdue to become an aeronautical engineer. I never looked back. When I got to Purdue, I switched to mechanical engineering.

"I don't know if I would have gone to college without the GI Bill. My father once told me he'd pay for me to go to seminary. But I wasn't interested in that.

"In March of 1946, we lived in the field house. They had big double-decker bunks lined up row after row. I don't know how many there were. A couple thousand of us must have been staying there. But it was fun. You got to know people. I never resented it. It was an adventure. After six or eight weeks, the university got these defense-housing buildings and moved them onto campus. In these, we each had a single room about ten by twelve feet with space for a bed and a desk. It wasn't terribly uncomfortable. It was fun. I enjoyed it.

"There weren't a lot of girls on campus. In the fall of 1949, I was living in Cary Hall, and a guy named Fred Hopkins lived across the hall. He and I were dating the same girl, Mary Lou

139

Boy meets girl

Kull. We were both very much infatuated with her. She knew our feelings and that she was going to have to make a decision. She elected to stay with Fred.

"Mary Lou was a member of Sigma Kappa sorority, and she fixed me up with another girl in the house, Doris Roberts. Doris and I were married in October of 1950. I graduated in February of 1950 but she didn't graduate until June. Her family was in Indianapolis, and since I was in love with her, I got a job in Indianapolis.

"Thinking back on that time, the war was behind us, and we had a definite purpose in college. A couple years of our lives had gone to the war, so we were very serious students. We were very intense about our studies. But on weekends, we did have our little social get-togethers. We drank beer and solved the world's problems.

"We experienced a very interesting part of the history of this country. We were born predepression and lived through the depression. We came through the war. Afterward, we were able to participate as engineers in rebuilding the world. We lived in a fantastic period. We went through tremendous turmoil, and we got to enjoy the rewards that followed our work.

"I never did get my private pilot's license. I never flew an airplane again after I left the Army Air Corps in 1946, even though flying had been my number one ambition in life. As I said, I reached my lifetime ambition when I was nineteen or twenty.

"So I just moved on from there."

Mary Lou Kull Hopkins

Mary Lou Hopkins is a woman who loves to tell stories. The memories flow from her as easily as pages turn in a photo album.

A strong Lutheran, she went to Saint James Lutheran School in Lafayette and was in the class of Alfred B. Kirchhoff at the time he was writing the "Purdue University Hymn."

"I told her I'd give her a call"

"He taught fourth, fifth, and sixth grades at Saint James, and every room had an organ," Hopkins says. "He wrote the hymn while he was in class. Every so often he'd say, 'Sing these notes,' and we'd sing a measure or two of the 'Purdue Hymn.' I took piano lessons from him."

Now she lives in Brownsburg, Indiana, not far from Lafayette where she was born in 1928, the daughter of a dairy farmer.

"What I remember about my dad is that he would get up at three-thirty every morning and milk the cows," she says. "I had two older brothers who helped. My father did his own bottling, and he delivered that milk in the north end of Lafayette by 6 A.M. He was a good German. He did everything himself.

"We always had plenty to eat, even during the depression, because we had a garden. I do remember many of my dad's customers couldn't pay the milk bill, so they would come out and work on the farm to trade for the milk.

"We didn't get electricity on the farm until 1937, but because my dad was a dairy farmer, he had his own system that also provided lights in the house. They weren't always the best, but we had lights.

"We got indoor plumbing when I was very young. A fellow on Ninth Street by the name of Lahr put it in for us. My father traded Mr. Lahr one-hundred-dollars-worth of milk for a bathroom.

"I went to Jefferson High School in Lafayette. When I started out, I wanted to be a secretary. All of my courses were in business. When I became a junior, I decided I wanted to be a teacher, and my father said, 'You better try to go to Purdue.' So I picked up the college-prep courses I needed and enrolled at Purdue.

"I know not all fathers wanted their daughters to go to college in those days, but my father was pretty progressive. I was the first in my family to go to college. Neither of my brothers went. My younger sister came to Purdue two years after I entered. When my older brothers graduated from high school, the depression was still going on and things were tight. But when I graduated in 1946, we had come up out of the depression.

"Purdue was very crowded. I lived in Cary Hall East my freshman year, and then I moved to the Sigma Kappa sorority house.

"I met Fred Hopkins shortly after I arrived at Purdue. He was from a military family. He was at Purdue when I was a senior in high school. We were both taking piano lessons from Vi Murphy on north Ninth Street. She told me she wanted me to meet a young man who was a student of hers. She told me to call him. But my father did not allow me to date students from Purdue. So I knew better than to call.

"When I went away from home to live on campus, Fred and I were both still taking piano lessons. I wouldn't have called him except the piano teacher said he was trying to reach me and couldn't. So I called him first and we started to date. We also stopped taking piano lessons. That teacher lost two students at once.

"About a month after I started dating Fred, I met George Benko at University Lutheran Church, and I started dating him, too. It became very complicated. These guys lived across the hall from each other. Sometimes all three of us went places together.

"They were both mechanical engineering students. They had both been in the Army Air Corps. They were really quite similar. I had to make a choice. I chose to stay with Fred. There was just that electricity when we were together.

"But I really liked George, so I introduced him to a sorority sister, and they married.

"Fred graduated in January of 1950 and went to Ohio State to get his master's, which he never finished. He took a job in Ohio. He was tired of school and war and everything else. He was ready to make a little money.

"Of course, engineers were a dime a dozen at that time because so many of the ex-GIs graduated with engineering degrees

142

"I told her I'd give her a call"

at the same time. The country was swarming with engineers. Fred earned $225 a month in his first job. But it was money. Those guys had been to war, and they hadn't ever made any money.

"I graduated in June of 1950 and took a job in a township school in Benton County, Indiana. It was in Freeland Park—ninety kids in grades one through twelve with a wonderful basketball team. I taught home ec, which had been my major.

"Fred and I were married at Saint James Lutheran Church on July 7, 1951. We moved to Brownsburg in 1954. I wasn't working. We had three children in all, the last born in 1959.

"Brownsburg was under a trusteeship school system. The trustee heard I was a teacher and one day he came knocking on my door. It seems they couldn't find enough teachers. Even though I had a degree in home ec, I taught sixth-grade elementary for five years on a permit, starting in 1962. I was also going to Butler working on a master's in elementary education. By the time I had earned my master's, they had built a new junior high, and they offered me a job as a home ec teacher there. I taught for twenty-three years until I retired.

"It's kind of interesting. The first six or seven years we lived in Brownsburg, none of the women worked. But about the same time I went back, they all seemed to go back to work."

Fred Hopkins

Fred Hopkins's father was a pioneer in aviation who, in 1940, was called to Washington, D.C., by Henry "Hap" Arnold, who was chief of air staff. A firm believer in the importance of airpower in warfare, Arnold persuaded industry to step up production of planes.

Small wonder that Fred Hopkins, an only son, grew up yearning to fly.

"My dad was in Germany after World War I," Hopkins says. "He flew all those planes that were held together with bailing wire. The Army was far behind in its thinking about air power. They didn't know what the airplane could do.

"He became a general in 1942, the same year I graduated from high school in Washington. I wanted to fly. My dad had been my first flight instructor.

"There were four Purdue University grads in Washington at that time, and I got to know them through my dad. One was Ed Elliott, the son of the president of Purdue. The men from Purdue worked with my father and they impressed me. So I thought I'd go to Purdue.

"I went for one year to engineering school in Virginia after high school, and then I enlisted in the summer of 1943 when things really got hot. I trained as a B-17 ball turret and waist gunner.

"I was scheduled to go overseas, but the war ended. When I was discharged, I went to Purdue on the GI Bill.

"I loved music. So when I got to Purdue, I decided I wanted to learn to play the piano. I took lessons in town from a woman named Vi Murphy, God bless her. I told her I wanted to meet a nice girl who liked music. She lined me up.

"I tried to reach this girl but she was always out. So I left a message and she gave me a buzz. We started dating.

"I had a buddy, George Benko, who lived across the hall. He started dating her, too. He was a fine guy. But I out-maneuvered him. What did I do? Let's just say I offered her a Hollywood contract and she went for it.

"I graduated from Purdue in the winter of 1950 and entered Ohio State to get my master's degree in business. But I didn't finish. I went out to work in industry. I was tired of school. I wanted to go to work.

"The depression has influenced a lot of my thinking. You know, my family didn't have it so bad during the depression. My dad was in the Army, and he always had a job and a paycheck.

"I told her I'd give her a call"

"But I saw what was happening on the outside. And that's what has made me very conservative throughout my life."

Doris Roberts Benko

She is the wife of George Benko. Born in 1928, Doris Roberts Benko grew up on a farm in Marion County, near Indianapolis, Indiana, the only child of a farmer and his wife.

"Both my parents had gone to two-year colleges and were teachers," she says. "But after my dad started farming, he quit teaching. Being a dairy farmer was a good business, but he also had to drive a school bus and do his regular crop farming in addition to the dairy.

"I graduated from Broad Ripple High School in 1946. I went to Purdue because I wanted to get into home economics.

"There were a lot of men on the Purdue campus. I didn't date a lot my freshman year. I was still adjusting to being away from home. I wasn't eager to get socially involved at that point. Sometimes I would get homesick and overwhelmed, but I adjusted.

"In home ec, my major area was interior design and my secondary area was major equipment like ranges and refrigerators. Most of the girls on campus were in home ec and science. There weren't many girls in engineering. At that time, women didn't have that many options.

"I joined Sigma Kappa sorority. I met my husband in the fall of 1949. I think I went to a Cary Hall dance with him. I guess he didn't sweep me off my feet that night. I don't remember its being that exciting. But we kept on dating.

"After I graduated, I went to work with Indianapolis Power and Light as a home service adviser. I went into homes and demonstrated electrical equipment that had been sold by dealers in town. I also gave public demonstrations in an auditorium. One of the popular appliances then was a mangler that did ironing.

"We had two children. I stopped working when our first child was born. Some women still do. Our daughter-in-law did. Women, back then, weren't as career oriented as they are today. We didn't have to have everything. We were contented to live on just one salary.

"Growing up, I never expected to have to work outside the home. I always expected that I would get married, have a family, and stay home. And that's what I did."

Jack Martin

The year 1950 had its ups and downs for Jack Martin. It was the year he finally graduated from Purdue at the age of twenty-seven— a college education that had been interrupted by war. It was also the year he was recalled to fight in Korea.

Now the owner of an insurance agency in Lafayette, Martin also owns an apple orchard and has become known as a Johnny Appleseed to thousands of area children who have visited the farm every fall on a tour he provides.

He has a deep voice and a love of telling a story. As he sits in an office in his agency, he leans back, and the springs squeak in the cushioned, metal desk chair.

The depression never bothered his family, he says. His father worked on the railroad as a conductor. Men were let go according to their seniority. Martin's dad was next on the list to be laid off. But they never got to him. He never lost a day's pay. His luck was good.

Martin remembers living in Terre Haute, Indiana, and the bums coming to the house for handouts.

"Dad always gave them something," Martin says. "They were just down on their luck, as he put it. They never caused any problem. Most of them were nice people. They just didn't have jobs.

"We moved to Indianapolis. In 1941, I graduated from Ben Davis High School. I had always planned to go to college. My

"I told her I'd give her a call"

father had encouraged me all my life. Dad thought I should be a professional and do something on a level above his own. There was nothing wrong with what he did. He just wanted something better for me.

"The plan was that Dad would help me through college, and when I graduated, my brother would be ready to go. Assuming I had a decent job, I could help send him through college.

"I entered prelaw at Butler University in Indianapolis in September of 1941. I planned to be a lawyer. But Pearl Harbor came and changed all that.

"We didn't even go to classes that Monday after Pearl Harbor. We just drove around and listened to the radio. We knew we were going to war. We were apprehensive. We felt patriotic, but we wanted to pick the branch we were going to be in, rather than get drafted and arbitrarily assigned to something. I certainly didn't want to be cannon fodder. We lost three of our high school classmates that first year.

"I enlisted in the Navy within six months after Pearl Harbor and waited to be called. It didn't make any sense to stay in school knowing I was going to be called, so I left Butler and took a job with the railroad while I waited. I was a brakeman.

"I had a lot of fun. There were plenty of girls around. I worked a great deal. I probably had more money back then than I've ever had in my life. I was paid $175 every two weeks, and I didn't know what to do with all that money. For the most part, I just had a good time and bought some clothes. I roomed with a family.

"For awhile, prisoner-of-war trains came through Indianapolis. They were mostly Italian prisoners and were very friendly. When you walked by the train, they leaned out the windows and asked for cigarettes.

"Finally, everyone who signed up with the military when I did had been called but me, so I checked on what was going on.

147

They had lost my file. If I hadn't called, they probably would have forgotten all about me.

"In 1943, I finally entered the service. They sent me to DePauw University for preflight school and then to Purdue for flight training. At that point, I decided I loved aviation but had no stomach for flying. So I got into control towers and spent the war in New Orleans at a Navy air-training command.

"I arrived at Purdue in the fall of 1946. I was on the GI Bill. I received fifty-six bucks a month, and the government paid for all my books and fees. Four of us, all men, lived together, and we did our own cooking—a lot of macaroni and cheese.

"I wanted to stay in control-tower work, so I had to take freshman engineering classes like chemistry and physics—stuff I had always avoided. I had to do surveying for one class—start at one point and go from point to point to point around campus and back to the starting point. When I got back, I had the elevation twenty-seven feet higher than when I started. I transferred to the school of education.

"People were serious about their education. I joined Alpha Chi Rho fraternity. They had a good grade-point average. Most of the guys in the house were back from the service. They had a good time—weekend parties—but they were there to get an education. There were quiet hours at night for study, and if anyone got noisy, he was told about it and was fined.

"Some of the guys were getting married. They had these old Army barracks where married students lived. They weren't very nice. I had a friend who, every time he thought about getting married, went down and looked at those barracks. He would come back and say, 'There's no way I'm ever getting married.' It didn't work. Now he has six children.

"I met my future wife, Fern, the last part of my sophomore year. She belonged to a sorority but lived at home with her par-

"I told her I'd give her a call"

ents in West Lafayette. The summer after my junior year we got married.

"After graduation in the summer of 1950, I decided to go to grad school in industrial recreation. I worked part-time in insurance.

"I was called back for service in Korea that summer. When I left the Navy, they told me to enlist in the reserves. They said I'd never be called back unless the president declared war. I was foolish. I was called back for active duty and told to report to Indianapolis. I said there was no declaration of war. They said that didn't matter and there was nothing I could do about it.

"I had a history of ear problems dating back to my service during World War II, so I got all my medical records together and took them to Indianapolis with me. I gave them to the doctor. He took one look at my ears and said, 'Rejected.' That was the one time in my life I was glad to be rejected.

"It wasn't that I was unpatriotic. I was very patriotic, but I had served my time. It wasn't fair. I had already done my duty."

Fern Honeywell Martin

It was a happy day in 1928 when Earl R. Honeywell, a professor of floriculture at Purdue University walked into his class and approached the blackboard. "Fern Marie Honeywell," he wrote in bold letters, announcing the long-awaited birth of his daughter. "Purdue University Class of 1950."

And so the die was cast. On the day Fern Marie Honeywell was born in West Lafayette, the decision that she should attend college where her father taught seemed a foregone conclusion.

What was not known that happy day was that the stock market would crash within a year of her birth and that there would be depression followed by war—events that would shake the world and affect the lives of everyday people in everyday places like West Lafayette, Indiana.

149

She is moved when she talks about the end of the war. She was working for the Purdue Library in 1945, and one of her assignments was to clip and file newspaper articles about the atomic bombs.

"We did feel good about winning," she says. "But there were some questions in the back of my mind. We were greatly concerned about the bomb and the devastation. Yet, we also talked about how many American lives would have been lost if we hadn't brought that war to an end.

"I had a very strange feeling as I sat there clipping those stories. I felt I was sitting in on history, and I wondered where it was going to go from there."

Martin still lives in West Lafayette and is director of public relations for the Tippecanoe County Historical Association. She is a slender woman with long graying hair that she usually keeps pinned up in back. She is a pleasant woman—friendly, well read.

"I was an only child," she says. "When I was young, growing up in West Lafayette, we did not feel as much insecurity about the depression as some others felt. I can remember there were things I wanted to do, but my parents wouldn't let me. They said there wasn't enough money.

"We lived in an old home with big trees. My father didn't keep a garden at home. My mother would chastise him about that, and he'd say, 'Dr. Quackenbush is a chemist and I don't see him coming home to play with a chemistry set.' That was the way he felt. We had a nice yard, but he felt he worked all day with flowers and that was enough.

"On Pearl Harbor Day, I was at an Abbott and Costello movie with one of my girlfriends. When I returned home, my father told me about it, and we sat by the radio and listened constantly to the news. I was in a state of absolute dismay. How could this have happened?

"Growing up in high school during the war was certainly a different experience. Several of my classmates left school early to

"I told her I'd give her a call"

enlist. There were, I believe, only two cars in the whole high school class. Gasoline was rationed very tightly. Automobiles were no longer being made. Because no tires were available, kids were not cruising around in cars.

"When the football team played out of town, some parent would save his gas all week, and we'd all pile into his car and go to the game. We didn't have easy mobility. We all lived with rationing. And we lived with the idea that we were mortal even though we were nowhere near a war zone.

"Some of my classmates had parents in the service. In high school, we were definitely aware of what was going on. Much of our conversation was about current events.

"Foods like sugar and meat were rationed. We received rationing stamps that we redeemed at the grocery store. It's amazing how we coped with things like that. My mother started cooking with honey instead of sugar. We cut back on a lot of things. There was no butter. We used oleomargarine, and it came in a yucky white blob. One of my jobs was to sit in the kitchen and mix the color into the oleo.

"Part of my allowance was put into war stamps and bonds. No one traveled much. One time, we were able to go to western Kansas to visit relatives who lived on a farm. Of course, they had beef there, and we sat down to one of the biggest steaks I had ever seen. During the war, we didn't see steaks much. My mother was irritated when my cousins ate just a couple of bites of this wonderful steak and gave the rest to the dog. And there we were with meat rationing at home in town. It was an entirely different way of life for relatives who were farmers.

"I went to downtown Lafayette to celebrate the end of the war. It was neat. There was great excitement—snake dances, music. Everybody was happy to have an end to the war and a new beginning. There were thousands downtown. People were hugging one another. Everybody was your friend. It was time for celebrating.

Boy meets girl

"I started college in the fall of 1946. I lived at home in the beginning. There was a housing crunch, and my mother rented out a room because the university made an appeal for people to open their homes to students.

"We went to college as eighteen-year-olds, and in college, eighteen-year-olds were in a minority. We were in class with men and women much older than we were, and they were much more intent on an education. These were not college-boy pranksters. The competition was fierce.

"I majored in English and social studies and minored in psychology, but a lot of the women students majored in home economics. I got a bachelor of science degree.

"I had some wonderful teachers. I wasn't used to making bad grades, but trigonometry was a disaster for me. We didn't have many teaching assistants, but we did have some. I had one in trigonometry, and the problem was she taught to the students who knew the most. She would say, 'Do you understand this?' All the guys in the room who had been radar operators in the war would nod, Yes. To myself I would say, Ugh. She was talking to the ones who understood, and I was totally lost.

"I ended up taking trig in summer school, and my teaching assistant was Arthur Hansen. He had this wonderful way of imparting knowledge, and I did much better. Although I had so much trouble the first time I took it, after the second exam in his class, he asked, 'Miss Honeywell, have you ever considered majoring in mathematics?'

"When we first went to school, we girls went out and bought whole new wardrobes. During the war, very little fabric was available. But after the war ended, fabric became available again, and the fashion industry introduced 'The New Look.' It was an entirely different style, and we all had to go out and buy new wardrobes again. The style was very long full skirts and very narrow

152

"I told her I'd give her a call"

waists—a lot of fabric. We wore bobby socks and saddle shoes or penny loafers. Poodle skirts were quite popular. Pearls, of course. You had to have pearls.

"I met my husband when I was a sophomore. He had dated two of my girlfriends, so I was aware of who he was. We started dating and we were married in the summer of 1949.

"When I started college, I didn't know what I wanted to do with my life. I thought I'd go into personnel and I had a love of history. The standard joke back then was that girls went to college to get their 'Mrs.' degree. And I knew some girls who got married right out of college and never really knew where a dollar came from. But I think that image has been overplayed.

"During our college years of 1946 to 1950, one of the things we thought about was what to do after a major conflict? How do we get our lives back together? Where do we go from here? Do we forgive the countries that fought against us or punish them?

"We felt that although we'd just been through a difficult period now it was time to put things back together. A lot of people went to college who would never have had the opportunity. It was a euphoric time. We felt good about winning the war. We were not, however, as realistic as we should have been, because we were all so high on the belief that we had also won the peace.

"And we were going to have peace forever."

Noisy celebration greets peace news; 2-day holiday here

Downtown Lafayette was the scene of a noisy peace celebration Tuesday evening, recalling the wild demonstrations which greeted the armistice ending World War I nearly 25 years ago.

Police estimate that at least 20,000 persons were on downtown streets between 8 and 9 p.m., with perhaps 30,000 to 40,000 present throughout the evening and night. The spontaneous celebration began a few minutes after 6 when President Truman announced that Japan had surrendered and continued until early Wednesday.

Despite the great throng of happy people who took part in the demonstration, there were only minor disorders. For the most part, people just stood about talking to each other and watching the many spontaneous parades and stunts. Paper littered the streets and about every imaginable noise making device was used.

Stores not already closed shut their doors upon receipt of the peace announcement. . . .

A number of local churches announced special peace services for Wednesday evening. . . .

All in all, the news of peace brought one of the greatest celebrations in the history of the city and one of the longest general suspensions of business. . . .

With receipt of the announcement church bells were rung and locomotive whistles let loose their shrill blasts as did some factory whistles. People began flocking downtown, horns on their autos blowing unendingly.

People carried dinner bells and cow bells, whistles, horns, tin cans, pans and other articles which could make noise. All were used for hours. Firecrackers were set off. The fire siren at Fourth and Main streets was turned on. People shouted, talked and milled about. Bits of paper were scattered over the street.

The celebration was not restricted to any age or group. Among the happiest were perhaps a number of men and women in uniforms of the various branches of the armed services home on leave, their faces were wreathed in broad smiles.

Youngsters formed impromptu snake dances and parades, winding their way up and down the streets. Old people cheered and babies in arms became frightened adding their cries to the din. Dogs barked. . . .

"I told her I'd give her a call"

Flags were carried by some and several autos had flags fastened to their hoods. Effigies of Hirohito were carried among the milling crowds with the throng jeering and cheering. In one neighborhood, youngsters burned such a figure. . . .

Sailors at Purdue routed out the Purdue Victory Bell and paraded it throughout Lafayette, ringing the bell and shouting merrily as they drove along.

JOURNAL AND COURIER, AUGUST 15, 1945

Arthur Hansen

He was president of Georgia Tech University in Atlanta until 1971. That year he came back to West Lafayette to become the first and only Purdue alumnus to be the university's president.

Well-liked and respected on campus and in the community, he held the job for eleven years, the period of time he said he would stay when he accepted the position. Soon after, he became chancellor of the Texas A and M University system.

He started his career in 1948 with NASA in Cleveland where he worked in jet engines and wing design. Then, at the Cornell Aero Lab in Buffalo, New York, he did research in nuclear aircraft. Next, he went to the University of Michigan to set up a new area in fluid mechanics in mechanical engineering. He left Michigan to go to Georgia Tech as dean of engineering.

Art Hansen is a man who talks engineering, physics, math, literature, painting, or music with equal ease. He has a sparkle in his eye and a way of letting people know he is interested in what they are saying.

Retired from his university positions, he is on four corporate boards and does consulting work and community projects in his Zionsville, Indiana, home.

He received his B.S. from Purdue in electrical engineering in 1946 and his master's in math in 1948. He was a teaching assistant during the time the class of 1950 was going through Purdue. As with many people, it was the war that first brought him to West Lafayette.

"I was born in 1925 in Green Bay, Wisconsin," he says. "My father had a corner grocery store. It was tough running a store during the depression, mainly because people did not have money. We had a good day if we sold thirteen-dollars-worth of food. Charge accounts were common because cash was not handy, and those accounts became a serious problem. We knew our customers. They were neighbors and friends. We couldn't turn them down. But we had bills to pay, too.

"It was a family neighborhood-store and our family ran it. I delivered groceries on my bike. When people called in orders, I put the groceries on my bike, ran them to the house, and dropped them off.

"My dad attended school to about the tenth grade and then he left. My mother might have finished high school. I'm not sure. She died when I was thirteen.

"I was graduated from West Green Bay High School in 1943 and had a scholarship to the University of Wisconsin. But the war intervened. Recognizing that I was going to be drafted, I enlisted in the Marines Corps and was able to continue in school until graduation.

"I had been class valedictorian, and for some reason, the Marines thought I might be good officer material. After graduation, they shipped me off to a school I had never heard of—Purdue University.

"I was in a Marine V-12 program that prepared students in engineering. We finished a complete degree in two years and nine months, nonstop, three semesters per year, taking eighteen credit hours a semester.

156

"I told her I'd give her a call"

"In addition, we had our Marine Corps training. We got up at the crack of dawn and ran around the athletic field, now occupied by dormitories and intramural sports facilities. Following the morning run, we marched to the union, ate, and came back for inspection. At 8 A.M. we left for classes, so the schedule was hectic.

"The university was about one-third the size it is today, and there were a lot of people in uniform. In addition to the Marine V-12 program, we had a Navy V-12, an Air Force group, and a program for foreign flight officers from South America.

"Women outnumbered men on campus during those war years, which was fine from our standpoint.

"Many people in the V-12 program came from Big Ten universities and were outstanding football players. That's when Purdue had a year unbeaten and untied.

"By the time I was graduated in 1946, the war was over. Two moments I remember vividly. One was the start of the war. I was driving downtown in my dad's car when I heard the report on the radio about the bombing of Pearl Harbor. I also remember being in an electrical engineering lab when someone came in and said that something called an 'atom bomb' had been dropped on Japan and done enormous damage. Some of us pooh-poohed it. It sounded like hype. We found out later what had really happened.

"In 1946, I was commissioned and put in the Marine Reserve. I remained in the reserve until 1950. After graduation, I continued at Purdue, working on my master's degree in mathematics.

"There was a real switch in enrollment at the university from the years before 1946 and the years afterward. Suddenly there were more men on campus than women. Many of these veterans were in their mid to late twenties and early thirties. They were serious students, and they came for an education.

"I was a teaching assistant in 1946. Teaching for the first time was difficult. Here I was a little over twenty-one years old

157

and I had these veterans twenty-five and thirty years of age in class. Twenty-five looked old to me! These were seasoned veterans returning from the South Pacific and the European engagements. It was a challenge. They weren't like young men out of high school.

"There was a lot of construction of temporary buildings during this time. In the summer, I worked as a laborer on one of those temporary buildings. It is still being used. I had to join the plumbers and steamfitters union, and I went to the union office wearing a suit and tie. Those union members looked at me like I was from another world. But I got my union card.

"When I began work, I was befriended by a big, husky fellow who wanted to be helpful. He said, 'Hansen, I'll help you with easy jobs.' The first 'easy job' was unloading radiators. They weighed about two hundred pounds. He was so muscular he could almost pick them up with one hand while I almost got a hernia trying to lift them. It was then that professional work seemed more attractive.

"I first met Nancy, who is now my wife, when I was an undergraduate. Her older sister was dating my former roommate. While I was in graduate school, Nancy came to Purdue as an undergraduate. I first met her in the living room of the Phi Gam house.

"However, she did not know that I was a graduate teaching assistant in the math department. As an undergraduate, she was taking beginning algebra. The first time I walked into her class Nancy was surprised to see me. She said, 'Why don't you sit here by me?' I said, 'I can't. I'm teaching this class.' Little did either of us know what lay ahead many years later.

"There was a seriousness to my generation. It was a seriousness we all felt. In part, it was the depression. I remember many times people coming to our house asking for food in exchange for cutting the grass or some other work. There was a railroad track not far from our house, and we saw people who had been traveling in the boxcars to find work. Life, for many, was grim.

"I told her I'd give her a call"

"When the war came along, everything changed. There was now a focus, and we pulled together—all working to win the war. Those who joined the service felt very unsure when they left school or graduated from high school, left a girlfriend behind, and went off not knowing where they would be sent. You grew up very quickly.

"But we had some good times along the way. It was probably hardest on the parents who knew their kids were going off to war .

"Families were different then. The nuclear family was still intact. Mothers did not often work, until the war came along. The strong family unit was intact, perhaps more so than today.

"It was a sober time filled with expectations. We wondered what the future would hold for us. I lost some dear friends in the war. One of my high school classmates, one of my closest friends, died at Normandy. He was about eighteen or nineteen years old. To lose someone like that so young was hard. His father was a doctor, and he had planned on going to medical school. He was class vice president. Others in my class died—it didn't seem possible. Also, some guys from Purdue died at Iwo Jima. One fine football player and a friend died at Iwo. When news of these deaths came back, the war became very real.

"These were your colleagues, your friends, the guys you had lived with. And when they died, something changed in your life. Hopes, aspirations, and perceptions were altered."

Nancy Hansen

A native of Indianapolis, she went to Purdue University in 1946 and met a young man named Arthur Hansen. In 1971, he became president of Purdue University. In 1972, they married.

For Nancy Hansen, the years at Purdue were good—the early ones and the later ones.

"I had two older sisters," she says. "My mother went to Miami of Ohio University, and my father, who worked in the main downtown post office in Indianapolis, went to the Cincinnati Conservatory of Music.

"He played all instruments except strings. He was a fine clarinetist, saxophonist, and pianist. He had a band in Cincinnati with some famous people in it. Harry Basin was his drummer, and his vocalist was Sophie Tucker.

"My oldest sister went to Miami of Ohio, and when I went to Purdue as a freshman, my second oldest sister was there as a senior. I majored in chemistry and biology with a minor in English. I wanted to be a teacher and I became one.

"It was wonderful at Purdue. The vets were all coming back to campus. My future husband was there in the Marine V-12 program, and I saw him many times in his uniform. He was my algebra instructor. He was a graduate assistant, and we dated. He was a wonderful teacher. He still is.

LET THEM EAT CAKE. *In the 1950* Debris, *this photo of women having a late-night party in a sorority house was coupled with one of men quietly reading newspapers in a fraternity house.*

"Purdue was crowded. I pledged Kappa Kappa Gamma, but in the fall of 1947, I had to live in the temporary Quonset huts on the west side of campus. The next spring when room became available, I moved into the sorority house.

"The huts were really cozy. A little, black, potbellied stove stood in the middle of each study room, and on either side of the study room were two bedrooms. Each bedroom held two or four girls, I can't remember which. My bed, against an outside wall, was cold. At night, we sat and studied with our slippered feet propped against the stove. We had to hold to study hours. Rules were strict, and lights went out at 10 P.M.

160

"I told her I'd give her a call"

"With all the returning vets, there were more men than women. I remember having three dates in one day. On Sunday, you'd go to church with one fellow and then to his fraternity house for lunch. After the main course, a brother would come up and tap him on the shoulder. The first fellow left, and another sat for dessert. You'd go to a matinee with him. Then, you'd go back to the sorority house, and someone else would pick you up to go out for a sandwich.

"It wasn't at all unusual for women who were friends to date the same fellow because the social situation was so different. One of my sorority sisters came and asked if I minded if she went out with someone I had been out with the night before. I told her to beware if he said, 'I can see you in a white wedding dress.' After her date, she came to me and said, 'Guess what! He said, "I can see you in a white wedding dress."'

"People were very happy at that time. Of course, I was born a happy person.

"Those days students sent their laundry home to be done. My sister and I had brown laundry cases for our dirty clothes, and we put the cases on a bus or train to Indianapolis. My mother picked them up, did the laundry, and sent clean clothes back in a couple of days. Mother always put something like brownies or Canadian bacon in with the clean laundry, so we had something to eat on Sunday night.

"I remember one student who made a lot of money. Out past Cary Quad, he put up a sandwich stand just big enough for himself. He had a telephone, and on Sunday nights, he took orders and delivered the best sandwiches to the residence halls. There weren't many restaurants in those days, and no one else delivered. He must have done well.

"I remember programs in the Hall of Music. The biggest names in show business came, people like Bob Hope. He came to the Kappa house for lunch and left his chewing gum on his plate. When he left, everyone dived for that chewing gum. They put it on paper and displayed it on the bulletin board. In our house was a gorgeous girl named Jeanne Wilson who was a swimmer. Bob Hope told her she should go to Hollywood and substitute for Esther Williams.

"Let's see—I'm free a month from Friday night."
(From the Purdue Exponent*)*

"At the end of my sophomore year, I left Purdue. My father had become ill and my mother was taking care of him alone in Indianapolis. I felt I had to go home—so I did, and I went to Butler University. I'm glad I did that because my father died during my senior year. He did not get to see me graduate.

"In those days, people were well behaved. They had a code of ethics. Morals were better. I'm not saying it was such a virtuous generation, but there weren't the opportunities to be anything other than pretty chaste. We lived by strict rules.

"When the fellows brought their dates back to the dorm, the lobby was well lighted. Everyone kissed goodnight and that was it. Now it's different when students can visit each other's rooms.

"The doors to the sorority were locked every night, and the girls visited with one another while they put hair curlers on. If a girl got pinned, her boyfriend's fraternity stood outside the sorority house and sang their fraternity songs—the girls sang, too. It was beautiful. Now those things are gone. Everyone has lost.

"It's a different world today. I'm not sure if it's a better world."

Virginia Warren

Virginia Warren has a gentle southern accent and a way of speaking that relaxes those who hear her.

"I told her I'd give her a call"

She is a historical interpreter at Colonial Williamsburg. With five children and four grandchildren and her husband retired, she sounds like a woman who is very happy with her life.

She was born in Wilmington, North Carolina, in 1927.

"I graduated from high school in 1945 and entered the University of Richmond that fall. A Navy unit was stationed there the first semester, and during the second semester, all the service men began coming back.

"My future husband was one those who came back in January of 1946. We had a class together, started dating, and got married in 1948.

"He went to Purdue to get his master's degree. I, too, went to Purdue, finished my bachelor's, and graduated in February of 1950. I majored in English and got a degree in general science. I had no plans for a job after graduation. I just wanted the education.

"Indiana weather was cold. In the very beginning, I wanted to go home to Virginia on the weekends.

"The people we stayed with when we first arrived at Purdue lived twenty miles out in the country. They had children our age who were away in the service. We made good friends with that couple and stayed friends until they died.

"Later we moved into an apartment in town at 2717 South Street, where we became friends with a student couple next door. They were on an even tighter shoestring budget than we were. We went to the grocery store once a week with them. Their budget was so tight that when they bought a head of lettuce they picked up the extra leaves lying around and patted them onto the head they were buying.

"It was a delightful time. There were many young couples like ourselves. Every Thursday night, we ate at the student union or one of the little inexpensive nearby restaurants, and then we went to a free foreign movie at Purdue's Hall of Music.

Sweet times. Tables were pushed together so big groups could gather and talk at the Sweet Shop, where students sometimes found one Coke with two straws could be a sweet experience.

"My husband was a Kappa Sigma. Hoagy Carmichael came to the fraternity house once and played the piano and sang his hit songs.

"When we came back to Purdue in the 1960s, student rebellion was spreading on campus. I remember the condition of the student union as I walked through it after the Kent State shootings. Trash was strewn on the floors. The furniture was soiled and had been abused by people who were expressing contempt for the way things were happening in our country.

"It was a frustrating time, but, thank goodness, our children survived it and are successful and happily married."

William H. Warren

Retired from the School of Business Administration at the College of William and Mary after twenty-two years as a professor, William Warren went to college during two of the most unusual times in the academic history of the United States.

He did his undergraduate and master's degree work in the post-World-War-II era. He came back to Purdue in the 1960s to receive his doctorate after years of working in industry.

Warren lives in Williamsburg, Virginia, with his wife, Virginia. He was born in 1924 in Newport News, Virginia, an only child. His father was a harbor pilot. Both of his parents died while he was young, and he went to live with an aunt.

He was listening to the Metropolitan Opera on the radio when they broke in with the news about the Japanese bombing of

"I told her I'd give her a call"

Pearl Harbor. He was seventeen years old. He knew what it would mean for him. That night he and his aunt went to a movie to try to put their minds on other thoughts.

"I had no aspirations to go to college," he says. "I didn't think we'd have the money. After high school graduation in 1942, I worked in the shipyards, mostly on aircraft carriers that were built in Newport News.

"I joined the Navy in early 1943, the same day that Eleanor Roosevelt christened the second *Yorktown*. I spent most of the time in the South Pacific with a supply group that serviced the fleet. We were bombed a few times, but nothing of great consequence happened. I was a machinist.

"I was discharged on January 7, 1946, and in college on January 20. I entered the University of Richmond on the GI Bill. I completed a bachelor's degree in June of 1948 after two years and one semester. I enrolled at Purdue in September of 1948 to work on a master's degree in industrial psychology and finished in 1950.

"My wife also went to the University of Richmond. We were married September 11, 1948, and had to report to Purdue for classes on September 13. We had a two-day honeymoon on the way out.

"Purdue was crowded. There was no place to live. We finally located a place advertised in the local paper. It was with a family who lived twenty miles out in the country in a farmhouse. Living there was a nice experience. We stayed there until we found a place closer to town.

"For entertainment we went to the movies, and that was about it. I had been in Kappa Sigma fraternity at Richmond, so we did some things with the chapter at Purdue.

"We needed money, so I got a job at the local newspaper, the *Journal and Courier*. I talked to a guy there, and he asked, 'What can you do?' I said I could sell ads. He hired me on the spot. I did real well. The publisher came by one day and asked,

'How much are they paying you?' I told him twenty dollars. He said, 'Next week you start at sixty dollars.'

"I decided to stay on at Purdue for my Ph.D., but in September of 1950, I got a call from the University of Richmond. They offered me a teaching job and needed me in a hurry. We went. My wife was nine months and one week pregnant with our first child.

"I taught at Richmond for three years and then took a job in industry, where I remained until 1966. With a wife and five children, I was at a crossroads. At forty-two years old, I decided to go back to Purdue in the summer of 1966 to finish the Ph.D. We bought a nice home on Cumberland Avenue and stayed in West Lafayette until 1971.

"It was an experience! Much of the material I had learned nineteen years earlier was outdated. The students and professors of the 1960s with all the new philosophies were different from those I had known earlier. It took patience, but we kept our perspective.

"You know, when we first went to college after the war, we were older and mature, and we did a lot of 'adult' things. I think the younger students at that time looked up to us, and we got those kids started in the wrong direction. When I went to high school, nobody drank except a few on the outer fringe. But after the war, everybody did. The kids learned from us. They grew up too fast.

"My generation came through the 1930s and the 1940s when it was rough. We learned to play it close to the belt and not spend money. We learned how to get pleasure from the simple things of life. Then came the 1950s and the 1960s—the golden years for my generation with lots of opportunities. We, of course, had to see that our kids got what we ourselves didn't get.

"I think my whole generation may have spoiled the next one."

166

"I told her I'd give her a call"

Maier contends educational focus misplaced; Urges return to moral and religious ideals

By Don Meyer

"We have misplaced the whole focus of education" was the charge of Dr. Walter A. Maier against our country's present educational system when he addressed the Convocation for Worship Sunday night. . . .

The eminent radio speaker believes that today we are "living in an age where there is a great stress on amorality." By producing a philosophy of life in which the "after-office hours" have no relative importance, man's very existence centers around the making of money with no emphasis on religion and morals. . . .

And what are the responsibilities of the educated man? Social conditions which have allowed one of every 27 Americans to be actively working as criminals in 1947; one of every 29 had no belief in a God; one of every 12 children was illegitimate; one of every four marriages ended in divorce; and one of every two Americans was not a member of any church.

The destruction of the American home through divorce, race, suicide and abortions is the tragic reality confronted by students today. If the leaders of today do not reproduce, the leaders of tomorrow must be chosen from the children of large, poor families who will not go beyond grammar school. Besides divorce and small families, the curse of abortion claims 800,000 unborn children every year, according to conservative estimates of social experts.

"There are no less than 27 million persons under the age of 21 in our country who have had no religious instruction at all. Consequently, we are bringing up a generation that does not know God. "Thus," continued Dr. Maier, "We have misplaced the whole focus of education."

Purdue Exponent, March 22, 1949

167

Boy meets girl

Larry and Jane Martin Lane

The Lanes' house sits on a wooded ravine in West Lafayette, not far from the Purdue University campus. It is an ideal place for entertaining, and after many Purdue football games, it has been filled with happy people.

In the family room, which faces a wooded ravine, a fireplace takes up an entire wall. Sitting in that room, the Lanes talk about years past as if they were not so long ago.

Larry Lane

He is the owner of two companies: Lane Engineering Specialties Company and Environmental Improvement Enterprises. He is a big man with a deep voice that has a take-charge sound. He has always been in leadership positions. He is a happy man. When he laughs, his earlobes jiggle.

Born in 1922 in Rensselaer, Indiana, Lane lived on a farm for a short time. His family moved to Gary, and in June of 1941, Lane graduated from Lew Wallace High School.

The world was very close to changing, but Lane had no idea how quickly events would direct and shape his life. Still, he was getting ready for the future without even knowing what that future would be. In high school, he belonged to ROTC. During his senior year, he was cadet colonel of the entire Gary unit.

After graduation, he took a job at U.S. Steel. On December 7, 1941, the radio was on in the plant where he worked. Lane listened to the news all day. He knew what it meant for him. He left the steel mills to take a job more closely related to the war effort at the Kingsbury Ordnance Plant.

"I worked there a few months, but I really wanted to enlist. However, enlistments were frozen. The services weren't letting anyone enlist at that time. I also wanted to get some school in, so I came down to Purdue, where I ran into my old sergeant from

"I told her I'd give her a call"

high school. I told him I was coming to Purdue because they wouldn't let me enlist. He told me to go to Fort Knox where my high school teacher of military science and tactics was.

"I went to Fort Knox. This man was a colonel. I told the MP at the gate whom I wanted to see, and he started laughing at me—an Army colonel was going to come out and see me? But the colonel drove out in his jeep with a driver and asked me to dinner.

"The colonel asked, 'Why aren't you in the military?' So I told him. He said, 'We'll take care of that.'

"The next morning he went to see the adjutant major. He said, 'I've got a guy here who wants to enlist.' The major told him enlistments were frozen. The colonel bristled and said, 'There's a war going on, mister, and nothing is going to stop this man from enlisting.'

"He sent me back to Gary and said I'd be hearing from them. In ten days, I got a telegram. I still have it. [He shows it. It says, "Permission to enlist hereby granted. The War Department." It is dated October 29, 1942.]

"After I signed up, I was given a two weeks' leave. I went home, and my mother was in tears. The draft board had been after me. I had gotten my draft notice. I went in uniform to the building where the board was located. The offices were caged in. I went up to one of the cages and told the woman who I was. She didn't even look up. She said, 'You're one of those draft dodgers we're looking all over for.' She was yelling so loudly the whole office was looking, and the other people started to laugh. She finally looked up at me, and there I was standing in uniform. She just said, 'Okay. Good-bye.'

"I knew I was bound for officers' school. I went through all sorts of training. I became an artillery officer. I later went to the tank corps. I was in the United States the whole time, but when VJ Day came along, we were getting ready to move those tanks.

"It was a happy earth on VJ Day. I was on leave, and I got caught in Indianapolis. I couldn't even get out of the Circle area downtown. Everybody was having a good time, and if you were a guy in uniform like I was, it was heaven. Nobody would let you do anything. They wanted to do everything for you.

"I involuntarily went to three parties. I finally told the people I had to go, and they got me out a back door. Everybody was having such a wonderful time. It was indescribable! I had my share of kisses that night. Most of the girls were kissing first. I was so dog-tired I couldn't see straight, but that woke me up in a hurry.

"I got out of the service in late 1945. I had a lot of friends who liked Purdue, and I liked that it had a good reputation for engineering and was involved in agriculture. One of my buddies from the tank corps was from West Lafayette, and he told me about his fraternity at Purdue. I joined Phi Gamma Delta. I did my freshman year at the university's Gary branch, then transferred to the West Lafayette campus.

"I knew Jane from high school in Gary, but I had never dated her. We had met and talked, but there was never anything serious until we got to Purdue. I was driving back to Gary from Purdue at Thanksgiving, and a friend of mine told Jane I might have room in the car for her to sit in front with me. Six or seven of us were in that car. Jane and I hit it right off. We were married in July of 1948."

Jane Martin Lane

"After I graduated high school, I went to a girls' school in Virginia for a year, then I worked in the office of the steel mill for eighteen months. There wasn't too much else to do. There weren't many guys around. Gary was just boring at that time.

"So, I joined the WAVES, the women's branch of the Navy. The reason I joined the Navy was that a woman had to be

"I told her I'd give her a call"

twenty-one to be a WAC and join the Army. It was fine with my father that I did this.

"I went to boot camp at Hunter College in New York City, then I went to Bloomington, Indiana, and finally to Pensacola, Florida. There were a lot of sailors in Pensacola. It was a lot more fun than Gary.

"I got out of the Navy in 1945. I wasn't really sure what I wanted to do, so I came to Purdue in September of 1946 to study home economics. The ratio of men to women at Purdue was five to one and six to one, so it was a great time to be a woman. It is great to be a woman anytime.

"That ride with Larry at Thanksgiving was totally unplanned. He was the only person that I knew from Gary who had a car. At the time, I didn't even know he was on campus. A friend of mine told me that Larry was on campus, had a car, and was going home. He didn't have room for me on the way up, but I rode back with him.

"After we were married, each of us was on the GI Bill. We each received up to $120 a month. We lived better then than we have the rest of our married lives—on a rather different scale.

Larry Lane

"After we got married, we moved into a little farm apartment in the country. Later we moved onto campus.

"During my senior year, I was president of the Purdue Student Union. We sponsored a lot of big bands, and I got to know some of the musicians, like Tommy Dorsey. Tommy was a great guy. He played trombone, and that's what I played. He was a nice guy to talk to.

"Part of my job was to entertain performers who came to Purdue. A top violinist was to perform at Elliott Hall of Music, and just before the performance, his sidekick said they would like to have dinner right then. I just about fainted. We had six thousand people waiting for him in Elliott Hall, and he wanted to have dinner. The sidekick said, 'Don't worry. All he has for dinner is a cup of coffee.' We got that for him in a hurry.

"Also during my senior year, a convention for the National Student Union Association was held in Massachusetts. I tried to persuade R. B. Stewart, who was vice president of the university, to take the entire Purdue Student Union Board to the convention. I told him we'd get a lot out of it. He approved the money. I had a big grin on my face, and he said, 'Don't smile so fast. What you don't know is that I'm going to be the principal speaker at the convention.'

"When we arrived at the conference, we found in attendance many representatives between twenty-three and twenty-five years old as well numerous younger students. It looked like there might be some rip-roaring parties, and that possibility wouldn't sit well with the hotel owners. The building had a ballroom, so I went to the hotel manager and told him I wanted to use it for a dance. He laughed and said the rent for the ballroom was incredibly high. I said that I wasn't thinking about the rent. I was going to help him protect his property by keeping the students occupied. We talked for a while, and he finally said, 'Okay. It's yours from six to twelve o'clock.'

"We gathered up a few musicians and had a little band. We charged the first hundred people in the door one dollar. We used that money to pay for booze and beer. It was a very successful night. Halfway through the evening, R. B. Stewart came in. He danced the hokey-pokey and had as much fun as the kids.

"A week later when we got back to campus, R. B. came to my office in the Memorial Union building. He said he owed me some money. You know that if R. B. ever said that it was a miracle. He could handle money like no one else. He pulled out a twenty-dollar bill and said, 'Take this. I went to your party and didn't pay.' I told him, no, because I wouldn't know what to do with the

"I told her I'd give her a call"

money. He said, 'If you don't know what to do with it, you're dumber than I think you are.' I kept the twenty.

"In 1948, I bought a popcorn machine near Crown Point for $150. I spent a whole winter polishing it. I went into Chicago and discovered that parts for the machine were still available. I brought the popcorn machine to campus and set it up. At noon, I stocked it with change and bags. I paid married students to run it for an hour or two or whatever time they had. I went back at midnight to clean up and collect the money.

"One night while I was there, I heard a peck at the window. I opened the door and saw several of the most beautiful women I had ever seen. We had girls on campus, but these were women. I found out they were all with the show *Brigadoon*, which was on campus as part of a road tour. They wanted something to eat, and there was no place to go.

"I gave them some popcorn, loaded them in my Plymouth coupe—there must have been five or six of them—and headed for this greasy spoon restaurant. But, then, I thought, Wait a minute. What am I doing. I have all these beautiful women here and a house full of fraternity brothers.

"I asked, 'Have you ever been to a fraternity house?' They said, 'No.' I said, 'Well, you're in for a treat.'

"We walked into the living room of the house, and there were some guys sitting around in their pajamas and reading. I told the women I'd try to get some food going and took them to the kitchen. In that house was a back stairway leading to the kitchen. By the time the women walked into the kitchen, a line of guys was standing on that stairway staring at them in complete silence.

"I thought, Holy mackerel! Let's have a party. We took the chain off the refrigerator, opened it, and found some cheese and crackers. We got a big punch bowl, and everyone started pouring something in it—beer, gin, whatever.

173

"At that point, I left. I found out later that two of the women didn't get back to their company for two days. They missed their train. A couple of the guys were with them. And I suspect the rest of those women were late getting back, too.

"The Class of 1950 turned into one huge force to get things done. The class was fantastic. I love every one of them."

Lane's ears jiggle when he says that.

"I told her I'd give her a call"

chapter **6**

" I was an aviation bug "

Some were flyboys

Jim Blakesley

He is the current president of the Purdue University Class of 1950—a group of people scattered around the country united in a belief that this World War II generation is up to any challenge. They were years ago. They are today.

When they were children, they survived a depression. When they were young, they won wars. When they became adults, they changed the world with their technologies and unflagging spirit.

Jim Blakesley never left Purdue once he arrived. He is a director in charge of space management and academic scheduling. Under his leadership, Purdue became the first university in the country to computerize its student course scheduling, and he received a master's degree in industrial engineering for this accomplishment.

His office is dominated by photographs of his four daughters, and he talks about them at length. He talks about his wife, Rosemary.

Tall, trim, and still a pilot, he leans back in his chair and sometimes places a foot on the low table before him. He enjoys talking about this period of time. Only other appointments stop him.

"I was born in 1924," he says. "My claim to fame is I was born in Los Angeles in Watts. I was born at home. My grandmother delivered me because the doctor couldn't get there in time.

"At that time, a lot of orange groves grew in the L.A. area. Now it's all houses and streets and super highways. Later we lived in Altadena near Pasadena.

"Dad was a baseball player. At one time, he was going to be a member of the New York Yankees. A newspaper had even set a headline about it, but the club owner who had rights to Dad demanded more money from the Yankees and the Yankees said no.

"He played triple A with the New Orleans Pelicans, the Vernon Tigers (the Los Angeles Angels), and teams in the Western and Eastern leagues. He was a heavy hitter. He led the league twice, hitting .384 for Omaha, Nebraska, and .382 for New Haven, Connecticut. His thirteen-year lifetime average was .333. He enjoyed baseball. I never traveled with him, but my mother did. I stayed with my grandmother while Mom and Dad were on the road.

"Grandma was the entrepreneur of the family. She invested money. We owned apartments. But all that was lost in the depression. Mom didn't work outside the home. When the depression hit, Dad became part owner of a gas station, and that's what pulled us through. I helped out in the service station.

"The focus in the family was really on education. My mother taught English in college. Every letter I ever sent to her was corrected and sent back. I enjoyed climbing trees, making model airplanes, and reading comic books about landing on the moon. Maybe comic books are the things that dreams are made of.

"My parents sent me to Loyola High School, a Jesuit school, with rigorous discipline in college prep courses. It was math, chemistry, physics, Latin, and English—all the way through.

"I had to drive thirty-five miles each way every day to take part in this educational experience. My day started at six o'clock in the morning. Classes started at eight-thirty. I had a half hour for lunch. At four, I got in the car, drove home, and studied until midnight.

"I was an aviation bug"

"Initially, I drove to school, but eventually my grandmother did the driving. She would drive me and three other boys there in the morning, wait all day for us, and drive us home in the evening. This went on for two solid years. Where she got her money at this time I don't know. I wondered if she was the little old lady from Pasadena who robbed banks.

"During this period of my life, I started to perceive what education was all about, and I started applying myself. I became very interested in math and used the time while we were driving back and forth in the car to do some of my studies.

"Next, I went to a boys' academy in Arkansas where my uncle had gone to school. It was a tough school. You had to attend church and you had to do all your studies. In my senior year, I went to Pasadena City College, which didn't have much discipline, so I sort of had fun.

"I became an assistant manager at one of the theaters in town. Motion pictures were dominant in the Pasadena area. I met my future wife, Rosemary, while working at the movies. She was the cashier and I was the ticket-taker. Once, we teamed up to sell tickets to a sneak preview, and we sold the most. So we won a prize—tickets to the premiere of *Yankee Doodle Dandy*.

"Our first date was to that premiere. We got all dressed up. I wore a tux. I borrowed my mom's car. We got out at Grauman's Chinese Theater, and I discovered I'd forgotten my money, so I didn't have a tip for the guy who parked the car.

"Rosemary and I thought our tickets would be on the main floor. They were in the top balcony, last row. From up there, *Yankee Doodle* was about the size of a postage stamp. But it was great fun. James Cagney starred in that movie. We saw him on TV the other night and it drew tears.

"The war came, and in 1942, I turned eighteen. I wanted to enlist and become an aviation cadet. My mom didn't want me to

177

go and I argued with her. I told her as a pilot I'd either come back whole or I wouldn't come back at all. Dad finally signed for me. I took the cadet test. You had to pass the equivalent of a two-year college preparatory test, and I just breezed through it because of my demanding high school curriculum.

"Before I left for the service, my mom made breakfast and served it to me in bed because that wouldn't happen again.

"My cigarette is the MILD cigarette... that's why Chesterfield is my favorite"

Ronald Reagan

STARRING IN
"THE VOICE OF THE TURTLE"
A WARNER BROS. PRODUCTION

It takes ABC
TO SATISFY ME!
says Picture Star Ronald Reagan

When you change to Chesterfield
THE FIRST THING YOU WILL
NOTICE IS THEIR MILDNESS
Also because of their Right Combination
World's Best Tobaccos

A ALWAYS MILDER
B BETTER TASTING
C COOLER SMOKING

ALWAYS BUY CHESTERFIELD

THE RIGHT CHOICE. Movie star and president-to-be Ronald Reagan is featured in this advertisement for Chesterfield cigarettes that ran in the Purdue Exponent *in 1948.*

"I had been playing junior college varsity basketball and had developed athlete's foot. It had even spread to my hands. When they called me up to the service, I asked the lieutenant if they still wanted me. He said they did. I was given a private bunk in the train because no one wanted to be around me. They put me in the military hospital at Buckley Field in Denver, and the only treatment was rest, relaxation, and Ivory soap.

"I liked the Air Force and became a B-24 pilot. However, I had one bad flaw. I was always volunteering. However, because of that, I ended up on the cutting edge of a lot of things.

"While pilots were training, they had to be single. When I completed my training, Rosemary and I got married, and she was able to go with me.

"One time we were stationed in Liberal, Kansas, and we lived in the home of a couple there. We got the daughter's bedroom. I'll never forget how that room was plastered with Ronald Reagan photos. Ronald Reagan was the last thing we saw when we went to sleep at night.

"I was an aviation bug"

"In 1944, I was nineteen, almost twenty years old, and at that age, I commanded a bomber with a crew of nine airmen. They didn't tell us we couldn't do things back then. If people don't know what their limits are, they go ahead and do what they're told. I'm sure there was some apprehension about putting a nineteen-year-old with nine other people in a bomber and saying, 'Do this.' But we had been well trained. We knew what to do. We were told to serve our country and do the job we were trained to do.

"I never went overseas. I eventually did patrols off the West Coast looking for Japanese subs. Once in awhile, one would pop up and we'd go out after it. I don't think we ever hit anything.

"When I was twenty-one years old, I was asked to be the commander of a two-thousand-man base that was being deactivated. Half the men had already left before I got there. But I had a good top sergeant, and we brought all but three or four back to the base to be properly discharged.

"I was discharged in late summer of 1947. We had two daughters, Susan and Roseanne, by then. Both were delivered at the Fifth Army's beautiful Vista del Arroya Hotel/Hospital, which overlooks the arroya the Rose Bowl is in. Rosemary enjoyed those extended ten-day vacations between delivery and release—times have changed!

"With a family to support, I needed to prepare for a job. Rosey and I decided, Let's get an education with the GI Bill. I contacted Cal Tech and talked to a counselor there. He asked me, 'Do you want to work with men, money, or ideas?' I answered, 'People and ideas.' He said Purdue University was that kind of place whereas Cal Tech focused on ideas. I chose Purdue.

"Rosemary had an uncle, Chalmers Zufall, a professor of pharmacology at Purdue, who lived in West Lafayette. When we called him, he said if we couldn't find a place we could stay with him at 617 Waldron Street.

"Rosemary and I drove across the continent with all our belongings and two infant daughters in our 1939 two-door Mercury convertible. It had twin pipes, a Carson top, and a Columbia rear-end overdrive. With the engine I rebuilt, it averaged twenty-five miles to the gallon. I wish I still had that car!

"When we arrived in Lafayette, our first meal was at the Sarge Biltz restaurant. We got lost trying to find the Piggly Wiggly—a grocery story—and Waldron Street. Getting around West Lafayette hasn't changed much.

"Rosemary's uncle had made arrangements for us to be considered for temporary housing. The waiting list gave priority to families with children by student classification. We had two kids, so that put us at the top of the list. We got a two-bedroom married-student Federal Project Housing Administration unit—FPHA 229-2.

DARN GOOD, IF YOU COULD GET IT. Married student housing was short on luxuries, but in the late 1940s, those who were able to get an apartment considered themselves lucky.

"These housing units were wooden structures with a roof. They did have inside plumbing, and the floor had nice openings in it. If there was dirt, you just swept it in the openings. They had iceboxes—real old-fashioned iceboxes. Every time the man came with the ice, Rosemary would put down newspapers for him to walk on because he would drag in cinders from the cinder paths onto our only carpet. He avoided walking on the newspapers. So we bought a refrigerator.

"Some of the other living units had potbellied stoves, but ours had gas heat. If you put a lot of caulk in the windows, you

"I was an aviation bug"

could keep warm. The unit was not soundproof. You could hear what was going on next door. We were in the center unit.

"We made many friendships there at the barracks. We'd have card parties so we could keep an eye on the kids. We didn't have much money. We enjoyed the companionship of people in the same area—getting together and sharing children stories. We also got together and played basketball. Our team played the University of Chicago and beat them. We blew out three tires driving up.

STAYING IN. Married students—always short on money—often had friends over for games and conversation on weekends. Pictured are (left to right) Glea and Larry Kreider, Peg and Bob Miles, Rosemary and Jim Blakesley, and Mary Benoit. Bill Benoit took the picture.

"I was always helping to take women to the local hospitals to have babies when their husbands were away. I remember the woman next door knocking on the wall and saying, 'It's time to go.' In one short period, with my help, four wives were admitted to two different hospitals—Saint Elizabeth and Home. The nurses must have wondered about my involvement except for Rosemary, who was about to deliver our third daughter, Carole, in 1948.

"Much credit must be given to Rosemary—and all the wives—for the love, companionship, and support given. We were carrying eighteen and nineteen credits of course work each eighteen-week semester plus overloads during the summer sessions in order to graduate in three years and start our careers, and they made it endurable and possible.

"Similarly, the overloaded and dedicated staff of Purdue also helped the returning veterans reach their goals by accepting class workloads of twelve to fifteen hours per week with class sizes bulging.

Some were flyboys

"It was an all-out effort by everyone to change the world.

"In June of 1950, I graduated with a bachelor's degree in mechanical engineering. President Hovde hired me to determine the university's current and future space needs and to serve as executive secretary of Purdue's scheduling committee, which masterminded the university's schedule of classes. It was a great challenge involving all areas of the campus.

"A year later we moved into our first home in the center of campus, 506 Waldron Street, along with our fourth daughter, Nancy, and we have seen the family and campus grow and change for forty-five years. In contrast, my brother, Jack, joined the Navy, went overseas before college, married, and had three sons. He still lives in Altadena at the old homestead.

"As a continuing military commitment, I served in the Air Force Reserves, but I didn't get called back for Korea. However, a member of the adjutant general's staff threatened some of us. He talked to us one-on-one and told us if we didn't volunteer he'd strip us of our captain's rank and send us overseas as buck privates. Those of us who were being threatened were working on our master's and Ph.D., and we said, 'No, we won't volunteer. If we're called up, fine.' Well, we weren't called up and they didn't bust us.

"At that time, we were all focused on future accomplishments. We had a strong drive to do things that were brand new. We were trying to make the world better. And the opportunities were there.

"The Purdue campus has changed—yet is unchanged. In the half-century since our graduation, the university continues to be one of the premier land-grant institutions of higher education. Student enrollment is now almost 36,000—up from our peak of just over 14,600. Less than 25 percent of the buildings from our era remain on campus. They stand out in our memory with only the 'Purdue Red Brick' tying them together with the many unfa-

"I was an aviation bug"

miliar newer buildings that punctuate the skyline. Because of the additional buildings, we might expect the campus to be less crowded than it was in the late forties. But it isn't. Despite the significant growth of the campus and student enrollment, the total amount of classroom facilities and the overall academic/administration space per student have remained *unchanged*, benefiting from conceptual changes in resource scheduling and space reallocation processes. But there is wonderment at the 50,000 square feet of *temporary* FWA—Federal Works Administration—structures still standing in support of academic programs.

"Things have changed—yet have remained the same. Purdue continues to operate with an efficiency that other schools envy."

William Moffat

If you want to talk to the owner of a company, call the office on a weekend. He will be the guy who answers the phone.

That is the case with William Moffat, owner of RADCON, Radar Control Systems, in San Francisco. It was during World War II while stationed at Pearl Harbor that he got to test some of the earliest radar equipment.

Moffat comes from old-line work ethics. He has a love for his work that not many people get to experience. Consequently, he works on the weekend.

Moffat's university years spanned 1940 to 1950. His education was "World War II interrupted."

"As they used to say in Russia, our World War II curriculum was the 'Twelve-Year Plan,'" he says, and he laughs.

Moffat is a fast-speaking man who talks about the technology of his business as though everyone who listens understands as well as he does. But his speech slows when he talks about the war, some experiences he had, some people he knew.

"I could go on and on with these stories," he says. But he doesn't.

Moffat was born in 1921 in Berwyn, Illinois, west of Chicago, to a father who was a salesman and who took his son along on trips to factories and businesses of all sorts.

"My father didn't even graduate from high school," he says. "He was an immigrant from Scotland in 1887 when he was seven years old. My grandfather lived until I was twelve years old. His Gaelic brogue was so thick I could hardly understand him. He was emotionally hostile to the English and to soldiers. In his day, soldiers had the right to come into anyone's home. That's why he came to this country.

"As far as my grandfather was concerned, you learned reading, writing, and arithmetic in school, and then you went to work as an apprentice. He was a skilled carpenter. I have his immigration papers. I'm very proud of one of the things he told me. He said, 'With citizenship come responsibilities, not entitlements.'

"I graduated high school in 1939 and I wanted to go to college, but I didn't have any money. So I went to junior college for a year and entered Purdue in the fall of 1940.

"To live in Cary Hall on campus at that time cost $440 a year. The issue for me was how to get $440. I met Red Mackey, who at that time was the line coach on the football team. I was six feet tall and two hundred pounds, so I was a pretty good size, and he wanted me on the football team. I played defense and got my freshman numerals.

"I was awarded an athletic scholarship, which I thought would give me some money. What it gave me was the opportunity to wait tables at Cary Hall every day for three hours. In addition, I was spending three more hours on the athletic field, plus I had three or four hours of class every day—I was majoring in engineering—and I wasn't getting any sleep. I had a hell of a time my first year. It was very tough.

"I remember a professor at Purdue in 1941, K. D. Wood. He gave us a demonstration of the fundamental principle of flight.

"I was an aviation bug"

He took a three-by-five card, held it up, and let it fall to the floor. He said if we could properly balance the center of gravity of this card it would fly. He reached into his desk drawer, pulled out a paper clip, and showed us the secret of aerodynamics. He folded the card very slightly, put the paper clip on the proper spot, held the card up, and gave it a little push. It flew to the back of the room and hit the wall.

"On the day Pearl Harbor was attacked in December of 1941, I was waiting tables at Cary Hall. This was in the Midwest, and we had just finished Sunday lunch. When the room was almost empty, we turned on the radio, and that's when we heard. We said, 'Here we go!'

"At the end of the semester in February of 1942, I went off to almost a year of Navy flight training. I graduated in January of 1943 in Jacksonville, Florida, the top student in my class.

"They shipped me out to the Pacific. I did two tours over two years—144 tactical missions on two aircraft carriers, the old *Enterprise* and the *Bunker Hill*.

"We got shot at a lot, between long time intervals of trying to keep our marbles. I was almost shot down over Okinawa. I got the airplane back to the carrier and landed it. It was so badly damaged they just shook their heads and pushed it over the fantail.

"We did dive bombing. We'd start at fifteen thousand feet and drop down vertically for accuracy. We had twenty-millimeter cannons. You could sink a ship with those things.

"In 1943, I was stationed on Ford Island in the middle of Pearl Harbor, and I got to fly with the first radar. This equipment was the result of the work of a handful of very dedicated scientists. Because I had an engineering background from Purdue and was a qualified carrier aviator, I am the guy who got to do operational evaluation testing.

"I'll tell you, I have some eye-opening stories to relate as I flew that Grumman airplane and realized the all-weather potential.

Some were flyboys

Unfortunately, we never really utilized radar much during the war. Few understand it yet.

"The best intelligence we had was *National Geographic* magazine. We all carried twelve-inch-long machetes with us in case we were shot down. No guns. We didn't want to make noise and attract attention.

"I always got back. But we lost some guys on every mission. A typical strike would involve twenty or thirty aircraft. We had a tactic where we'd drop something on the enemy with all twenty or thirty aircraft going in and out in twenty or thirty seconds. We'd have to execute this without flying into each other or shooting each other.

"The first targets we'd try to hit were the anti-aircraft guns. That was when we'd sustain the greatest losses. Maybe three guys would never recover from the dive and go into the ground. A couple of others would parachute out, and we'd find out later the enemy had chopped off their heads.

"One day following a strike, I was assigned to fly along the shore of Formosa, now called Taiwan, that bordered on the China Sea and look for friends who had previously been shot down. I was flying slowly—maybe eighty knots—and I was only a hundred or two hundred feet in the air when up ahead I saw a lighthouse. It was a dark-gray stone tower with the top glistening in the sun like crystal, and it was surrounded by a rock wall.

"As I came up on it, I was looking for electrical power generating capacity. I was within one hundred feet. I passed over it, made a circle, and came back. I didn't have any bombs left, just those twenty-millimeter cannons. I came back slowly and started shooting at what I took to be the electrical generator housed at the base of the tower. Pieces of rock bounced off, and the whole inside of the courtyard became a plume of dust.

"All of a sudden, out of the bottom of that tower came a string of people—I think three generations of people, young and old. I had no intention of hurting civilians. I saw their faces and

"I was an aviation bug"

they were terrified. I stopped shooting. I darned near flew into the glass top of the lighthouse.

"In 1945, they brought a guy who had been a prisoner of the Japanese and in the Bataan march to talk with us. He was so emaciated and feeble they had to help him onto the stage. He said he wanted to tell us what it was like on the day we made the first strike on Manila Bay and Clark Field. I had been on that strike.

"He said it was morning, and there was some unusual activity outside the prison walls. The prisoners had been cut off from all communication with the world. They had no idea what was happening. The prisoners could hear a rumbling sound, and it was different from the rumbling of Japanese planes. Next, they heard anti-aircraft guns fire. Finally they realized the rumbling sound was being made by U.S. aircraft. This former prisoner was struggling to stand and tell us this story. I don't have to tell you how emotional our response was. I'm becoming emotional right now just recalling this.

"One day our ship picked up about a half dozen Japanese survivors from a boat on the ocean. They were emaciated and scared to death. They must have thought we were going to cut off their heads. They were small—couldn't have been over five feet tall. We had Marines on board, and they all lined up with their rifles. The rest of us stood behind the Marines—looking.

"On that ship at that moment, if there was any emotion shown toward those guys, it was sympathy. The last thing anyone wanted to do was hurt them. They were well taken care of. It shows the dignity of man, even in war, and the extreme capacity of man to feel pity.

"In 1945 after the bomb was dropped, we were madder than hell. It was totally unnecessary. Everybody knew the war was over. We had the Japanese isolated—cut off from their fuel. They only had fish to eat. There was no need for that bomb. That was disgusting. We were on our ship in the Western Pacific when we heard

Some were flyboys

about it. We just couldn't believe it. It was so unnecessary, and it was a terrible thing to do.

"In November of 1944, I got a thirty-day leave after serving eighteen months in the Pacific. One time, we had gone six months without seeing a woman. Another time, we had gone three months. Let me tell you, movies are no substitute for seeing the real thing.

"So I had returned on leave from the Pacific—ten thousand miles. I arrived at Union Station in Chicago and called my dad. I told him I'd catch a train to our town and be there in fifteen minutes. He said he'd have a nice surprise for me. I figured he'd have ice cream. I never got much of that while I was in the Pacific.

"When I climbed off the train in Berwyn, there was only one person on the platform. It was a young lady I had gone to high school with and hadn't seen for a year and a half. After all those months of not seeing women, that was one of the most exciting experiences of my life. Her nickname was Mickey. I only had a thirty-day leave, so I figured the last thing I wanted to do was get married, only to be shipped overseas again. So I married her.

"When the war ended, there was no housing at Purdue, and my wife wouldn't live in a shack. So instead of entering Purdue at that time, I attended an aircraft design school that Jack Northrop had founded. I was in the fifth engineering class.

"In 1948, we came back to Purdue when we could get a nice place to live. On the GI Bill, I had a one-hundred-dollar-a-month gratuity, and my wife worked as a secretary.

"By 1948, the infusion of all the technological information from all the research done during World War II was really coming in—things like radar. There was some marvelous research going on. I went to Purdue to learn how to use these new technologies. I graduated in February of 1950, and I was absolutely exhausted.

"I went to work at Douglas and stayed ten years with them. They were very selective about what universities the engineers

"I was an aviation bug"

they hired had attended. There was a higher percentage of engineers there from Purdue than from any other school—by far.

"I formed my own company in the early 1970s.

"I know everyone talks about differences between then and now. But when I look back, there's really no difference between the kids when I was in high school and kids in high school today. Today there are unsolved problems—just like there were then—and great difficulties in communication, as well as financial concerns.

"The fundamentals haven't changed. That Purdue education was superb!"

J. Warren Eastes

J. Warren Eastes grew up in a farm family living in Mount Comfort, Indiana, fifteen miles east of Indianapolis. Those were depression years.

"I remember one day," he says, and laughs at the memory flashing before his eyes. "We were in the general store, and they had these candy bars—Butterfingers and Baby Ruths. They were a penny a piece. I asked my dad if I could have one. He said, 'If I had a penny, you could.' Think of that. Candy bars for a penny. And he didn't have a penny.

"We lived on a farm, so we always had something to eat—even if it wasn't candy bars. My parents had a thousand-dollar mortgage on that farm, and we felt it would never get paid off. You have that much on your credit card today.

"I graduated from Mount Comfort High School in the spring of 1942. There were only seventeen students in my graduating class, so it was pretty easy to be involved in everything. I was in the orchestra, I played first trombone in the band, I was the drum major, I represented the school in contests, and I was in school plays.

"On Pearl Harbor Day, I had been out riding my bicycle. We got the news in the afternoon. I didn't even know where Pearl

189

Harbor was. My brother was already in the Army. He had enlisted in 1941. He was the second guy from Hancock County to go in, and I knew I was undoubtedly going to wind up in the service, too.

"I guess I always had assumed I would be a farmer, like my father. After I graduated in the spring of '42, I bought a tractor and planted crops. I bought a couple of sows that had some pigs. I thought I'd stay around and take care of them. But by the fall of that year, I thought I'd better get in the service. If I didn't enlist, they were going to draft me into the Army, and I wanted to be an aviation cadet in the Army Air Corps. So I enlisted.

"I had always wanted to be in aviation and learn to fly a plane. I remember on Sunday afternoons when I was fourteen or fifteen years old, a guy with a plane would land in a field close to our house, and he would take people up for a ride for a dollar. I got a job and made seventy-five cents, so he said he'd take me up for that. Oh—I loved it!

"I got all the way through preflight and was ready to go on when they closed down the flight schools. I was supposed to graduate from flight school in the summer of 1945, but by that time, the Air Corps had more pilots than they needed, and they weren't going to train any more. I didn't do much but sit around and wait after that.

"I was stationed at Maxwell Field in Montgomery, Alabama, and that's where I met my future wife, Ellis. She worked as a bookkeeper for a dairy. I played in a dance band. We met one night when she came to the USO while I was playing there.

"We got married in February of 1946. One week later I started at Purdue. I wanted to be a mechanical engineer, and my brother-in-law, who was at Purdue, told me that was the place to go.

"I went to the university on the GI Bill. I probably wouldn't have gone to college without it, because I don't know how I could have afforded to go.

"I was an aviation bug"

"My wife and I lived with my sister and brother-in-law for six months near campus, until we got an apartment of our own in Lafayette on Sixth Street. The apartment was in an old house, but it was pretty decent. We had a living room, a bedroom, and a small kitchen. And it was ours.

"My wife worked at Ross Gear keeping records. It was not easy for the wives of ex-GIs to find jobs because so many of them were looking for work. But she got a job right away. I worked summers. I was too busy studying during the school year to work.

"I guess I wasn't very interested in campus life. I was newly married, I was twenty-two years old, and I had been in the service. I was thrilled to death to be at Purdue, but I was studying and my wife was working. When we had free time, we just tried to do things together.

"I was optimistic about our future. I thought I would get a degree from Purdue, find a decent job, and raise a family. It was a very upbeat time.

"I graduated in February of 1950, and our first child, Steve, was born that November. His brother, Dave, came along three years later.

"I went right to work with Eli Lilly in Indianapolis. I graduated on a Sunday and went to work on Monday. I stayed there thirty-five years before retiring. Afterward, I did some consulting. I finally hung it up in 1988.

"I was the first one in my family to get a four-year degree. Now, both of our sons have graduated from college, one from Purdue. Today, you just assume that everyone will get a degree. Our granddaughters are eight and five, and we're talking already about where they want to go to college.

"But you know, when I started out, I never had any big plans that it would end this way. This is just what happened.

"And I'm awfully glad it did."

191

Some were flyboys

Richard Wann

In 1990 while Richard Wann was away from home on a business trip, his wife received a telephone call from a German man. The man was making the call for his friend Andreas Rau, who was visiting in the United States. Rau wanted to meet with Wann.

Forty-five years earlier, during World War II, Rau had been one of seven German soldiers who captured an injured, starving, freezing Wann, setting him on a course that led to physical and mental torture and malnutrition.

Now, a lifetime later, Rau wanted to meet Wann once again. There were two things on his mind.

Wann was about to come face-to-face with a past he would rather have forgotten, an experience he would have never imagined growing up on an Indiana farm near Elwood in the 1920s.

"I grew up with a brother and a sister," Wann says.

"My father was a farmer. There was a lot of hard work and not much play on the farm in those days. Our house had no electricity and no indoor plumbing. The toilet was out back. In modern times, we talk about a five-room house with a bath. In those days, we had a five-room house with a path.

"We heated water for our baths on the old range that generally used wood as its fuel. It had a reservoir on the side that always had warm water in it. We'd bring a big tub in the kitchen, put some paper on the floor, and take a bath, which wasn't too private. In the summertime, we put the tub outside and let the sun heat the water. With all the rows of crops and lots of trees, we had a pretty isolated place to take a bath.

"I can remember working long hours during the depression years. We had our chores to do and no pay. But it was a happy life in the sense that we were close.

"We weren't nearly as formal about some things as we are now. If we got our work done and wanted to play cards at a

"I was an aviation bug"

neighbor's house, we'd just walk down there because we knew they'd be home. It was a good life.

"I remember going to town as a young man and meeting a friend who said he was getting twenty-one fifty a week for work. I asked how that could be. He said he got twenty-one meals and fifty cents.

"School was quite easy for me. Through eighth grade, I went to a one-room school. It was good in some ways. I never felt I was at a disadvantage in life because of it. I got to listen to all the other classes do their lessons. By the time I reached eighth grade, I pretty well knew what my lessons would be.

"There were four of us in my eighth-grade class. From there, I went to Elwood High School in the second largest town in the county. There were 620 students in that school, 118 of them in my class when I graduated in 1938.

"My plan was to go to Purdue University. I thought I would like to be a schoolteacher, and being a farm boy, I thought I wanted to be a vocational agriculture teacher. Not having the money for college, I set out to earn my way. I did farm work, and I got a night job at Delco-Remy in Anderson. I had enough money saved to go to Purdue when 1941 came along. I was twenty-one years old in '41.

"I enlisted on October 15, 1942. I wanted to be in the Army Air Force. At that time, you had to have a college education or pass an equivalency test to be a pilot. I went to Lafayette and took the test—and I passed.

"I'll tell you, I was an aviation bug. This was the era of the barnstormers. I had a friend who used to fly to our farm. He didn't have a pilot's license. He'd land his plane in a field, I'd fill his tank with five gallons of gas, and we'd fly that plane until we had to go to work in the evening. I thought flying was the thing of the future.

"I went through training in the Army Air Force, and in May of 1944, I was awarded my wings and I got married.

Some were flyboys

"I became a crew commander, a first pilot on a B-24 bomber—the Liberator bomber. In December of 1944, I was sent to England to the Eighth Air Force.

OFF TO EUROPE. Dick Wann is standing second from the left in this October 1944 photo taken after his crew completed operational combat training, just before they headed for Europe. (An Air Force photo)

"I didn't do very well. I managed to get shot down on my second mission in February of 1945. We were bombing a synthetic oil refinery at Magdeburg in Germany, and we were hit over the target. We managed to trade altitude for distance. We got hit at twenty-eight thousand feet and started heading back to our base. Right off, we lost power in one engine and couldn't stay in formation. We kept trying to get back, but we got hit again—we estimate at Frankfurt. In the meantime, we lost another engine. We couldn't stop that propeller from windmilling. It was a drag on us.

"Then, too, we were losing fuel. We had lost two of the four engines. Due to fuel problems, the third engine was running, then cutting off. We went down to nine thousand feet, and we weren't sure how accurate the altimeter was. We knew there were mountain peaks of eighty-five hundred feet. We were in clouds. We had seen one of the mountains peaks go by on the left side of the plane.

"The engineer told me we had fuel left for five minutes of flight. We decided the thing for me to do was order a bail-out while I held the plane level. Without someone holding it, the plane would have slipped into a pretty steep angle. We bailed out near Zweibrucken in Germany. I was the last one out.

194

"I was an aviation bug"

"We had almost made it back to our lines. Seven of my crew fell in American lines. Two fell on the German side. I came down in no-man's land, right in between the fronts.

"I broke my left ankle when I hit, and my shoes were torn off when my chute opened, so my feet were exposed. It was sub-zero weather.

"I could tell the difference in the sound of the fire, the Germans on one side and the Americans on the other, so I tried to get to the American side. I was trying to crawl on my hands and knees. But our artillerymen were throwing up so much firepower, I had to turn back.

"The snow and the artillery had knocked all the limbs off the big evergreens, so I could bury myself under them for some warmth. I didn't have any food. I lived on nothing but melted snow. My feet were frostbitten.

"I avoided capture for seven nights. The Germans knew I had parachuted out, and they came to get my chute because they needed the cords for shoestrings. They finally found me and captured me.

"I was in bad shape. And I was frustrated. I was thinking, Why me? I will say the first Germans who captured me treated me pretty well. They put me in a foxhole. When I was a kid back on the farm, I was taught that if you got frostbite you should put ice water on it. I asked for ice water, but the Germans misunderstood and brought me hot water. I put it on my feet and that was misery.

"From then on, the Germans' treatment of me deteriorated, and they were very abusive. I was struck. They played Russian roulette with me—they put a gun to my head and clicked. They were trying to get me to tell them how we bombed through the overcast weather.

"They took me out on the mountain and submerged my head in water until I was certain I would drown. This went on from the evening into the wee hours of the morning. They finally stopped.

I didn't tell them anything. The fellow who did all this said, 'Good soldier,' took me back to camp, and turned me over to the SS troops, who were Hitler's elite.

"The SS was the same group that had captured 125 Americans during the Battle of the Bulge and just machine-gunned them. We had been told to resist SS troops because if we were caught by them the likelihood of surviving was pretty slim.

"I had always been an optimist. But this one German soldier told me, 'Why do you think you're going to win? We're going to fight until we die.' I had always thought the Germans were humane, but if they were going to fight until they died, why would they let me live?

"They took me to a prisoner-of-war camp, Heppenheim. It was a horrible place. I weighed 164 pounds when I was shot down. In two months, I was down to 129 pounds. Heppenheim was an absolute horror camp. That was the nickname given to it. The German major hated Americans' guts and acted accordingly. We estimated we were given about five hundred calories a day. The physical abuse continued. They took you out in the cold and pistol-whipped you. About as painful as anything was, when your face was almost frozen, they slapped you with leather gloves back and forth across the face.

"They just wanted to point out that they were still in command, the superior race. I felt patriotic and proud to be an American.

"There were 290 Americans in that camp. There were also British, Dutch, Belgians, and a number of Russians. There must have been seven hundred of us in all.

"The camp had been a mental institution. A group of about thirty of us were held in a room. Each group lived separately, and we saw each other only out in the yard. But we never saw the Russians. They were kept in a basement. If it's possible, the Russians were treated even worse than we were—like animals.

"I was an aviation bug"

"We had no heat or medical treatment, but we had lots of lice, which were bothersome, to say the least. Every day we each got a bowl of very weak soup, and they split a loaf of black bread and cut it into ten pieces. That's what we had to eat. On Wednesdays, we got one small potato.

"A lot of men died. There were people who died beside me in the room. I always felt I would survive.

"The front lines were not all that far away. We could hear shelling and our planes going over daily. We had hopes the Germans would leave, which is exactly what they did two days before the Americans arrived on March 27, 1945.

"The Germans had been very abusive. But in the last few days, when they knew the Americans were near, they took off their side arms and put on Red Cross armbands and brought us some food. They tried to make us believe they were good people. The major left twenty-four hours before the Americans arrived. It was a wonderful day when we saw the Americans coming to liberate us.

"When U.S. Gen. Jacob Devers came in, he and his men were shocked. Our country was shocked. We had been led to believe the Germans were humane and followed the rules of warfare. The German major was caught in a nearby wooded area. The only statement made to us about him was that he wouldn't be bothering us anymore.

"They told us they'd have us in a hospital by Easter Sunday, and they did. They brought in one hundred ambulances, and DC-3s flew us to a hospital in Paris. I learned that all my crew who had landed in the American lines were safe and the ones who had landed behind enemy lines had been able to walk to safety. I was the only one captured.

"The Germans did not set my ankle, and I received no further treatment for it after my rescue. My ankle has been bothersome my whole life.

"From Paris, they sent me to England where I was treated mostly for malnutrition. I arrived back in the States on May 8. The last time I had seen my wife was in Charleston, South Carolina, on December 3. They sent me to a hospital in Indianapolis, where I saw her again on May 9, the day after I arrived in the States.

"When I saw her, she was wearing a particular dress that I thought she looked pretty in. She looked like I remembered. But I looked quite different. We just hugged. I didn't cry. She cried. She had tears in her eyes because she was so happy to see me. And I was happy to see her.

"I got out of the Army on December 10, 1945. I went back to work at Delco-Remy in Anderson, Indiana, for awhile with the intention of going to Purdue when I could get in. But Purdue was crowded at that time, and I couldn't get in until January of 1948. I finished in August of 1950. I had some credits from study I had done in the service. I took heavy loads and went straight through. I studied vocational agriculture in the School of Agriculture.

"When we got to campus, there was no place to live. But the university had a trailer camp on Cherry Lane. We were told we could buy a house trailer and live there, which we did with savings my wife had. We lived there the whole time I was at Purdue.

"We were pretty active in campus activities. But we did not have a lot of money. On the $105 we were getting from the GI Bill, we were lucky if we had fifty cents left by the end of the month to go to the Triple XXX restaurant and buy a hot dog and root beer.

"After I received my bachelor's degree, I went on to complete my master's in January of 1952.

"I took a job as a vocational ag teacher in Kirklin, Indiana. But Firestone in Akron, Ohio, wanted me to quit teaching and come to work for them, so I left in August of 1952. We lived in the Akron area after that. I retired in October of 1982, and we moved back to Elwood. They say you can't go home again, but we did. I started doing consulting work.

"I was an aviation bug"

"In 1990, while I was in Akron on a business trip, a man speaking German called my wife at home. He was calling for one of the first soldiers who had captured me in Germany. He wanted to see me. There were two things he wanted to talk about. One was, he said he stole my wrist watch. That wasn't true. I gave him my wrist watch because I knew someone was going to take it.

"It was called a hack watch. Before you went on a mission, you synchronized the time of day. You pulled out a little pin that stopped the watch, and the commander said something like 'It's 7:01—hack,' and you shoved that button back in.

"The Germans were after our watches, cigarette lighters, and pens. They even took my wedding band, but I convinced them to give it back. They told me it didn't matter because someone else would take it later on, but no one ever did. I still have it.

"That German I gave my watch to was captured later by the Americans, and an American took the watch. The German thought the American would have returned the watch to me. I told him it didn't work that way.

"In addition to telling me about the watch, the other thing this German wanted to talk about was how I was doing. He wanted to know if I was alive. He had been the only good German I ran into when I was captured.

"My wife and I flew to Portland, where he was visiting, to meet him. I wondered what meeting him would be like. When we got off the plane, the man and his friends had signs with our names on them so we'd recognize them, and they had a bouquet for my wife. When I saw his smiling face, I knew everything would be all right. At first, he didn't want to talk to me directly. He had a relative talk for him. But he talked directly to me when he saw I wasn't mad at him.

"He has since been back to see the capture site. Now he thinks he has found the remains of my plane, and he wants me to go to Germany to see it. I hope to go. I've been back to the prison.

They've turned it back into a mental institution. It seems very much the same.

"The head of security at the institution had been in the German Sixth Panzer Division. He was severely wounded after D-Day. He was captured and was treated well. I told him what had happened to me in that place, and he just kind of froze up. I don't think he believed me.

"The name of this German who helped capture me is Andreas Rau. To this day, I can't figure out how he found me after all these years. He turned out to be a nice guy. We both agreed it's much better now between us than it was those many years ago.

"I don't hold any grudges. You can't live with bitterness. It was difficult living with the memories for awhile—to start with. And it still bothers me to buy German or Japanese products. I try to buy American. But I realize it's an entirely different world and about everything you buy will come from a mix of countries.

"I come from an era when you grew up early and accepted responsibility. It was a time when you knew, if you were going to make it, you were going to have to make it on your own. You gave a day's work for a day's pay. The war coming after the depression reinforced the feeling that you can live through some rough times and still get on with it. There was plenty to do.

"I remember when I was going down in my parachute after I jumped out of my plane. My plane was going down, I looked up at the other planes flying home, and I asked, Why me? When I found people dying around me in prison, I asked, Why me? Why am I alive and they're dead? I decided it was because of something I had believed in all along. I was put here on earth for some reason. The reason was to try to better the lives of the people around me.

"And that's how I've lived my whole life."

200

"I was an aviation bug"

chapter 7

"Everybody was going"

Into the Army, Navy, and Marines

Maurice Wann

He is the brother of Richard Wann. He is a retired educator but continues to tutor.

He works with several students—some in high school, some in college. More want his help. He does not have time. For twelve years, he was principal at Madison Heights High School in Anderson, retiring in 1985.

Born in 1924, Maurice Wann went to Purdue University at the same time as his older brother.

"I had an older sister too," he says. "But my brother—I followed in his shadow. He always made excellent grades. He was a tough act to follow. My brother, my sister, and I had a pretty good relationship.

"For one year, I went to Elwood High School where my brother and sister went. Then, there was a change in the township trustee. The new trustee wouldn't pay to bus kids into Elwood, so I went to Summitville High School. It was much smaller—only about a hundred fifty kids. But this was one place I wasn't Dick Wann's brother.

"On the day of the attack on Pearl Harbor, we heard the announcement over the radio. I had uncles who were ready—right then and there—to put on a uniform, which most of them did. I did too when I was old enough.

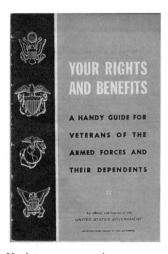

YOUR RIGHTS
AND BENEFITS

A HANDY GUIDE FOR
VETERANS OF THE
ARMED FORCES AND
THEIR DEPENDENTS

An official publication of the
UNITED STATES GOVERNMENT

You're out of the Army now. A booklet explaining benefits and rights was given to GIs when they left the service. At left are emblems of the military branches.

"I graduated in 1942, when I was only seventeen years old. I wanted to enlist, but my dad had to sign the papers for me. He wouldn't do it. I went into the Navy in April of 1943.

"I went to a service school to be a radioman. The Navy was recruiting people for the V-12 program, which was an officers' candidate school, and I was selected. I studied two semesters at Purdue and two more semesters at DePauw University in Greencastle, Indiana. Next I went to a pre-midshipman school at Princeton University. I was two weeks from getting commissioned when they gave me a physical and said my eyesight didn't qualify under new regulations. The war was winding down, and they didn't need all these officers, so they changed the regulations to weed people out.

"I was sent to a Navy repair base in New Orleans and then to San Diego. I was assigned to a destroyer escort getting ready to head for Okinawa when, wing-bingo, they dropped the bomb and everything stopped. I spent the rest of my time in the military waiting to get out, which I did in 1946.

"It was rough when we got word my brother had been shot down. I had just received the information that I was getting wiped out of the officers' training program. Then, this bad news came, and I had a feeling he was gone. I didn't tell my feeling to anyone in the family, but I knew from being in the military that 'missing in action' is almost always a death. I had a good friend who had been missing in action. He did not survive.

202

"Everybody was going"

"I prayed that my brother was all right. Finally, we heard from some of his crew that they had seen him jump from the plane and that his parachute had opened. So that gave us some hope.

"It was hard on our parents. You know how it is on parents with sons in the service. It's always harder on the folks at home. When you're the one involved, at least you know where you are and what you're doing. They have no idea.

"When the Americans finally reached him, I got a call from my parents telling me the news. When he arrived in Indianapolis, I got a seven-day leave to go and see him.

"When I was discharged from the military, I went to work in a General Motors plant in Anderson making pretty good money. However, my brother pressed me to go back and finish school, so I entered Purdue at the same time he did in 1948. I had two years of college credits from the Navy V-12 program.

"I majored in science—chemistry, physics, and math. I wanted to teach, which is what I did.

"I lived with my brother and his wife in their trailer. It was kind of crowded.

"At Purdue I was so busy trying to make decent grades that I just kept my nose to the grindstone. It seemed to me that 99 percent of the people in the class knew what they wanted to do. Everyone hit the books. It was very challenging.

"I think those of us from that era owe a lot to our parents. And I think the one-room schools helped us. If you were fairly bright, you could learn a lot simply by listening to the teacher working with the older students.

"We talk about the depression years—but I think something was different in those days. There were some tough times, but we all pulled together. We had the feeling of being wanted and cared for, and there was a closeness we don't often find nowadays.

"Nobody turned anyone away."

Into the Army, Navy, and Marines

Those ingenious ex-GIs
foil psychology professor

Besides initiating a much publicized anti-hair cut campaign, the ex-G.I.s at the university have exhibited a number of other clever talents. For instance, in a psych class held early (8 a.m.) yesterday morning, the professor became rather irked, to put it mildly, at a number of sleepy eyed stragglers who began wandering into the room after the bell had rung.

Ah-ha

His solution to the problem was to lock the door, leaving six or eight surprised students standing outside. They held a short organizational meeting and elected one of the boys for a reconnaissance mission, whose duty it was to slowly open the transom door, take a running jump and peer through just to make sure the rest of the class was really there.

Then followed a silence outside; the door was lifted suddenly completely off its hinges, leaned against the wall, and the victorious students entered. It took the rest of the period for the class to quiet down and the poor professor could be heard mumbling in his beard from time to time, "these ingenious ex-G.I.s."

PURDUE EXPONENT, NOVEMBER 13, 1946

William Hufferd

"It is possible that I graduated at an older age than anyone in the class of 1950," he says.

William Hufferd was thirty-three years old and a veteran of World War II when he received his degree in agricultural engineering in March of 1950.

"My life has been a little messed up. A little different than most people's life," Hufferd says.

"Everybody was going"

He was born in 1917, during World War I, the son of a rural mail carrier in Rush County, Indiana.

"I spent most of my young boyhood on my grandfather's farm," he says. "I don't remember much about the 1920s. But the 1930s were rough. My grandfather and I farmed all through the thirties, and we never made any more than what we had to have to eat and pay the taxes. My father being a mail carrier actually had one of the best jobs in Rush County.

"In those days, school ended in April so the kids could farm, and I helped with the harvest in the fall after school and on weekends.

"I graduated high school in 1935. It was a small school with the elementary and high schools together. There were twenty kids in my graduating class—ten boys and ten girls.

"My father and I bought a farm in 1935. I guess I exaggerate when I say we bought it. We put a few hundred dollars down and took over the mortgage. What we bought was seventy-one acres. I farmed it and my grandfather's 134 acres. We had tractors, but we used horses a lot. I planted corn with horses the first two or three years. At that time, I thought farming would be my life.

"Pearl Harbor was attacked on December 7, 1941. I was sitting in a restaurant that Sunday evening shooting the breeze with a bunch of guys. That was an unbelievable thing we were hearing. But I knew right then and there I was going to be drafted.

"So on December 9, I enlisted in the Army Air Corps to try and control my destiny a little bit. I can't remember if I was sworn in on the ninth or tenth, but I went right in. I was a month short of being twenty-five years old.

"I might have gotten a deferment for farming. But one of my close friends in high school stayed with farming and they drafted him. So you didn't know.

"I wound up in Iceland for twenty-eight months. Going over there, we were hounded all the way by German subs, and I saw some freighters sunk. Our mission was to keep the Germans off of Iceland.

Into the Army, Navy, and Marines

"When we left Iceland, they sent us to Scotland, and we returned to the United States on the *Queen Mary*. We carried a thousand ambulatory patients who had been cut up pretty badly in France. Those of us with no war experience were told to keep our mouths shut and not to complain about anything around those guys. And we didn't. Fred Astaire and Bing Crosby were on that ship, too.

"We got back into New York on October 8, 1944, and the newsboys were hawking papers about Wendell Willkie's death. He had run for president in 1940, and he owned farmland near ours in Rush County. His national campaign headquarters had been right there in Rushville.

"I spent the last year of service in Charleston, South Carolina, working on B-24s. I was discharged October 29, 1945, so I spent all but a day or two of the war in the service.

"I went back to the farm, and I became aware of this GI Bill. I had always had an ambition to go to college, but I never had the money. So we sold the farm, and I started off for Purdue at the age of twenty-eight. I wanted to be an engineer, and when I discovered ag engineering, I went for that.

"I started in March of 1946 and graduated in the winter of 1950. In four years, I spent a total of forty-five hundred dollars, including my own money and what the government gave me.

"I lived all four years in Cary Hall. In my first year, my roommate and I shared a room that had been for a single student. There were a lot of GIs, but most of them weren't as old as I was. The GIs outnumbered the young fellows two to one, I expect, but we were all one big family. The only thing was, those young guys liked to do some things we had outgrown, like fraternity hazing.

"I'll tell you, it had been eleven years since I got out of high school, and I had pretty much breezed through that. But when I got to Purdue, I found things weren't going to be so easy. I found out you had to work at college. I was permitted to make up minor

"Everybody was going"

deficiencies in my high school education as part of the freshman curriculum.

"Rita Henley and I got married in August of 1950. I had known her before from back home. She was the cousin of a buddy of mine. I was thirty-three when we got married and thirty-seven when our oldest child was born. We have three sons and one daughter. Three of our children have college degrees.

"Jobs were scarce in 1950. After working a few months as a salesman for a farm co-op, I hired on with Public Service Indiana as an agricultural representative. I spent most of my thirty-one years with PSI as an adviser to farmers on the application of electrical energy to agriculture.

"I guess with the experiences I've been through, I'm a little more conservative than a lot of young people today. I'm not too much for government handouts. But I was delighted to go to college on the GI Bill.

"If there ever was a government program that worked, that was one."

Harold Michael

When Gordon Kingma was with the Indiana Chamber of Commerce on a visit to Washington, D.C., he asked federal officials for the top man in urban traffic.

"I'd like to see the best man you've got here for some fresh advice about urban transportation," he said.

No problem, he was told. In fact, one of the top people in the country happened to be in Washington that very day and a meeting would be set up.

Not long after that, Kingma was presented to the expert. It was Harold Michael, head of the Purdue University School of Civil Engineering and a fellow member of the Class of 1950. They knew each other quite well.

Kingma still laughs when he tells the story.

Michael has been closely involved with Indiana State Highway projects, including the interstate system, throughout his career and consults internationally. He retired as head of civil engineering in 1991.

He still spends weeks at a time in Washington, D.C., with various traffic committees.

In 1992, Purdue presented Michael with an honorary doctorate—his first Ph.D. In a circumstance that no doubt will never happen again, Michael served as head of a department at a major university without a Ph.D. He did not get it done early in his career. And in his later years, there seemed to be no need for it.

"They told me in the early 1950s if I didn't get my Ph.D. I wouldn't advance," Michael says. He smiles because they were wrong.

Michael—people call him "Mike"—was born on a small farm outside Columbus, Indiana, in 1920. His father died when he was five years old, and his mother took Michael and his younger brother to the farm of her bachelor brother.

The warming aroma of soup simmering in the Michaels' kitchen fills the house while he talks.

"My uncle had 250 acres, which is all you can handle with teams of horses," Michael says. "He was happy to get two boys. We were young, but we soon started doing things.

"We picked the corn by hand. It was a hard job. You had to shuck the corn. You had a hook in your hand and you pulled. You could do about an acre a day. It was slow going. I turned out to be a pretty good shucker, as far as that goes. I even entered some corn-shucking contests that were held all over the state.

"Everything we ate we grew on the farm, but some things on the farm my uncle wouldn't let us eat because they were too valuable. We used them to get money, which we used to buy sugar

208

"Everybody was going"

and flour. We never ate beef. We sold the cattle and sent them to people who had more money. We ate a lot of pork and chicken.

"I liked farming, and I probably would have been a farmer if the war hadn't come along. I wanted to go to college, but my mother didn't have much money. Everybody wanted me to go to college because I had good capabilities. I was toward the top of my class. I took a lot of math. The best teacher I ever had was my high school math teacher. She's still living. She thinks I'm the greatest thing that ever came along.

"When I was a freshman in high school my uncle had a serious accident and was put in the hospital. Who came to see him every day but an old girlfriend he hadn't visited since his high school days.

"When he got better, he married that woman. Under those circumstances, we had to find a new place to live. My mother bought a fifty-eight-acre farm. About six acres of it was woodland, and some of it was too wet to farm. But we farmed what we could and raised cows, pigs, and chickens. We always had something to eat, but we didn't have much else.

"I graduated from high school in 1938 and went back to farming. Then I got a job at Westermeier Hardware Company in Columbus and soon became the person in charge of repairing all small appliances. In 1942, I was drafted.

"When I joined the military, I went to officers' candidate school and did well. They sent me to officers' survey school. That was when I got my first taste of civil engineering.

"I ended up a second lieutenant, a forward observer with an artillery unit. It wasn't long before the commander of the unit, a lieutenant colonel, found out I could read maps better than anyone else in the battalion. He decided he wanted me beside him so that he would know where he was. He didn't want to be anywhere near the Germans, and he kept me with him at all times.

"I landed in Normandy a few days after D-Day. There was a storm. We were supposed to land on Omaha Beach, but part of our group landed on Utah and the other part on Omaha.

"We finally got things settled, but we had to pass through French towns that the Germans controlled. However, the Germans had pulled back from them when we went through. Our superior officers told us to keep on moving. The Germans later came back to those areas. A week after we landed, we had to turn around and fight for those towns we'd passed through.

"The maps we had from aerial photos were so good all you had to do to fire the guns on target was measure distance and angles from a visible point in the photos to each of our howitzers.

"We were the first unit over the Elbe River, and we captured a bridge over the Rhine. We wanted to be the first to capture Berlin, but they decided to let the Russians have it. They told us to go back, but we refused. It had been too much trouble to get where we were. We had done a lot of hard fighting. We had lost a lot of men. I wouldn't want to go through it again.

"In October of 1945, I got sick. At one point I had a 107-degree temperature. I was sent home in December of 1945.

"Before going overseas, in December of 1943, I had married my high school sweetheart. By the time I got home, we had been apart for two years. I wrote her a letter every day, and she wrote to me.

"When I got home, I was sent to a hospital in White Sulphur Springs, West Virginia. It was a rehabilitation center, but I didn't need rehabilitation by that time. They kept me there for six months and told me I had to be in bed in the morning when the doctor came by.

"My wife came to White Sulphur Springs, and we rented an apartment in town. I spent the night in the apartment, and every morning I'd go in to the hospital to be there when the doctor arrived. When he left, I left and went back to the apartment I had with my wife.

"Everybody was going"

"I got out of the military in July of 1946, and we returned to Columbus. I went back to Westermeier Hardware, and in the fall, I started at Purdue in an extension center in Columbus. I took freshman engineering there.

"I came to the West Lafayette campus in 1947. The GI Bill paid tuition and books. My wife, Elsie, got a job at Lafayette National Bank as secretary to an officer. She developed kidney problems and died in 1950.

"I was twenty-six years old when I started college on the GI Bill. I was thirty when I graduated.

"The students at that time were the best Purdue ever had. They knew what they wanted, they were willing to work, and they did work. They had experienced much in life and were mature. There weren't very many who took longer than four years to get through. I made it in three and a half years majoring in civil engineering.

"That was an exciting time. Highways really started developing after the war. There was no money to spend on them during the war, and they were in such bad shape they had to be rebuilt. Highway construction was going on everywhere. And we knew a lot more about building highways by that time. Everybody got a job who wanted a job.

"The first year of the interstate system was 1956. They were looking for engineers to do this. There was no problem finding engineering jobs—good jobs, high-paying jobs.

"I've traveled all over the world advising people. Most of my time, however, has been spent here in the United States.

"I remarried in the 1950s. She was a widow with four children when we married, and then we had one more. She died in 1989.

"The legacy of the Class of 1950 is this: we were a group of people, many of whom had been in World War II, who came to

211

college generally knowing what we wanted to do. And then we started working on the redevelopment of this country.

"And we still are."

Bob Mitchell

Bob Mitchell's voice is weak. His days are hard now. Just six months before the February afternoon he told this story, he had been diagnosed with cancer.

"It's the worst one," he says. "I have it in the stomach. I've had chemotherapy. I'm off it right at the moment. I have good days and bad days. It's not a fun trip."

"Bob Mitchell, a fellow graduate, and I went to southern Indiana . . . and we worked in a log yard. . . .

Along toward August, Bob came in one day and said he was leaving to go back to the Marines. I tried to find him for years after that but couldn't. I finally figured he'd been killed in Korea."

—JIM RARDON, PURDUE, 1950

Mitchell, who got his degree from Purdue University in forestry, lives in Lake Oswego, Oregon. He worked for Weyerhaeuser and then went to the Federal Bureau of Land Management where he stayed until he retired.

Born March 28, 1924, he grew up on a little farm in Scottsburg, Indiana, about thirty miles north of Louisville.

He graduated from Little York High School in the spring of 1941— six months before the Japanese attacked Pearl Harbor. A good student, he entered Indiana Central College in Indianapolis and studied one semester, working his way through.

"In fact," he says, "When I left, the college owed me thirty-eight dollars. I hauled coal, and I was fireman for the heating plant. We made good money. They furnished us with little short-bed, half-ton Dodge trucks, and we loaded the coal by hand off a gondola car, hauled it, and dumped it in a pile.

"Everybody was going"

"There was a lot of talk about what was going on in the world. Like now, you couldn't tell what was going to happen by listening to the politicians. Roosevelt said, 'I'll never send your boys to Europe to die.' That wasn't exactly true, was it? Pearl Harbor was bad news. It looked as if there was going to be a war. I didn't enlist for awhile. I went into the Marines in June of 1942.

"In August or September, they sent us to the Central Pacific. We never even had a liberty. I was in amphibious reconnaissance. We checked out places to make sure it was safe for the Marines to land. There were many, many islands in those Pacific chains, and our officers relied on intelligence about whether or not the islands were occupied. But intelligence was frequently wrong. Usually when they told us an island was occupied, no one was there, and when they said it wasn't occupied, it was.

NOT SO PACIFIC. Dense jungle growth surrounds the photo lab for the Twenty-sixth Photo Reconnaissance Squadron in New Guinea. (Photo courtesy of Robert Peterson)

"The work wasn't too safe. We had two guys on Iwo Jima thirteen days before that invasion. I don't think the information they got was worth the risk they took. We already knew the information they got, and their presence alerted the Japanese. They knew we'd been there. All those guys took with them was swimming fins, a knife, and a capsule—cyanide.

"We also did a lot of patrols behind our lines. They used us for security at night. Here's how the Marines operated. When they went through an area, they didn't bother to clean everything out. They bypassed a lot, so the enemy was out roaming around at night. We went looking for them. It wasn't easy, but we had it better than a lot of people.

213

"At the end, we were getting ready to go into Japan for the invasion. They were going to land six Marine divisions with no support other than what they had. It would have been pretty bad.

"I went to Japan with the occupation. The Japanese didn't have much stuff left. A lot of their guns were just terrible. But they were intending to fight for it. They wouldn't have given up. They didn't know those words.

"I was sent home in January of 1946. I decided I wanted to study forestry. I don't know why. I guess since I'd grown up around trees in southern Indiana I just decided I'd like to study forestry.

"I worked part of that summer in construction and went to Purdue in the fall on the GI Bill.

"Purdue was just full of veterans—and it was crowded! I was assigned to Cary Hall, but I didn't get a room the first year. I ended up in the attic. There was sort of a dormitory up there. It was all right, but you didn't have any place to study—just a bunk. You could sit on your bed and study, but there was a problem with light.

"I wore my Marine Corps dungarees a lot—khakis. You heard war stories all the time from all those guys. People going to school then were of many different ages. One guy in our class was retired from the Navy. He'd had at least twenty years in the Navy before going to college. Most of us just wanted to get done and get out.

"After I graduated, I got a job with a classmate, Jim Rardon. I had stayed in the Marine Reserves and was called back for the Korean deal. I went back for another year.

"The Marine Corps had used the reserves for the Inchon landing. Some of those guys had just been in the service for a couple months and, bang, they were dead. So Congress passed a rule saying no one could be taken overseas without a year of training. I was signed up for only a year, so that was the end of it for me. I was with a recon battalion at Camp Lejeune. All we did was train. It

214

"Everybody was going"

was kind of strange. It didn't make much sense, but we did it. You know, it could have been tougher.

"We could have been sent to Korea."

On March 15, 1994, thirty days after this interview, Bob Mitchell died.

Erwin Michalk

They used to call him "Red" because of the color of his hair. Some still do, but the red is long gone from Erwin Michalk's hair.

A retired electrical engineer, Michalk is now an adjunct professor at Pima Community College in Tucson, Arizona, where he lives. The son of a Lutheran minister, he has a son who is a Lutheran minister.

Born in 1924 in Texas, Michalk grew up during the depression.

"We were able to exist because we lived out in a farming community and we could raise our own food," he says. "But it was very tough. The house along with a small plot of land was paid for by the congregation, and we raised cattle and cows for milk.

"We didn't have electricity. We couldn't keep food fresh, so every day we had to get what we were going to eat. We collected water from the rain that ran off the roof of the hog house.

"My father was paid the princely sum of one thousand dollars a year. There were seven of us children and Mom and Dad and a grandparent all living together, so ten people had to live off that thousand dollars a year.

"I remember it was always my job to clean the henhouse, and one day something in the manure pile caught my eye. I thought it might be something interesting, so I dug it out, got some water, and cleaned it off. It turned out to be a gold dollar. I have no idea how it got there. I saved it. Then, of course, not long after that, the government called in all the gold.

215

"I was the son of a minister. I had to do what was right and turn it in, but I sure didn't want to. When I took the gold coin to the banker, he took one look at me and my long face and said, 'Let me see what the law says about this.' He did a few 'harumphs' and said, 'Well, you do have a coin collection, don't you, son?' I looked at him and didn't know what to say. He nodded his head for me to say yes, so I said, 'Yes.' Then he said, 'The law allows you to keep this coin if it's part of a collection.' I still have that coin.

"In June of 1941, I graduated from Concordia Lutheran College in Austin—it's what today we would call an academy. We lived on the campus. That was another thing that made everything very tight for the family. My brothers and I chose to go to Concordia, and that meant six hundred dollars a year out of the one thousand dollars the family had to live on went for our education. One brother did it because he wanted to be in the ministry. Two of us just wanted to have an academy education.

"By the time I graduated, war clouds were looming, and I couldn't find work no matter how hard I tried. Employers didn't want to hire a seventeen-year-old because they figured he'd get called into the service.

"So I decided I was going to try one of the courses called ESMWT, Engineering Science Management War Training, at Southern Methodist University in Dallas. The program prepared people who had been farmers to go onto the production line. The idea was to try to improve our nation's industrial production capability for the coming war. It was obvious the United States was going to be in that war sooner or later.

"Then, I became aware of another school. Not much was said about it but that we'd be paid for going to school. I thought, Great, I'll give it a try. They needed people in training so badly the school was being run twenty-four hours a day, six days a week. I went from eleven at night to seven in the morning.

216

"Everybody was going"

"Next, I went to another level of training—back at SMU—and again I was placed on eleven at night to seven in the morning, six days a week.

"What was being taught was very secret. One night they showed us a movie about radio direction and ranging. That was the first I ever heard of radar. They told us we could not divulge what we had seen. It was quite new. But that's what we were training for.

"Eventually, they said I had to put on a uniform. Since we already had all this training, I went in as a tech fifth grade, T5.

"I happened to be at home one weekend, and I was milking the cows when my dad walked down from the house. He said he'd just heard over the radio that the Japanese had attacked us that morning. I said, 'Well, I guess we're at war.' He said, 'Yes, I think so.'

MARCH OF A GENERATION. Acres of Cadets *are pictured in this San Antonio Aviation Center photo. Many young men set their sites on the Army Air Force and the excitement of flight.*

"We prayed. By that time, a lot of my friends from the neighborhood had been taken in the one-year conscription in 1940 and 1941. As they left, those guys said they would be back in a year. All those guys I knew were sent to the Philippines and were killed. I lost an older brother in the war, too.

"When I was ready to be assigned, the need for radar men had decreased a bit. Quite a few had gone through radar training. We were given an opportunity to take a test to see if we could qualify for a college training program, ASTP, Army Specialized Training Program. I took the test, and they said, 'Why don't you go to the Citadel in Charlotte, South Carolina, and join ASTP.'

"So I went to the Citadel and was there for three weeks, and they moved me to Clemson. I was there a total of nine months and the program ended. We didn't find out for six months why. It was because they needed warm bodies for the invasion of Europe. I was one of twelve men from the two-thousand-plus group at Clemson who went to the signal corps. All the rest were assigned to infantry and artillery and sent for the invasion.

"In the signal corps, they put me in training, but they didn't say much about what I'd be doing. It wasn't until I found myself on the way to India of all places that I found out we were to test a new type of communication, what we called 'Stinky Link.'

"This communication link was being used to support the OSS operation in the China-Burma-India, or CBI, theater. OSS was Office of Strategic Service. Now it's call the CIA. It was an outstanding success. One of the rather obscure stories of World War II was how effective the OSS was in preventing any shipping from reaching the home islands of Japan.

"I got out of the service in 1946, and I decided to enroll at Valparaiso University in the fall because some friends had spoken very highly of it. I thought I'd check it out. It was also a Lutheran university. I went on the GI Bill, which was marvelous—probably one of the best things the government ever did.

"After two years, I made the move to Purdue. We didn't have time for much nonsense at school. We all felt four years had been taken away from us—four to six—and we had to do something about it. So, much of this Joe College business was absent from our lives.

"One thing, though, the GIs did get involved with was a bicycle race. It was held just before the Indianapolis 500. The married male students would have a race. They would start with a tricycle and go around the course twice before making a pit stop.

"At that point, they could do mechanically whatever they wanted to the tricycle, so long as for the last two laps they returned

218

it to its original condition. They were all inventive. They would bring in bigger wheels and have the big wheel driving the small wheel. It was very interesting.

"That was the kind of stuff we engaged in—rather than the Joe College stuff."

Charlie Sanchelli

Charlie Sanchelli, the grandson of Italian immigrants, owns a Lafayette real estate company specializing in restaurants and businesses.

Born in 1924 in Newark, New Jersey, he was the oldest of four children. The family moved to Irvington, New Jersey, in 1928.

"We lived in a two-family house," he says. "Our family had the first floor, and my mother's brother and his family had the second. It was like one big family. We only locked the doors at night.

"I entered high school in 1938. During my senior year in 1941, my father was fixing up a nice room in the attic for my cousin and me to live in. On Sunday of Pearl Harbor Day, he put down his tools and never picked them up again to fix that room. He knew what was going to happen to us. We wouldn't be using that room.

"I graduated from high school in the spring of 1942. I thought I was going to be mapmaker. I tried to get in the Navy Air Force as a pilot, but they turned me down because of a heart murmur. I went home to my doctor, and he told me not to worry about it. He said, 'If they don't want to take you, fine.'

"I ended up getting drafted into the Army Air Corps, flying on B-17s. During my whole military career when they checked me, they always stopped and listened a little longer to my heart. But no one ever said anything. When I finally got back home from Europe after flying fifty missions, the doctor said, 'Do you know you have a heart a murmur?' I replied, 'Yes, I do.'

219

"I was an engineer gunner on a B-17 and was sent to Italy. Our crew flew practically every day. We were there less than six months before we got our fifty missions in. The Air Corps wanted to send us someplace to rest after those fifty missions and then bring us back for another fifty. But the flight surgeon said they weren't going to do that. He said, 'I'm not going to let them keep sending you back until they finally kill you.'

CATHEDRAL AT ULM. U. S. planes devastated parts of Germany during bombing runs over major cities. Landmarks of religious and historic significance were spared, if possible. (Photo from the private collection of Dr. William Sholty)

"We went on bombing missions, a lot of them over the Ploestia oil fields. We also bombed targets in France and Germany. One time we flew to Russia, and on the way, we bombed in Hungary.

"We stayed in Russia for ten days and bombed a couple targets from there. The people in Russia were very nice. Everyone went to the park at night and walked around. They kept the streets free of rubble, even though they were being bombed. When we came back from a mission, young Russian kids, fourteen and fifteen years old, would jump on our planes to wipe off oil. If they did that satisfactorily, they didn't have to go to the front, so they were very eager. When we went to town at night, we saw elderly men with machine guns walking along with their wives. They were on their way to the front. It was very sad.

"The bombing missions in Italy didn't bother me. One time I wrote back to my father, 'Dad, don't tell Grandma, but we just

"Everybody was going"

bombed her town today.' She got a little upset that we did that. But I was born in the United States. I was an American.

"I went overseas in 1944 and I came home in 1944. I can't remember the dates, but I was there less than six months.

"When I got back to the States, I joined the cadets to learn to fly, or to navigate, or to be a bombardier. I was heading for pilot training when I found out if you had eighty-five points you could get out. I had that many points. I figured, The heck with being a pilot. I went to the colonel and told him I wanted to get out. He said, 'You can't get out. You're a cadet.' I told him I had eighty-five points. I said, 'I quit the cadets.' I got out on September 25, 1945.

"I went back home to Irvington and checked with the VA about going to college on the GI Bill. I wanted to be an engineer, and I tested well for engineering. I was accepted at Georgia Tech and four other schools, including Purdue. I decided to go to Purdue.

"I got to campus in the fall of 1946. We lived in the gym for about four weeks—in bunk beds lined up just like in the Army.

"The university finally put up some housing. I moved into a building called Seneca. Three other buildings like it were constructed. Each one had seventy-two or seventy-six single rooms. I spent my whole four years living in Seneca. We had a very good softball team. We were champs every year. There were a lot of former GIs in those four buildings. We formed an organization called 'Dunroaming,' which kind of described us all.

"In my senior year, I was invited to join a fraternity, but I decided not to. Having gone through the war, I didn't feel like going through the hazing and so forth.

"The GIs were at Purdue for a purpose, to get an education, so we didn't do much fooling around. We were glad to have the opportunity to go to college and we took advantage of it.

"We didn't go on vacations to Florida during spring break in those days. During the summers, I went home and worked. One summer I worked two jobs. Starting in the morning, I delivered Coca Cola, and at night, I'd get two or three hours of sleep and then work at a bakery.

"However, we did have fun while we were at Purdue. We used to go to town and raise heck, but we never got into any trouble.

"I remember eating places, such as the Blue Blazer, the Gun Club, the Circle Drive-In, the Park-and-Eat, and the Wagon Wheel. We'd go to the Knickerbocker once a week for dinner for a dollar and a quarter. There were so many restaurants in town— so many more than there are now.

"I remember on weekends we walked downtown, and there were a lot of people walking around. The drugstores with their soda fountains were busy. It was real nice.

"I graduated in February of 1950, and I went to work in Decatur, Illinois, for Wagner Malleable Iron. I was paid a dollar and a quarter an hour and was very glad to get it. Jobs weren't too plentiful in 1950.

"I got married in June of that year to a girl from Lafayette. Every weekend we went back to Lafayette to see her folks. Her father liked a drive-in restaurant along the way between Decatur and Lafayette called Dog 'N' Suds, and he told us to stop there. Coming home one weekend, we did stop. I didn't know a thing about the restaurant business, but when we left that restaurant, we had a franchise for a Dog 'N' Suds in Lafayette.

"We opened in 1953—the Patio Drive-In. It was located on U.S. 52 South, on the bypass where Wendy's is now. We sold pizza, too. Actually, we gave it away. We were the first Lafayette restaurant to offer pizzas, and we used to give out a slice with every order we sold. People didn't know what it was. The only ones who knew were the students from bigger towns.

"Bruno's Swiss Inn and Pizza King came to town and they sold pizzas, so I decided to get out of that business. A young fellow named Eddie Pearlman—fourteen years old—worked for me.

222

He said it would be a mistake to get out of pizzas. I told him, no, I had a good drive-in business.

"It turns out he knew what he was talking about."

Bogdon Mareachen

The son of immigrants, "Bogie" Mareachen is a born storyteller. In the nineteenth-century house in Lafayette that he bought while going to Purdue, and where he still lives, Mareachen's eyes sparkle as he remembers and tells stories. He pauses for effect and enjoys the response of an audience.

He's a small man with a big heart. He would find it hard to tell you no if you asked a favor.

Born in Hammond, Indiana, in 1923, he never expected to go to college. In fact, after his service in World War II, when he was in his twenties, he had to return to high school to pick up some credits before he could get into Purdue on the GI Bill.

"I originally went to Hammond Technical Vocational High School," Mareachen says. "My dad was a blacksmith. He worked in the New York Central Railroad yards. He kept his job through the depression, thank God. I was lucky, very lucky.

"During the depression, most of the parents in our neighborhood were unemployed and had a lot of time to devote to kids. It was one of the blessings of being born at that time. We'd make sandwiches and go on field trips or fishing along the rivers—no organized events. The movies were five cents. I didn't go very often because it was so expensive.

"My parents were immigrants. My father was born in Austria and my mother was born in Russia. My name, Bogdon, is Russian. My parents spoke with accents. We were a close family. We enjoyed being together.

"At the age of fourteen, my dad was told he had to leave Austria or my grandfather would lose his job overseeing the farm.

223

You see, my dad had killed the landlord's dog because the dog had attacked and bitten him.

"My dad went to Czechoslovakia, then spent time in the Balkan countries, the Ukraine, Russia, Poland, and, finally, Germany. He could see that the kaiser was getting ready for war. He went to a seaport and asked a German captain in a tavern where was the best place in the world to live. The captain went over to a map and pointed to Argentina, and then he pointed to the Great Lakes. My father came to Hammond.

"When I was in high school, in about 1938, because my first name was Russian, I was offered membership in the Communist party in Hammond. Since my last name was Austrian, I was offered membership in the Nazi party. I went home and told my dad I'd been offered membership in the Communist and Nazi parties. He looked at me and said, 'Do you know why I left Europe?' I didn't join either.

"In my neighborhood, I had to learn to speak German, Hungarian, Italian, Polish, Russian, and Yugoslavian. My mother spoke very little English. Usually she spoke Polish or Russian. It's very simple to learn all those languages. The real challenge comes in your dreams. If you dream in a particular language, then you really know that language. I always dreamed in English.

"My high school, Hammond Technical, was not accredited as a high school for entering college. When I graduated in 1941, I was able to get a job for two years at the Pullman Standard Ordnance plant. We built tooling for the tanks, the howitzer 105- and 155-millimeter shells, 81-millimeter mortars.

"The Army conscripted me in the spring of 1943. I was about twenty years old when I was drafted. Because of my background in machine shops and welding, I was put into an aviation engineering battalion. We were sent to the Pacific. Our battalion would go in by ship with the invasion force. Our job was exclusively to go in and rebuild.

224

"Everybody was going"

"We were hit by suicide aircraft. I lost 117 buddies with one bomb. I was always on the deck of the ship during an attack. Nine planes would come at us—eight suicide planes and one that would return. Two would come at the ship from each side. The two coming in from behind would try to hit the screw—they'd try to knock off the propeller. Another would go for the bridge and another for the engine room. I've seen that tactic repeated and repeated and repeated.

"We had fifty-caliber machine guns strapped onto the deck, and we'd go after the planes. I could see those eighteen- or nineteen-year-old pilots in those planes. They were so close I could take off my sunglasses, throw them up, and hit those guys in the head as they flew by. As a plane went by, our guys would let him have a burst of fire. It would hit his canopy, and he'd go down in the water without doing any damage to us.

"When those planes came in, they winked at you. They had guns in the wings. As they came in, they fired one after another, and it looked like they were winking at you. Three minutes after those attacks started, it was all over.

"I got back home in early January of 1946. I had been in active combat areas for two years. Our battalion was on the ground, so we saw what the bombers did. We encountered children who were orphaned, and we would take them in. I didn't see that this was a clean victory because of what we had caused not only to ourselves but also to others. I thought, My gosh, it's horrible. It's no lasting solution. I think war is the last thing we want.

"I had worked with a great many engineers in the service, and they knew so much more than I did that I wanted to be like them. I wanted to go to Purdue but I lacked high school credits. I was admitted to Purdue with the stipulation that I get those credits.

"I was twenty-three years old when I went to high school classes to catch up on my deficiencies. The principal approached me and said, 'You are a veteran and a male, and the girls will take to you. I only ask one thing: you do nothing with the high school kids, especially the girls.'

"In September of 1946, I started Purdue at the branch in Hammond. In 1947, I came down to the campus in West Lafayette. I was on the GI Bill, and I majored in mechanical engineering.

"When I came to West Lafayette, I lived as a tenant in a little apartment in the same house that I'm living in now. The owner of the house was interested in selling it, so I talked to my brother. My brother had half the money and I had half the money, so while I went to school, I bought this house for eighteen thousand dollars. That was a lot of money back then.

"I rented out ten sleeping rooms. This is what I did while I was going to school—I was very mobile. I had a bed, a desk, and a light. I would move into one apartment and work on it. When I finished that apartment, I rented it. Then, I moved into another one and worked on it. I made money while I was going to school.

"I would go down to the Wabash Tavern with a bunch of guys, and they would start talking about the war. You could tell when somebody was lying, saying more than he'd done. I kept quiet until one of them said, 'Bogie, what did you do during the war?' So I outdid them.

"I said, 'It was very simple. Have you read about Mac?' I was talking about MacArthur. I had seen him many times. So I said, 'Before every invasion, he would have the entire beach lined up with people ready to embark. He would drive up in a Cadillac driven by a sergeant. The sergeant would open the door, and Mac would step out with his corncob pipe. He would look at the men in readiness. Then, he'd sort of put his hand over his mouth while he lit his pipe and say, 'Is Private Mareachen here?' I pretended I didn't hear him. Finally he'd remove his pipe, cup his hand around his mouth, and say, 'Is Private Mareachen here?' I always answered in the same way. I said, 'Yoo hoo, Mac.' Then he would give the order—and let the battle begin.

"Everybody was going"

"After I told that, I didn't have to listen to another war story from someone else for years. Many of the guys started calling me 'Private Mareachen.'

"While I was at Purdue, I got to know Dean Potter. I would take the Monon Railroad to Hammond. He had a daughter in Chicago, and we would be on the same train. Sometimes we would sit together. We would talk, and I would complain about school. One time, he said, 'Bogie, don't waste your time griping. You've got a full schedule. You haven't got the time to gripe about Purdue. The col-

A MEETING OF THE MINDS. *A university can only be as great as its faculty, and the Purdue professors of the late 1940s were excellent. At this faculty meeting, President Frederick L. Hovde speaks to an audience that includes Verne Freeman, agriculture; Jane Ganfield, library; George Hawkins, mechanical engineering; Frank Hockema, vice president and executive dean; Margaret Nesbitt Murphy, family life; A. A. Potter, dean of engineering; Louis Sears, history, economics, and government; and Max Steer, speech.*

leges in this country are young and we're still learning.' Here he was the dean of engineering, and he said he was still learning.

"I wanted to get out of school as soon as I could. In 1948, I met my wife on a blind date. We were supposed to play tennis but

227

it rained, so we went to a movie. I fell in love with her. We got married in 1950. She had started at Purdue in 1944, but she quit.

"While I was at Purdue, there was this dog, Boozer, that was enrolled and attended classes. He was a huge dog. Boozer would come in a building, pick a class, and sit down in front. When this dog did that at the beginning of the year, it meant he would be in that class every session. If you tried to remove him, he growled.

"Boozer was admitted to Purdue under a fictitious name. The fraternity that had him did all this. Boozer took tests, had a grade-point index, and had an ID number. Guys in the fraternity would take the tests for him. It came time to graduate, and through some little technical glitch, the dog forgot to pay a fee. The university asked for the person to come forth—and the whole thing exploded.

"Years later, I asked, 'What happened to Boozer?' The fraternity guys said, 'Well, we transferred him to Indiana University.'

"I enjoyed college. I found out I knew nothing about anything. What I thought I knew I didn't understand. A lot of people when they get out of Purdue think how great they are. When I started to design machines, I asked the question, Have you considered what new problems your solutions will create?

"I met two Purdue students once and talked to them for about an hour. When they left, I said they would never finish Purdue. And they didn't. People asked me how I knew. I knew because out of the whole time they talked to me they spent 95 percent griping, griping, griping. If they did that 95 percent of their time, that only left 5 percent for studying.

"As Dean Potter told me years ago, don't waste your time. You don't have that much time in this world to waste it by complaining."

Veteran protest limited purchase rule

Vigorous protests of the VA ruling that veterans allowances can be applied only to purchase Pickett and Eckel

"Everybody was going"

slide rules were voiced yesterday by many veterans in the engineering schools.

In the past, the $16.50 allowance for slide rules could be applied toward any slide rule. However, a recent letter to the bookstores from the office of the Chief Accountant refers to the Veterans Administration ruling prohibiting veterans from sharing payment with the VA on any purchase.

According to W. A. Knapp, associate dean of engineering, objections to the selection of the P and E slide rule are that markings are not cut into the metal and may wear off and that the scales are arranged differently than other rules. The P and E is the least expensive of the rules now approved as 'sufficient' by the heads of the engineering schools. . . .

In accepting students under the G.I. Bill, the university automatically commits itself to abide by the VA rules.

PURDUE EXPONENT, FEBRUARY 11, 1949

Robert Sparks

In February of 1946, an old factory on the outskirts of Lafayette became the new home for Robert Sparks, a young man from the Pittsburgh area fresh out of the Navy. Other than the fact that no one was shooting at him, living conditions were not that much better than what he had experienced the previous years aboard ship in the Pacific.

Born in 1924, he was an only child. His father worked in middle management at Alcoa.

On the day Pearl Harbor was bombed, he was driving with some friends to a drugstore where kids hung out. They heard the news on the radio.

"We knew we were all going to war," he says. "We said, 'This is it—we're all going into the military.'

"I graduated from high school in 1942 and went to work in a local defense plant for a year before I enlisted. Everybody was going. That was what you were expected to do. We had been attacked, and we wanted to get into it and beat the enemy.

"I was always interested in the Navy. Even before the war, I thought I might go in the Navy. So that's what I did. I was on fire control—gunfire control. That means we aimed and directed the guns and solved the problem of hitting the target. The ships were rolling and pitching while the target was speeding away. To aim the guns and put them on target was very complex.

"We did have computers on those ships, but they were mechanical, not electronic. They had gears and that kind of thing. We provided the input as far as a ship's speed and such, and the computer calculated where we should fire the guns.

"I was on a destroyer, the USS *Hale*, in the Pacific. We were in seven major engagements—the Marshalls, the Gilberts, the Marianas, the Philippines, Tarawa, Leyte, Okinawa, and we bombarded Japan. We were the first destroyer to shell the mainland of Japan. I was at sea for three years. I went home one time in that entire three-year period.

"The quarters were very close. We had bunks stacked three high. There were about three hundred guys on the ship.

"It was especially difficult when the kamikazes came. One of the ships in our squadron took a hit. Thirty-eight guys died. Our ship was very close to that. We never got hit—just one near miss. The kamikaze crashed into the sea not far from us.

"We went into Japan at the end of the war. The place was completely devastated. Everything was bombed out. We were amazed. The people didn't resent us. They just accepted the fact. They didn't give us any problems.

"We arrived home in December of 1945, just after Christmas. We always had a turkey dinner on the ship on Christmas, regardless of what we were served the rest of the year.

"Everybody was going"

"I was interested in metallurgical engineering. Purdue was one of the best three schools in the country as far as I was concerned. I had been discharged from the Navy for only two weeks when I had a wire from Purdue notifying me of my acceptance for the February 1946 term if I would accept emergency housing.

"Having just been released from three years on a destroyer, I didn't think there was any kind of housing that could phase me. When I arrived on campus, I was told that about a hundred of us veterans were assigned to the Duncan housing facility. This building turned out to be a windowless factory made of cement located on the outskirts of Lafayette. The building had been constructed to manufacture some sort of military product by the Duncan Meter Company and was now war surplus. Transportation to the campus was by bus early in the morning and late in the afternoon.

"Sleeping facilities were double-deck bunks in one large space. Lavatories were those left over from when the factory was in use. One locker was provided for all your possessions. You had no real study facilities. Studying was done in the library. As far as living conditions, this wasn't much better than the military. I escaped after a couple months to Cary Hall.

"When I got the opening in Cary Hall, everything there was doubled up. One-person rooms became two-person rooms, and two-person rooms became four-person rooms.

"But we were so glad to be out of the service and back in school that we didn't complain much. We just wanted to get into school, get a degree, and get to work.

"Everybody had just gotten out and had war stories to tell until the wee hours of the morning. Guys were saying, 'There I was at twenty thousand feet and had to bail out.' When the lights were out in the dormitory, they were still talking about it.

"I married my wife, Nancy, in 1948. She was from Boston. I met her in the Navy. While I was in school, she worked in

Lafayette, and we lived in an apartment at 424 North Grant Street in West Lafayette. It's a parking lot now.

"I'm semi-retired now. I was manager of research and development for Wyman Gordon in Worcester, Massachusetts. I worked for many other companies before that—Pratt-Whitney on airplane engines and rocket engines. My first job was in a tractor plant in Iowa.

"While I was working for the tractor company in 1950, I was called back into the Navy during the Korean War. I spent a year and a half on active sea duty. We didn't go to Korea. The ship was in and out of Boston, so I got to be home with my wife fairly often. My initial thought when I had to go back in was, Oh, no! But then I thought, If they really need me, if the country is in trouble, I'm willing to go. It just bothered me that I had to delay a little longer working in my field.

"What with the depression, World War II, the GI Bill, Korea, and everything that's happened since, I think ours was a unique generation. I don't think any generation will have to go through something like this again.

"I hope not."

John F. W. Koch

John F. W. Koch was born in Evansville, in southern Indiana, nine days before Christmas in 1925. There were four children in the family, two boys and two girls. It was a perfect storybook tale to their parents.

Koch's father had a good job. He was an office manager for a metal bed company. Life was good. But life takes unexpected turns.

By 1940, the company Koch's father worked for folded, and his father spent several months out of work before getting a job at the shipyards. In the 1930s, the family experienced some hard times, but so did many others.

232

"Everybody was going"

"When we children went to school, we wore clothes made by our mom," Koch recalls. "We wore socks that were darned in the heels. The darns were a quarter of an inch thick. We didn't throw socks away just because they had holes in them.

"I remember Pearl Harbor Day. We had just returned home from church, and we heard on the radio about the attack. I was sixteen years old.

"As young men, we pretty well knew right then that this was going to be a big war, and we all wanted to do our part. Dad had served in World War I. He said, 'You don't go in until you are eighteen years old and get drafted.' And that is what I did. Several classmates volunteered at seventeen to go into the Marines.

"I graduated from high school in June of 1943, but I started at Purdue in May of 1943. The university was running twelve full months, three sixteen-week sessions. One session started in May. Even if you had not finished high school, if your grades were satisfactory, you were allowed to start college. I was able to get requirements such as English and speech out of the way.

"My dad didn't have to pay my expenses. I had a job at International Steel Company during my junior and senior years in high school and was able to pay my first-year expenses at Purdue.

"I was drafted on June 6, 1944. I was eighteen years old. I remember the day I left. My mom was standing at the front door of our home. I can still see her there. She said, 'Now that the invasion is on, you'll never have to go overseas.' She was at least relieved about that. Four and a half months later, I was on my way to Europe.

"I was in the infantry, the Sixty-sixth Infantry Division. We were on the high seas on Thanksgiving Day of 1944. First, we went to England. Then, on Christmas Eve, we shipped out to France. At that time, things were confused and moving fast because of the Bulge. We boarded the wrong troop ship at Southhampton. The one we were supposed to be on got torpedoed. We were right next to that ship within sight of the harbor lights of Cherbourg. We lost about a thousand men that night.

"From France, we were sent to Germany, and after the war, we ended up in the occupation forces in Austria. I returned home July 1946.

"I returned to Purdue in September 1946 on the GI Bill. I majored in civil engineering—structures.

"It was an interesting time. Most of us at Purdue were veterans, and we had just one goal: get that degree and get out. I was twenty years old, and I thought I was in school with a lot of young kids. Of course, we didn't realize how young we were ourselves.

"I joined Kappa Sigma fraternity. Most of us in the fraternity were older veterans. There was some hazing in the fraternity, but it was tempered by our past experiences. Drinking was not a major problem, and drugs were unheard of.

"The ratio of men to women on campus at the time was about five or six to one. There was one girl in our civil engineering class. It was very unusual then for girls to be in engineering.

"I graduated in the first week of February 1950. I was married on February 18. We left Evansville on the day of our wedding in a car I had borrowed, and we drove to Chicago. In Chicago, I went to work for Swift and Company, a meat-packing firm, in their engineering department.

"I don't know why I wasn't called for Korea. I was called for a physical examination by the Army in June 1950. The only reason I can determine I wasn't called is that my MOS—Military Occupation Standard—was that for a machine gunner. The Army must not have needed machine gunners.

"We have two adopted children, John II and Amy Jo. John II missed serving in the Vietnam War by one day. He had a low draft number, but they just quit calling. If they had called one more number, he would have been drafted.

234

"Everybody was going"

"I felt sorry for the troops in Vietnam. I couldn't comprehend the combat conditions in the Pacific in World War II, and I felt the combat conditions in Vietnam must have been much the same or worse. I had never experienced that type of combat.

"I felt that it was right for us to be in Vietnam. I couldn't understand or condone the violent antiwar demonstrations by so many people who had never experienced war to defend the freedoms we take for granted.

"I have my own engineering practice in Evansville now. If I were to say anything about the Class of 1950, the primary observation would be that everyone in the class seemed very close. We all had experienced the depression and wars. I never felt we had been deprived of life's amenities. It has been a good life. We have seen so much that we have been able to accomplish.

"It was true then and has proven to be true over the years: we are a class that has been challenged.

"And we have met that challenge."

Jim McCarty

When you look at a guy like Jim McCarty, it is easy to see he is successful. Sitting in a chair at the Purdue University Memorial Union on a Saturday afternoon, he is relaxed and dignified and talks with self-assurance. There is an aura about him that tells you he is satisfied with life and what he has done.

He has returned to campus for a reunion of Acacia fraternity brothers. The rainy May day has not spoiled their excitement.

McCarty is retired founder of Colonial Garden Centers in Evansville. There were three stores with 150 employees when he retired and turned the business over to his son. It is among the top one hundred garden centers in the United States.

"We've enjoyed great success," McCarty says.

Success has not come easily. He started in the popcorn business with his father, who had become one of the biggest popcorn producers in the world. But his father got leukemia, the business was liquidated, and McCarty went off on his own.

"The best years to be alive have been during our lifetime," he says. "It's been a period of remarkable changes. With our generation's background from Purdue and the other experiences we have had, it's been a wonderful time to be alive. We've seen the development of computers, television, and transportation, including jet aircraft—it's been a great time for growth and discovery of all types.

"I was born in 1925 in Evansville, Indiana. We did well during the depression. We all had to work very hard, but we had a strong work ethic that carried us through the tough times.

"I graduated from high school in 1943. I served on an amphibious ship in the Pacific for a year and a half. I saw little action. Most of the action was over in that area by the time I got there.

"I came to Purdue in the fall of 1946 on the GI Bill to study agriculture, business, and horticulture. Purdue was a big place—crowded. A lot of people were coming back from the service. I was married between my freshman and sophomore years to Bonnie, a girl from home.

"I lived in the Acacia house the first year, and then we got a place in the tar-paper buildings out by the dairy farm. They were pretty breezy places, but we made them work. We had little money, but we had a lot of enthusiasm and desire to get an education.

"The apartment had a living room-dining room combination and a little kitchen. We cooked on a gas stove, and in the middle of the floor was a furnace that heated the place. We had one bathroom and one bedroom, both small. There was not much to the apartment.

"To save money, we played cards, ate peanuts, and drank beer with friends on Saturday nights.

"Everybody was going"

"I worked part-time for a professor. I always took a full load of courses and went to school in the summer. I finished in three and a half years. I was in a hurry! When you're broke and going to school, you need to get to work.

"Between my sophomore and junior years, our first daughter was born. Eventually, we had another daughter and a son—and now six grandchildren.

"I didn't think my studies at Purdue were very difficult. I'm convinced almost anyone can make it through a university if he has any desire at all. But I had an advantage. I was married. I'd go home at night and study—that was the program. We didn't have a lot of extracurricular activities.

"After graduation, I worked for my father for seven or eight years, then started my own business from scratch in 1958. I hocked my life insurance for five thousand dollars, and I borrowed twenty thousand dollars from the bank. That was a huge amount of money back then.

"I had experience working with my father, a background in horticulture, a little knowledge of numbers, and huge desire. It's the American dream to own your own business. But I wouldn't recommend it to everyone. A lot of guys I've talked to this weekend have worked for large corporations and done quite well. Having your own business is more personal, but there's a lot of sacrifice.

"I retired in 1990. I stay away and let my son run things. But on special projects if he says he needs me, I'm happy for activity.

"I would say my generation is pretty work oriented. In our business, we worked hard to get going. We had the first television program on gardening in our area. It was thirty minutes long and all ad-libbed. I wrote a garden column for the local paper and also wrote for *Flower Grower* magazine.

"You don't have to have a lot of money to enjoy yourself. I sometimes think I had a better time when I had less money than I do now.

"I've enjoyed life. It's been great. And there's going to be a lot more to come."

Bill Popplewell

Retired, Bill Popplewell and his wife live eight months of the year in Myrtle Beach, South Carolina. The rest of the time they are in the mountains of western Maryland.

"I feel a little spoiled," he says. "We hate to leave both places."

It is a far cry from his youth. Popplewell was born in Anderson, Indiana, in 1925. His father was an itinerant builder through the depression years. Popplewell went to eight elementary schools and five high schools.

He says over and over how lucky he was.

"Actually, it wasn't as hard as they make it sound today," he says. "Authorities talk about the psychological problems that moving causes a teenager. But we did all right. I realize now it was probably tougher than I thought at the time. However, in those days, we seemed to appreciate life and what we had more than people do today.

"The depression wasn't tough on everyone. My wife's father was salaried, and she doesn't remember its being so difficult. But it was difficult for our family.

"My dad had some time on the WPA. When he was on the WPA, he supervised the building of a gym at the high school that I was attending in Alexandria, Indiana. I was proud of my dad, and I was proud that he was the supervisor of that project.

"A lot of people thought the WPA was a handout, a make-work program. And some of it might have been, but not this gym. I was proud of Dad, and I didn't realize the negative aspects of working on the WPA until he told me he didn't want me to tell my friends that he was supervisor of this project. He was ashamed to be on WPA.

"Everybody was going"

"Those were pretty poor days. Many people weren't doing well financially. But we made it through somehow.

"In 1943, I graduated from Franklin High School in Franklin, Indiana. I was first in my class and won a scholarship to Purdue. I can't remember if the scholarship came from Purdue, the state, the county, or where. Because I was draft bait, the scholarship went to an alternate.

"I went from high school into the Navy. In those days, you could sign up before you were eighteen for the branch of service you preferred, and they took you when you came of age. I went in the summer of 1943.

"I spent a lot of time at some very good electronic schools, and then I went overseas on an aircraft carrier to the Pacific. I didn't ship out until the tail end of 1944 and early 1945. We were involved in the Iwo Jima and Okinawa invasions. Iwo Jima was the worse.

"Later at Iwo Jima, I was in a heavy-bomber squadron. Previously, I had been in carrier-based torpedo bombers as a ball-turret gunner. It was a little scary.

"In that Iwo Jima invasion, I was glad to be up there flying, instead of on the ground with those poor Marines. It was horrible. We left a lot of Marines buried there. Some of those islands were made of volcanic ash, and all the landing equipment was designed for sandy beaches. The equipment bogged down, and for those guys, it was like being a target in a shooting gallery.

"Our ship got 'kamikazed' badly. We had three twin-engine bombers come at us all at once, and we got hit hard. It was at night, and they came in over our fantail. Two missed, but one actually hit. It went right through our aft bulkhead and exploded on the hangar deck. It was the loudest noise I'll ever hear in my life—I hope!

"In those days, you couldn't even put the word *kamikaze* in a letter. The censors would cut it out. The kamikaze almost turned

Into the Army, Navy, and Marines

the tide of the war. Our defenses weren't designed to handle that kind of thing. They still aren't.

"My torpedo bomber also did some sorties over the Japanese empire. I never got hurt. I was lucky, very lucky.

"I enjoyed the action of being on an aircraft carrier. We lost almost as many planes to normal takeoffs and landings as we did to enemy action. We used to call landing on a carrier a 'controlled crash'—this wasn't funny because that's what it amounted to.

"Toward the end of the war, I was on a plane that was designed to seek out and obtain intelligence on enemy radar. This was in the early days of electronic counter measures.

"You know, at our age at that time, I guess we were too naïve to be really scared. Most of the guys had a fatalistic attitude. You were either going to get through it or you weren't. The problem during the war wasn't wondering if you were going to get hurt or killed. The problem was wondering when you'd be able to get back home. My biggest problem was being homesick.

"I returned home in the spring of 1946. I elected to study electrical engineering at Purdue, one of the top engineering schools in the country. I was lucky to be a Hoosier student and fortunate to have the GI Bill.

"One of the criteria for going to Purdue in 1946 was that you needed a local address that could be verified. It was almost impossible to find housing. As a last resort, I went to a church rectory and found a note on the bulletin board from someone in Lafayette looking for a student boarder. So I got a room there. I was lucky. I lived there until I married my bride.

"My wife, Xena, and I met at a Lafayette short-order grill where I worked. We met when she came into the restaurant for supper one evening. She was a long-distance telephone operator. In those days, you didn't have to push all those numbers to make long-distance calls. You just called the operator and gave her the number.

"Everybody was going"

"We were married in July of 1948 and got an apartment for sixty bucks a month. I think every apartment in town was sixty bucks a month. We both kept working.

"I had gotten that job in the short-order place when I was in there with a bunch of other ex-GIs. The new owner, George Davis, leaned over the counter and said, 'How would you like a job?' We asked which one of us he was talking to. He said, 'All five of you,' and he hired us all on the spot. He needed waiters and cooks and dishwashers. That was the kind of confidence people had in ex-GIs. George and his wife were like Mom and Pop away from home to us. They even asked us out to their farm on weekends.

"We took school seriously, especially those of us who had been in the service, and probably some of the guys right out of high school, too. I think we were driven by the tough times of the depression. In general, depressions build national character and individual character, and the good times have the reverse effect.

"I looked at school much the same as going to work. I turned down a chance to be in a fraternity. I was in school just to get an education. I wanted to get out as fast as I could and get work.

"I graduated in February of 1950. Engineers that year were a dime a dozen. There were 440 electrical engineers in the February class of 1950, and as I recall, RCA tendered only one offer—to the top guy in the class. Lord knows how many engineers graduated in the spring that year. There must have been a carload of them.

"Being married when I graduated, I had to find work quickly, so I took my first job as a mechanical engineer in Ohio with an outfit that employed my dad.

"By the end of 1950, I had gone to work for IBM. I started as a customer engineer, which is what they called the field technicians who installed and maintained the old punch-card equipment.

"This era was the beginning of the electronic revolution. I was fortunate to be in on the ground floor of a lot of developments.

I was in on the early engineering and programming of computers, and IBM was a great company to work with. I retired in 1983 as a senior systems engineering manager. Throughout my career, industry's favorable reaction to the Purdue sheepskin made me proud to be a Boilermaker!

"In the early days, IBM, MIT, and the Air Force designed the Sage Computer System for the air defense system. That computer was the size of a basketball court and had fifty-five thousand vacuum tubes. It cost millions of dollars. Our home computers today are more powerful, smaller, and faster at a fraction of the cost.

"I look at these comparisons, and I think, My gosh, it's almost impossible to even imagine the advances!

"We had three children, sons born in 1951 and 1953 and a daughter in 1954. My sons were of draft age in the Vietnam era, but the older had a school deferment and the younger, unfortunately, had a medical deferment. And I considered that a big break. Do you want to know why?

"Most of us who were involved in the World War II era— and not just those of us who were in the service but the whole country—were pretty patriotic. That was a well-defined war. We knew who the enemy was and that they were bad guys who were at our throats. It wasn't too hard to understand why we had to be at war.

"But Vietnam, that was just the opposite. It was very difficult to understand why we were involved and why we did the things we did. From my vantage point, being from the patriotic World War II generation and a veteran, it was very difficult because I wondered about and even doubted why we were in Vietnam.

"Someone once asked me what the difference was between World War II and Vietnam. I said, 'In World War II, teenagers were afraid they'd be 4-F. In Vietnam, teenagers were afraid they wouldn't be 4-F.' That sounds corny. But it's true.

"Everybody was going"

"In the Vietnam era, my boys were subject to being called. I often look back at those days and wonder how I would have responded if one of my boys had come to me and said, 'Dad, I want to go to Canada.' I'm glad I didn't have to answer that.

"Because I don't know what I would have said."

30 percent employment drop is seen for 1950 engineers

NEW YORK, N.Y., March 17, ASCE Public Information Service—A 30 percent drop in employment of this year's engineering graduates is predicted by leading industrial concerns, government and state agencies and engineering colleges canvassed in a recent study. . . .

A decrease of 28 percent in employment by industrial companies and of 33 percent by government agencies is indicated by the survey. Engineering colleges, polled concerning teaching and research positions available, report a probable drop of 44 percent from last year's employment figures. . . .

Graduates in physical science also face reduced employment opportunities. . . .

Average starting salaries of $255 a month for graduates with bachelor's degrees are about the same as for last year. For graduates with master's degrees the average will be about $320 a month and for those with engineering doctorates, $445. . . .

Purdue Exponent, March 18, 1950

Jim French

Jim French always thought he would be a good teacher. He was right. After nine years in the classroom, he became a principal at Murdock Elementary School in Lafayette and stayed there for twenty-nine years until he retired.

He lives in Delphi, Indiana, the town where he grew up. He was born in Louisville, Kentucky, in 1925.

He is a happy man with a ready smile and a ready hand if you need help. He knows what hard times and needing help are like.

"I grew up on a farm, and it was a tough life during the depression," he says. "I remember when corn sold for ten cents a bushel and a lot of people were burning it, using it for fuel. It was cheaper than buying coal.

"I graduated high school in 1945, and I really wanted to go to college. But that wasn't the way it worked. I graduated on a Wednesday, and on Friday, I was in Camp Atterbury in Indianapolis going into the Army.

"The war in Germany was already over by then. They trained us for jungle warfare, and they were going to ship us to Japan for the invasion. But they dropped the bomb. I have to be thankful. I was probably one of those saved by that. We were all headed to be replacement cannon fodder in the invasion of Japan.

"Instead, I was sent to Germany for occupation duty for thirteen months. The people were friendly, but the place was totally devastated. You had a feeling of, Why? It made me think there must be an easier way to resolve problems. This was total destruction.

"When I returned home, I started right in at Purdue on the GI Bill in January of 1947. In order to finish by 1950, I took classes every summer.

"You couldn't find a place to stay on campus. I lived with a relative in Lafayette until I finished Purdue.

"Girls were very scarce. I had to go back to Delphi to date Francie. We got married in 1951 after she finished at Indiana University. Her father had a small newspaper, and I worked for him to make some money.

"Back then was a friendly time—a time when people would help one another. I remember I had trouble with physics. I went

244

"Everybody was going"

to a couple of guys, and they said, sure, they'd love to help me. I guess after the war, we were striving to make the world a better place and to take care of each other. The feeling was that we needed to do well in school and become better doctors or teachers or whatever.

"There was a feeling of euphoria after we won the war. The United States was the big power. Our country had great strength and strong people, brave people, people who were willing to try and make the United States a great nation. It was a hustling time. It wasn't a time of apathy. After we won the war, we felt, Hey, what else can we conquer? Conquer our own lives. Make the country better. Build highways. Make things go. It was a big growth period.

"There wasn't this feeling now prevalent that the government had to take care of everyone. You took care of yourself. If you weren't making enough money, you got two jobs, you worked longer shifts.

"With the feeling we had after World War II, I just never could imagine, during the Vietnam War, how people could ever question serving their country when they were asked. I guess I'm more capable of imagining that now. Maybe we were hoodwinked when we were young. You read some troubling things now, such as how everyone collected lard during the war, and maybe it wasn't even needed. However, it did make us all feel that we were involved."

Poll shows student plurality favors Stassen; nonvet draft supported by 68 percent of students

By Harry Smith

Thirty-two percent of all students favor Harold A. Stassen for the Presidency of the United States. Regardless of their preference, 45 percent think that he will actually be elected to this post.

Sixty-eight percent of the students favor a draft which excludes veterans, while 93 percent oppose such a draft if veterans are included.

These are the facts of the results of a recent poll of student opinion carried on by the Exponent. . . .

Harold Stassen is the students' favorite choice for President of the United States . . . his closest competitor being Gen. Eisenhower who lags behind with 19 percent. Only 7 percent have no opinion. Gov. Dewey is third with 15 percent and President Truman runs fourth with 9 percent. . . .

<small>Purdue Exponent, May 13, 1948</small>

"Everybody was going"

chapter 8

"Look at all those free people"

The African-American experience

Sally Papenguth Bell

A member of the class of 1950, she moved to West Lafayette in 1939 with her family. Her father was the Purdue University swimming coach.

"West Lafayette was pretty small when I got there in 1939," she says. "It was a friendly place, a place where you could walk around at night. But it was also a community that was closed to blacks. Blacks who came to town with visiting athletic teams or choirs couldn't even stay in the Purdue Memorial Union. They were housed in Lafayette.

"In fact, even years later, the prejudice existed. One of my friends in college was a black woman. One day a sorority sister came to me and said that I shouldn't walk with my black friend because it just wasn't done.

"Our family would leave in the summer and go to Canada where my father ran a girls' camp. One year my mother decided we ought to rent the house while we were gone. This was during the war, and some service people rented it.

The Whoopurdoo   By Sandy

"Awright, awright, so you do look like Little Eva. You still don't have to dress that way just to see the Minstrel Show." (From a 1946 Purdue Exponent)

247

"The family who rented our house came from a southern background, and they had a small baby who was cared for by a black nanny. When people saw the black nanny pushing that baby around, there was quite a to-do. It was against an unspoken law. They were shocked that she was living in West Lafayette."

Winifred Parker White

Her father was a graduate of Amherst College in Massachusetts. He did graduate work at Harvard and Indiana University. He taught math at a high school in Indianapolis. Her mother was a graduate of Butler University in Indianapolis. She was a social worker and a teacher. There was no question what Winifred Parker White would do when she graduated from high school.

WINIFRED PARKER WHITE. Winifred White's senior photo shows her positive attitude in a smile of confidence and determination that has served her well in life. (Photo from 1950 Debris*)*

"In our family, it was assumed all of the children would go to college," White says. "That was a fact of life."

White and her sister, Frieda, both were accepted to Purdue University for the term starting in the fall of 1946. The university brochure said all freshman women would live in the women's residence halls, so they applied there.

They were refused. They are African-Americans.

They had come from a segregated school system in Indianapolis. White had never gone to school with white children. She never even had much contact with white people. Then, she came to Purdue.

"Frieda had graduated from high school in January of 1946, and she went to West Virginia State," White says. "But she didn't like it and left. Our father decided we would

"Look at all those free people"

both attend Purdue. My father felt the program at Purdue was one that was very good. It taught the technical areas and critical thinking methods, and he liked that.

"In 1946, there were only five black women on the campus and twenty-three black men. Out of all the thousands of students at all different grade levels, that was it. Many of the black males at Purdue were returning veterans.

"We were not allowed to live in the dorms. The university did not allow minorities to live in the dorms—not blacks anyway. Some black males lived in the men's residence halls during the war, and a few lived in International House student housing, but that was it.

"During our first semester, Frieda and I lived with a family in Lafayette. It was an African-American family. The first page of the Purdue catalog stated that all women must live in the residence halls, but we weren't accepted. They said that didn't apply to us. There had never been any black students in the women's residence halls.

"So my father and some of his influential friends went and talked to the governor. By the second semester, we were allowed to live in the Bunker Hill (barracks) residence hall. My sister and I shared a room.

"Before we moved, the dean of women came to the house where we were living in Lafayette. She tried to discourage us from moving into the dorm. She said we wouldn't be happy there. Although she was very nice in the way she carried herself, her mission was to discourage us from wanting to move into the women's residence hall. But we wanted to be with the other freshmen on campus.

"I also remember very well that a questionnaire was circulated to women in the residence hall to see what they thought. A small percentage did not approve of our moving in. I don't remember what

The African-American experience

the numbers were. Another small percentage said it would be all right. The majority said they didn't care one way or the other.

"How did I feel about that? We were hurt. I think it had a lot to do with the approach I ended up taking towards education. However, I did survive, and I do not regret the education I got at Purdue. I majored in microbiology and chemistry.

"After we were accepted into the residence hall, several other black women enrolled, and they were able to live in Wood Hall. But my sister and I spent all three and one half years in Bunker Hill.

"At that time, the city of Lafayette was very segregated. We could not eat anyplace off campus. If we went to the movies, we had to sit upstairs in the balcony. I can remember my sister standing up one day, looking down at all the whites below, and saying, 'Look at all those free people.'

"There was a group of people at Purdue, faculty and students, who helped us get through. We formed an organization called the Social Action Group. We worked on changing some things.

"We did make some very good friends, and we did get the good education that my parents wanted us to have. I hope we helped to clear a path that many others followed.

"Our social life was rather difficult. We socialized with the other black students—usually over in town. Sometimes we attended university dances, but we went to all of the football and basketball games at Purdue. However, there were no black athletes. It seems to me in my senior year they finally let a black player wear a uniform to scrimmage with the football team.

"For the most part, the faculty was very good. Because the emphasis was so scientific, we certainly were exposed to first-class studies. But some professors didn't have high expectations for us, and we felt that from them. I had some difficulties. I went on academic probation my third semester because all that was going

"Look at all those free people"

on did have an effect on me. But I overcame it. I didn't graduate with honors, but I had a decent grade-point average.

"I met some very fine people at Purdue. As I look back on it, I'm glad I went to Purdue. It prepared me for the real world. By the time I graduated, I wasn't reluctant to face whites, and I learned to know and respect them as individuals. I had come from a segregated school system. I had never attended a 'mixed' school in my life. In fact, before Purdue University, my association with whites was minimal.

"I think one of the reasons our father sent us to Purdue was for this experience, although it was a cultural shock for me. Our parents had fought their battles, and they wanted us to fight ours. I'm glad more minority students are attending Purdue today, because the technology of the world has just skyrocketed, and African-Americans should be a part of it.

"There was a lot of pressure on us while we were at Purdue. We represented black people. We felt we had to make a name for ourselves.

"And there were other pressures. One of the things we faced was curiosity about us. There were so many people who had never lived with minorities before. It was a new experience for them, too.

"You know, we used to wear those yellow cord skirts our senior year. Girls would run up and down the residence hall and play tricks on each other. They'd write things on those cords. I remember a group coming to our dorm to do something, and we heard someone say, 'Don't bother them, whatever you do. Don't disturb those people.' My sister and I said to each other, 'Why can't they come in here? We have yellow cords, too.' Our door was open, and we expected them to do something with our skirts. But they didn't. We weren't going to bite them!

"In some classes, the professors made a point of including material about the contributions of black people. Sometimes it

251

was overdone, but at least they were making an effort. At other times in classes, I felt the pressure because I was different. It was very confusing to me at that age.

"I met my husband at Purdue. He was a chemistry major from Gary, Indiana, and a veteran. He was staying in Lafayette. He graduated in 1948, and we were married. He went to dental school in Washington, D.C., and I stayed at Purdue to finish my undergraduate work.

"Today I am director of special services at Milwaukee Area Technical College, one of the largest in the country.

"I'm glad things have changed, that they're not the way they used to be. I still believe Purdue is one of the outstanding universities in the country, and I'm glad I went there. I learned to treasure diversity.

"I've never been afraid of people since."

> Jimmy Joe Robinson . . . *flashy* Negro right half is perhaps the top runner of the (Pittsburgh) Panther squad. Though out shadowed in the total yardage department by his diminutive left side mate, the *dusky* speed merchant has no peer in the Pitt ranks as a broken field runner and power plunger. [Italics added]
>
> PURDUE EXPONENT, PAGE 1 PHOTO CAPTION, NOVEMBER 13, 1948

Frieda Parker Jefferson

She is the sister of Winifred Parker White and is a woman who loves to converse. Frieda Jefferson taught high school for forty years, almost all of it in the Milwaukee area.

"There was never any decision for me to make about whether I was going to college," she says. "I was going. I graduated from high school in January of 1946. From January of 1946 to June of that year, I went to West Virginia State College near Charleston.

"Look at all those free people"

"I did not like it. It was in the middle of nowhere. When I got home that summer, my sister was ready to go to college, so my father made the decision to send us both to Purdue because, he said, we were interested in what he called technical courses. My sister wanted to be a bacteriologist. I was interested in dietetics at that time. But I went into home ec, which today we call consumer education.

"My sister and I applied to live in the dorm at Purdue and were not accepted. My father wrote a letter to the governor. I still have a copy of that letter. He made it well known that Purdue was a land-grant school supported by state taxes and his taxes supported the school just like everyone else's, so why couldn't his children live on campus.

"The fact that blacks were not allowed in the dorms was a policy that had been set up in the housing office at Purdue. It was not a law. It was a policy. Someone had made that decision, and it had been passed on. My father also sent a copy of that letter to Fred Hovde, who was president of Purdue. President Hovde said he was surprised at that policy. I don't think he was, but he said he was.

"We moved into the barracks the next semester.

"I had come out of a segregated school system in Indianapolis. Once again, that segregated system was a policy, not a law. All the Negroes, as we were called then, went to a designated school.

"During the Second World War, there were changes in the Army. But it seems that as soon as the war was over our society put those changes aside and went back to 'as usual.' Lafayette was a good example. Black men had fought and died in that war, and people acted like they'd never heard of them.

"So the fact that we were not allowed in the dorm was not unexpected. It did, however, make us angry, and it did take away some of our self-esteem. You never knew what was going to happen next.

253

"I had a history class. I wasn't a freshman, but I don't remember what year it was. This history class was on Saturday morning. Everyone had to jump out of bed to get there, and everyone always had someplace else they'd rather be.

"In this class, we were discussing the Civil War. The woman in charge asked a question, and I answered it. The book had used the term *rednecks*. I also used the term when I answered the question, and it offended a veteran who sat in the back of the room. So he started talking and using the word *niggers*.

"The thing that made me so angry was that the woman in charge of the class never said a thing. She did not open her mouth. Of course, if this happened to me today, I would jump up and that class would be over.

"This man was not only in my history class. He was also in an education class I had. He had lost an arm in the war. I spent the whole weekend fuming. I finally decided I was going to have to say something to this man when I saw him again. I couldn't let it go. I couldn't suppress my feelings.

"He had lost a limb fighting for his country, but the next time I saw him I got close to him when we came out of the door of the classroom, and I said to him, 'You know, I'm very sorry that when you lost your arm that you didn't get blown up completely.'

"The man looked at me and didn't know what to say. His mouth opened in surprise. I shut him up for the semester. He never opened his mouth in class again. He never said another word to me, and I never talked to him.

"I think he was so used to using words like *nigger* that it never dawned on him that those words made people upset. He didn't think it was anything to get upset about. He was totally surprised by what I said. I could see the look of surprise on his face. He could have responded to me without anyone hearing a word because we were standing that close together. He learned something that day.

"Look at all those free people"

"And I learned a lesson, too. I learned the term *redneck* offended some people, and even though it was used in the book, I shouldn't have used it. If I didn't like being called names, I shouldn't have used names myself.

"Purdue taught me how to survive. It taught me how to think through problems. It opened my eyes to living with different kinds of people. It was a good experience for me.

"In the segregated school system I had come from, even though it was in a big city, you never had any contact with another race. I never had to interact with people I didn't know well. At Purdue, my sister and I had to do that, and some of the people we met were very nice. Some of them, once we sat down and talked with them, were very nice. It was a learning process.

FRIEDA PARKER JEFFERSON. Frieda Jefferson was one of the first two African-American women to live in a Purdue University residence hall. (Photo from 1950 Debris*)*

"In Lafayette, blacks could not go to a restaurant. They could go to Walgreen's, but they could not go to most places. My sister and I joined a small branch of the NAACP at Purdue. There were more white people in it than blacks because there were only about twenty-six black people in the whole university.

"A group from the NAACP used to go to Lafayette restaurants, and a black person would go in, sit down, and put down a coin for a cup of coffee. The man behind the counter would come up and say, 'You can't eat here.' The person from the group would ask, 'Is that your decision or the decision of the management.' Usually he'd say it was the decision of management, and the NAACP representative would pick up the coin and leave.

"Once a young man behind the counter at a restaurant really surprised me and said, 'Here, have your cup of coffee,' and he

255

took the coin. I was very upset because that was my last money, and I didn't really want the coffee.

"We went back to Purdue for a homecoming a couple years after we graduated, and by then, you could go anyplace. We didn't stay overnight, but I understand we could have. After the Supreme Court decision on school desegregation in 1954, things changed. When we attended Purdue, there were just a few places close to the dorm where we could eat. But by 1955 or 1956, things had changed.

"While we were students at Purdue, when we went to the movies, we had to sit in the balcony. Even in Indianapolis, by that time, you could go to the show and sit in any seat you wanted. But not in Lafayette. I think as things changed at Purdue, the town changed, too.

"My sister and I really did not socialize with people in the dorm. They were nice, but once again, being the products of a segregated school system, I don't think we felt that comfortable. If everyone was going to an Easter Sunday service, we'd go. But to a party in the dorm—no. Sometimes we were asked and some-times we went, but usually—no. We went to Lafayette to parties and dances with the black people. Really, we didn't have a lot of time for socializing. We studied hard.

"My most interesting experience was my last year when, as a home economics student, I had to live in and help care for a home. I had to leave my sister and our room and go live in this home with other students for six weeks. I dreaded it. But it was very nice. For the first time, I was the only black living with these white students. It was an interesting experience. Very good.

"When it came time for student teaching, I was assigned to Jefferson High School in Lafayette [she laughs]. The black chil-dren in Lafayette went to a segregated school through eighth grade. Then they went to Jefferson High School, but there weren't many of them.

"Look at all those free people"

"My whole class at Jefferson was white, and I was a black teacher. I taught there for six weeks. As the next step in teacher training, I was allowed to practice teach out of town. I went to Gary in a black setup. They were both good experiences.

"Most of my teachers at Purdue were women, and they didn't pay attention to race. I didn't have any problems. But some of the black fellows in engineering had some bad experiences with teachers. When I graduated I got very good recommendations from my teachers.

"My sister and I felt we had to do well. That came from home. My father used to give us lectures. He'd say if we did a project we would have to do it twice as well as anyone else just to be recognized. He'd say if we wanted a *B* we'd have to do *A* work. But I can honestly say I never got a grade I didn't deserve.

"You always felt like you had to do well and be good. When we went into the dorm, we had to be quiet even though everyone else was making noise and jumping up and down. Everyone would expect the Negro girls to be noisy and be having sex with everyone on campus, so we had to be especially good.

"My father always told us, 'When you're in college and you go someplace with black friends, don't sit all together, spread out.' So I'd go to concerts, and I'd sit way away from my friends. I finally decided that wasn't any fun, and I quit doing it. I made that decision on my own.

"Dating—now that wasn't a problem. There were twenty-one black males on campus and five black females. We didn't have any problem getting dates. The problem was, where could we go on those dates. But really, I didn't date much. I didn't meet my husband until five years after I left Purdue.

"After I graduated, I moved to Tucson and taught there. I did not like the situation there. I was right back in a segregated school system. I thought I had left that kind of system behind. I came back

The African-American experience

to the Midwest and went to Milwaukee. It was integrated, but there were so few blacks it didn't make any difference.

"I never felt like a trailblazer when I was at Purdue. But people said I was. In the 1970s, I sent two sons to Purdue to study engineering. I went back and people were saying, 'You were here in the late 1940s and 1950? How could you stand it?'

"I got to thinking. They were right. There had been others before me. There was one black man who finished in chemical engineering, and he stayed at the university and washed glassware. There had been two black girls who lived with a minister and his wife in West Lafayette. That minister received much criticism from people in his church and some left the congregation.

"It was a period of change. And I guess we were trailblazers."

Coffee and prejudice

Dear Editor,

While leisurely sipping a cup of coffee in one of our local snack bars in West Lafayette, I came upon a friend whom I had not seen for some time. Elated, I asked him to join me and ordered another cup of coffee for him. After two such requests for coffee . . . I was flatly told that the management forbade service to a colored person. You see, my friend, unfortunately, was colored. . . .

The above incident is but one of the many one sees on and off the campus. Colored students never have company at the dinner table. You can see them alone in a secluded corner, alone for lack of companionship. Sororities and fraternities close their doors to them. . . . Are they forever to be ostracized? Is it because of their odor? If so, let me inform you. A colored person's odor is not due to lack of soap or health. God has endowed him with very fine sweat pores, finer than yours or mine. He cannot prevent the fine pores he has. Contrary to what we may infer, he enjoys better health through them than you or I. . . .

"Look at all those free people"

I find them very polite, clean, immaculately dressed, ready to sympathize or help, self-respecting, sociable, intelligent, eager for friendship, ever conscious of their manners and never boisterous or disrespectful. While these poor souls are striving to better themselves . . . we show them every discourtesy. . . .

If . . . you feel superior to other races, I suggest that you join Hitler in his grave. He needs friends.

A sympathizing white student.

PURDUE EXPONENT, LETTER TO THE EDITOR, NOVEMBER 10, 1949

L. Orlando Starks

When he came to Purdue University in the fall of 1946, L. Orlando Starks was just like everyone else. He couldn't find a place to stay.

A three-year World War II veteran, he was twenty-three years old when he started at Purdue.

"It was especially hard for me to find a place to stay, you know," he says. "I am an African-American, and I had some difficulty finding a place. I lived for awhile with an African-American family in Lafayette. I later moved into a co-operative house in West Lafayette.

"You don't know what is was like back then unless you went through it. When I was fighting in Italy and we liberated a town and marched through it, the Italian people lined the streets and brought roses and bottles of wine to us. When I came back to the States, just off the boat, I marched in a victory parade in downtown Richmond, Virginia, and people there wouldn't even sell me a cup of coffee after the parade was over.

"What do I tell my children about all this? I never tell them anything about it. I don't want to belabor it. It's a different world now. We can't dwell on misgivings about the past. We have to look forward to better things. We have to be optimistic about the present and future. That's my philosophy.

259

"And my experience at Purdue was very good."

Starks lives in Los Gatos, California, where he has retired from a career in technical publications. He was the first person in his family to graduate from college. Born in Indianapolis in 1923, there were five children in the family during the depression years.

"My dad worked several odd jobs and retired from the Allison Division of General Motors in Indianapolis," Starks says. "It wasn't so bad. I graduated high school in 1941 and attended the John Herron Art Institute in Indianapolis. I received a scholarship and I aspired to be an artist. I got drafted into the Army in March of 1943.

"I received basic training in the Twenty-eighth Regiment of the Second Cavalry—last of the horse soldiers. They deactivated the cavalry, assigned us to a quartermaster truck corps, and sent us over to the European Theater of Operations. I went to French Morocco, and then we went to Italy—Anzio, Sezze, and the Battle of Casino, which opened the gateway to Rome.

L. ORLANDO STARKS. He fought to liberate Italy during World War II, but Starks came home to a nation that had not liberated African-Americans from discrimination. (Photo from 1950 Debris)

"We didn't have to fight for Rome because the Nazis pulled out. We went into Rome on June 4, 1944. It was very exciting. Two days later the Allies invaded Normandy. We thought going into Rome was a great triumph. But everybody was focused on Normandy.

"We saw quite a few aircraft flying over Gaeta on their way to Normandy to help with the invasion. I've never seen that many aircraft in my life—wave after wave after wave of them as far as I could see. They flew over for an hour.

"The Nazis made a counterattack near the town of Lucca on December 15, 1944. Christmas in Italy was very bleak at that time.

"Look at all those free people"

"I saw a lot of action. Up until the last few years, I never really talked about the war. We were in Genoa in northern Italy when the war in Europe ended.

"I went home on furlough. The plan was to bring us home, then send us to Camp Hood in Texas for amphibious training for the invasion of Japan, which would have occurred in November of 1945. But the war ended. They dropped the atomic bombs while I was home on furlough. I think President Truman did what he thought was necessary. It saved a lot of American lives—possibly my own life.

"I still had to go to Camp Hood. The service had established a point system, and you had to receive a certain number of points to get out. I got out in November of 1945. I came back home and decided I'd go to college.

"My high school math teacher convinced me to go to Purdue. I decided to attend adult school and take some refresher math and science courses first. The GI Bill made the difference for me.

"I enjoyed my professors, and I never did run into any major problems at Purdue. I heard other African-American students talk about problems, but I never experienced any significant problems myself. I was accepted by Iota Lambda Sigma, the trade and industrial scholastic honorary fraternity. I held an elective office in that organization. I was secretary. I was also a member of Omega Psi Phi social fraternity. And I was in the Purdue chapter of NAACP. A group of us students participated in the Social Action Committee over at the Wesleyan Foundation.

"I was quite busy. I was taking twenty-one hours a semester for the most part, and I worked for awhile. I majored in trade and industrial education, which later was changed to the School of Technology.

"Around campus, I wore my battle jacket and Army trousers along with my combat boots.

261

"I look back on those days as happy days. I have some fine memories—the camaraderie and the fellowship. I got a lot of encouragement from the professors and from fellow students that I knew. I felt I had people who were interested in me as a person and were concerned that I participate fully in everything. 'Hold your head up high,' they said. 'You don't have to bow down to anyone. You're at Purdue.' My spirits were bolstered.

"There were something like twenty-six other African-Americans on the whole campus. We figured there were five or six of us in our graduation class. That was an estimate. The school wouldn't tell us. They said they didn't keep any records of race, just nationality. There were a lot of foreign students on campus—a number of Chinese, Indian, and South American students.

"I have no complaints about my life. I've been very happy. I think the depression and the war made our generation more prudent in our endeavors. We're very conscious of family and security. We want to protect our home and way of life. We learned if we made a dollar we should save a dime, and we've adhered to that throughout our lives.

"My children sometimes ask me about my life during my younger years. They ask a lot of questions about the war years. But I don't like to look to the past. I'm optimistic. I like to look ahead. I recently received my black belt in karate. I might just go back to work as a bodyguard. After all, the Hollywood movies indicate this is an exciting lifestyle.

"You know, I'm only seventy-two years old—better late than never."

Color line

There is a news story on today's front page that should make a feeling of shame and embarrassment run through every university student and staff member.

"Look at all those free people"

A member of the all-Negro cast of "Anna Lucasta" who had come to the campus a few days before the date of presentation in order to supervise the erection of the sets and lighting was refused service in a store in Lafayette.

Moreover, when he asked the assistance of a Lafayette policeman, neither the policeman nor his superior officers had the guts to enforce the law and see that this man was able to buy what he wanted, where he wanted.

Unfortunately, we cannot say that this is a new development in Lafayette. Rather, it's been going on for a long time. . . .

Words are a poor substitute for decent treatment. But as the student publication of Purdue University, we would like to extend an apology to John Proctor for the embarrassment he was caused. . . .

PURDUE EXPONENT, EDITORIAL, AUGUST 5, 1949

chapter 9

"It was a fantastic time"

From radar through space

Bill Rose

Bill Rose looks like an executive, a man who is satisfied with life. Graying hair, bifocals, bushy eyebrows neatly trimmed—the corners of his mouth turn to a natural smile, and his eyes know where they want to focus.

He was interviewed on the forty-eighth anniversary of his discharge from the Navy after World War II.

He has spent more than forty-five years in the electronics business. It started fifteen days after he graduated from Purdue University in February of 1950, when he became the first person hired at the Joint Long-Range Proving Ground, Banana River Naval Station, Cocoa, Florida. It later became the Kennedy Space Center.

"Purdue is very well known for all its astronauts," he says. "But I was one of the lesser-known engineers who built the instrumentation that launched them, then kept track of where they were to make sure they weren't going to destroy property or injure people."

His first task as a project engineer was to build a chain radar system extending from Cape Canaveral down through the Bahamas and ending at Puerto Rico.

He laughs when he tells this story. This was not the job he had planned to take upon graduation.

"I had a job with Proctor and Gamble, and ten days before graduation I got a 'Dear John' letter from them saying due to circumstances beyond their control, they weren't hiring anyone. My wife and I said, 'What the heck.' We went to Florida on vacation and I found this job. Fate intervened."

Within six years, he and a couple of other engineers pooled their resources—a total of twenty-one thousand dollars—and started a company in Miami. Milgo Electronic Corporation developed and sold modems. Rose left shortly before that company was sold in 1967. By 1982, the new company had become the nation's leader in data transmission modems with six thousand employees and $276 million in sales.

His career continued with other companies. He speaks with pride of his accomplishments, but you have to ask to get the information.

It has been quite a life for a man born in Michigan City, Indiana, in 1925 to a father who was a chef. His mother had three children in twenty-six months, and they moved around between Michigan City and South Bend, struggling through the depression.

His father would never take charity. They often did without. Rose can remember the Christmas when there were no presents at home, so the children went to Saint Paul Lutheran Church where they were given a bag of peanuts, an orange, and a ten-cent gift. It was not so bad, he says. It was better than nothing.

"You're damn right it was better than nothing. I never felt badly about it. The only thing that ever bothered me was I can remember hearing my mother cry a few times because there weren't any presents for the kids. I was the oldest. I never felt envious of other kids or left out. There were so many of us in the same boat.

"Most of the time we had enough food. But we ate a lot of baking powder biscuits. We got those instead of regular bread.

265

From radar through space

"Things eventually picked up. My dad got his own restaurant in '38 or '39 and stayed with it. On Pearl Harbor Day, I was cleaning up there when I heard the news on the radio. I made my decision right there to join the Navy. I hadn't graduated from high school, but all I wanted to do was make sure I got in the service and got even with the Japanese.

"When the war broke out, I was too young to join. Everybody in my high school class was afraid it would be over before they got a chance to get in. I waited until I was seventeen, which was in the fall of 1942. I enlisted in the Navy the day I turned seventeen. I took an Eddy test to see if I was qualified for Navy electronics.

"Commander William Eddy came from Michigan City, and he set up the radar program for the Navy. A write-up about him had appeared in the local paper. I was taking electronic courses in high school. I passed the test and went into the service right after graduation.

"In 1944, I went to Pearl Harbor, then Guam, the Philippines, and New Guinea. There weren't a lot of us. We flew around and monitored the section we were in, looking for enemy radar signals. We passed this information back to the fleet so they knew what kind of radar the enemy had and could develop countermeasures.

"We were out in front. It was risky. The fatality rate for this kind of mission was high. But I was never even shot at. At that time I was disappointed. But I'm not today.

"We were scheduled to be part of the invasion of Japan, so we were quite happy when they dropped the atomic bomb. I think it saved many, many lives. It has been predicted the invasion would have cost a million U.S. casualties and up to ten million Japanese. They were ferocious fighters. They had determination.

"The only time I was ever homesick was Christmas of 1945. They showed us two movies, *Christmas in Connecticut* and Bing Crosby's *White Christmas*. Man, did we all want to get home!

"It was a fantastic time"

"The only communication we had with back home was letters. A lot of girls wrote to me, but I didn't have any special girl.

"I was discharged in March of 1946. I'd had a nice education in electronics in the Navy, and I thought I'd become an electrical engineer. They started an extension of Purdue in Michigan City, and thirty or forty of us veterans took our freshman year there. I lived with my parents and went to school on the GI Bill.

"I went to the West Lafayette campus my sophomore year. My God, I went all over looking for a room, any kind of a room. I finally rented a room in Lafayette in a person's home.

"My wife, Eileen, and I were married in June of 1947. We built our own first apartment on North Street in West Lafayette behind a bar, the Chocolate Shop. This guy had a garage there, and he said he'd put up the money if we'd do the work and convert it to an apartment. It was wonderful. It had two rooms. In November of 1948, our daughter, Karin, was born, and we added another room. We stayed there until I graduated.

"My wife worked until we had our first child. We eventually had four, and we have a grandson now at Purdue.

"After I graduated, I almost screwed up and got a commission in the Navy. But I had a test to take that day and couldn't go down to Indianapolis, so I didn't get commissioned. Because of that, I didn't get called up for Korea like a lot of other guys did.

"Ours was probably one of the most wonderful classes that ever graduated. The people who graduated in that era did a lot of wonderful things for this country because of the education they acquired. The guys from that era went off into industry and did all kinds of exciting things in engineering, science, medicine—so many different fields just exploded.

"We've moved from DC-3 aircraft to 767s. Electronics went from the vacuum tube to solid state. Our first computer had five thousand tubes. It filled half a house, and it wasn't as powerful as the computer on your desk. It's been a wonderful time.

From radar through space

"Those days were great times. I think it may have been one of the best times ever.

"It was a hell of a generation!"

Warren Opitz

He can tell you in one word what it was like to work for the Martin Marietta Corporation and to take part in the space race. That one word springs from his lips.

"Fantastic," says Warren Opitz. "It was totally unbelievable—tremendous opportunities, tremendous advances, and tremendous compensation capabilities. If you were willing to take responsibility, you could make your own position. I wouldn't change a minute of my life in those exciting, fantastic times."

Opitz is retired and now lives in Forest, Virginia. After retiring in 1985 from Martin Marietta as director of production operations, he went to work as a professor in the Defense System Management College.

During his years with Martin Marietta, he was primarily involved with missile development, ranging from the pilotless Matador/Mace program, to the development, installation, and activation of the safeguard system in North Dakota, to the vertical launching systems.

He went to work for Martin Marietta on April 16, 1953.

"I built the launching pads for the Titan ICBMs, later acted as a test director at Cape Canaveral, and ultimately led the activation for the *Mercury* program launch pad," he says.

"I also designed and built the launching pad for Vanguard missiles in 1956. If the Navy and Martin had not been unlucky and had an explosion on the pad, the U.S.A. would have been first with a satellite in orbit. As it was, the Russians beat us out, and it stayed that way for the next ten years.

"Later in my career, I pretty much got named the 'guy who could make it happen.' I moved approximately twelve times with

"It was a fantastic time"

the assigned work during my tenure of thirty-one years with Martin Marietta.

"It was a fantastic time. As I look back, the Vanguard program was breaking the threshold. The senior leaders weren't much older than I was. It was absolutely exciting—breaking the new frontiers.

LOOKING TO THE FUTURE. *Prof. Maurice J. Zucrow, a nationally recognized expert in jet propulsion, taught a graduate course in aerodynamics.*

"It was also long hours. I remember once the plant closed for two weeks for a planned vacation, so I returned to Chicago to work on the family home. When I got there, the phone rang. It was my boss. He said to meet him at the airport. We were flown down to Cape Canaveral. I have never seen that house since. I wasn't alone. There were a lot of Purdue grads involved in all of this."

Opitz was born in 1926 in South Chicago, the son of parents who had a bakery, a restaurant, and a catering business.

"Two times the family lost its shirt in the depression," he says. "But we came back, thanks to a lot of stubbornness from my mother, who could take success from defeat. She worked hard with my dad and they rebuilt the business. I did a little of every-thing, including cooking and baking.

"I graduated from Morgan Park Military School in May of 1943. I went into a military training program at Ripon College in

Ripon, Wisconsin. All of a sudden they needed troops, so the whole program was pulled and we were sent overseas. They pulled us at Christmas 1944, and I went to the Pacific in January 1945.

"I was strictly an infantry/artilleryman during the war. I served in Hawaii and the Johnson Islands—no combat.

"I returned home in August 1946. I was a civilian for ten days, and then I became a student at the Gary extension of Purdue. I started at the West Lafayette campus the following summer. I became the first one in my family to get a college degree. What a difference Purdue made in my life.

"I was not a good student. I took chemistry twice so the faculty was sure that I knew it. But at graduation, my grade point average was 3.1. I always carried nineteen to twenty-one hours. Naturally, I had a couple of hours to make up with my chemistry setback.

"I was married in 1948 to a girl back home. I took my summer exams in the morning, drove to Chicago in the afternoon, and was married that evening.

"Our first child was born in Lafayette in March of 1950. I was in class that day. The professor, E. M. Sabbaugh, called on me and I didn't have the answer. I had spent the evening in the hospital with my wife. One of my friends told the professor, 'His wife is in the hospital having a baby.' The professor pointed his finger at me and said, 'You get out of here and don't come back until you know what you have.' I loved that man.

"I was at Purdue on the GI Bill. Because I was married, I got $105 a month. In addition, I helped Red Sammons manage his bookstore. Also, on the corner across from the student union was a restaurant where I mopped the floor. That's how I made extra money. If you wanted your family to eat, that's what you had to do. I also worked at the student union to meet other students and be part of the many programs.

270

"It was a fantastic time"

"I was glad when the war was over. I was sad to see the gross destruction and huge losses. I had lost a number of friends and classmates from military school.

"To earn money, I had stayed in the reserves after I left the Army. The guys in the reserves had two distinct feelings during that period. There was the gung-ho attitude of the younger guys who had been untouched by the war. And then there were the older guys who had been through the war. They had a feeling of, I hope this doesn't happen again.

"It did. I graduated in June of 1950. My first job was junior engineer for the Michigan City Generating Station that was run by Northern Indiana Public Service Company. I worked with wonderful people. Within two months they gave me responsibility for co-ordinating and overseeing the building of a brand new coal-handling facility.

"In September of 1950, I got a letter in an envelope with a red border. The Army gave me ten days to report for duty because of Korea. We were the fourth group out of seventy-five called out of Indiana. Boy, was I mad! I had a wife, a daughter, and a brand new job with initial recognition. When I look back at it, I realize I had made money from the reserves, and it was an obligation I needed to fulfill.

"It worked out pretty well. Because I was a college graduate, I picked up forty-seven other graduates and reported to the Fort Bliss radar school. We became the new staff and instructed radar-training programs for Army people.

"My wife and daughter went to live with my mother-in-law. In August of 1952, I finally returned home without an overseas exposure.

"My daughter, who was six months old when I left, didn't know me. She called me 'the boy' for more than a year."

From radar through space

Frank Holt

Frank Holt grew up on an Indiana farm without electricity or running water. From that beginning, he went on to work in the space program. Technology might never change this much again in a single lifetime.

When he was born in 1920 on an Allen County farm, the family outhouse was out back. "It was cold in the winter," Holt says. "You didn't linger out there.

"My dad was a farmer. I had a sister and six brothers. I was born in the days before tractors. Most of the work back then was done by horses and mules.

"We grew corn, but we didn't have the hybrid seeds available now. You couldn't grow corn in what we used to call the muck ground—it froze too early. On that ground, we raised onions for the New York market—yellow onions. We did the weeding and the hoeing by hand, pulled the onions up by hand, cut the tops off them, graded them, and shipped them to New York.

"The depression hit, and by 1933, we couldn't sell the onions for as much as it cost to buy the bags to put them in. So that was the last time we raised onions. We changed to potatoes for awhile. When researchers came up with hybrid corn, we planted that.

"We didn't have any money during the depression, but we always had plenty of food. Whenever someone knocked on the door, we gave him something to eat. Once a week or so we got visits from what we called hoboes in those days.

"We moved to Whitley County in 1935. I graduated from Larwill High School in 1939. I won the Whitley County scholarship to Purdue when I was a senior. It paid for college tuition. However, I didn't have any money for room and board, and no one would lend me the money, so I didn't get to go. I went back to the farm and helped my dad until September of 1940.

"It was a fantastic time"

"I definitely thought we were going to get involved in a war. The war in Europe was already on, and I wanted to be sure I got into the Army Air Corps. So I enlisted. Congress passed a draft law, and it was put into effect on the same day I went in, September 16, 1940.

"Some people objected to the draft, but not many people tried to stay out. There were a few religious conscientious objectors, but they didn't run away to Canada or anywhere else.

"I trained as an airplane mechanic and was sent to France Field in Panama. On Pearl Harbor Day, a buddy and I were sitting in our bunks listening to the radio when we heard them announce the attack. We knew it was war. Some people I knew were over there, and I had friends in the Philippines when they were taken over. Most of them were listed missing in action.

"When the war started, they scattered our bomber group all up and down South America, as far south as Peru. We were doing sub patrol to keep subs away from the canal. I flew as a flight engineer on some of those sub patrols. I was on temporary duty in Ecuador and later on was sent to Peru. We were flying out into the Pacific. We never did see any Japanese subs, but they got some Germans on the Atlantic side.

"In June of 1943, they rotated us back to the states. I was sent to Tucson, Arizona, for training on B-24s and eventually was sent to England as a crew chief. I was in charge of the crew that took care of planes.

"Before D-Day, our planes were going out about every day on missions. We didn't know the invasion was on until that very day when the flight crew came back and told us. We had no idea when it was going to happen. We worked that day for thirty hours straight without going to bed. We loaded the planes with five-hundred-pound demolition bombs, just regular bombs full of TNT.

From radar through space

"I stayed in England until June of 1945 when the war in Europe was ended, and I was sent back to the United States. I was tech sergeant, and I stayed in the reserve.

"I had always wanted to be an engineer, but I didn't have the money to go to school. But now I had the GI Bill. I worked in the shop at the Pennsylvania Railroad for awhile. I married Treva, a girl from back home, on September 2, 1946. Two weeks later, I started school in Evansville.

"I wanted to go to Purdue, but I was told I had to have a local address, a place to live in the Lafayette area before they would accept me. And we couldn't find one in 1946. So I went to Evansville for two years and transferred to Purdue in the summer of 1948. We lived in Lafayette in an apartment in a big house, and my wife worked as a beautician.

"We didn't miss any programs at the Hall of Music while we were at Purdue. Also, we went to the football games. In fact, my wife and I were both in the card section our senior year.

"I majored in agricultural engineering and graduated in the spring of 1950, the first one in my family to get a college degree. They were all pretty excited about that. Now I have a daughter and three sons, and they're all college graduates.

"Of course, when the war in Korea started, because I was in the reserve, I got called back to active duty. I went to Georgia where they were training parachute jumpers. I was a flight chief— the boss of the crew chiefs.

"Because I was in the reserves, I had expected to get called back up. I had stayed in because I needed that extra money. My Korean duty ended in January of 1953, but I stayed in the reserves. In 1960, I was commissioned and retired as a colonel on my sixtieth birthday in 1980—forty years in the military all together.

"When I got out of the service, I worked for Ford in their tractor and implement division for three and a half years. I was

"It was a fantastic time"

laid off from Ford, but I found a job with Northrop, an aircraft company, as a test engineer.

"Northrop became involved in space work. I designed space simulation chambers, put them together, and started testing space stuff. We got the contract to operate the test facilities at the Johnson Space Center in Houston, and I spent the last eighteen and a half years of my career with Northrop working in the space simulation lab.

"We tested all the experiments that were put on the moon. It was pretty exciting work. Those experiments were designed to last five years. After twelve years, they were still working, but no one was using the data anymore, so we just shut them off. They're still up there.

"I started working for Northrop in 1957, so that was even before NASA. I got to know some of the astronauts. My favorite one was Edward White, who died in that fire down at the Cape. He was a prince of a guy. I knew Gus Grissom by sight, but I never did talk with him, even though he was in my class from Purdue.

"Who would have thought someone who grew up on a farm without electricity and plumbing would get in on the ground floor of the space program. That was a pretty big jump. I was very fortunate—very lucky.

"Even when I was in high school, I would never have dared to say things would change as much as they have. I just think it's amazing what's happened. Gee whiz, there's a computer at Purdue now that will do, what, 3.1 billion calculations a second. When I was there, we had to use slide rules. In fact, working in the space program, we didn't get use of pocket calculators any sooner than anyone else.

"We did a lot of our engineering on that program with slide rules."

275

From radar through space

Joseph Eng

Joseph Eng was born in 1926, the son of Chinese immigrants. He grew up in Newark, New Jersey, and never planned on going to college.

"I was in the Navy from 1944 to 1946," Eng says. "I spent that time in the United States on the West Coast. Most of my time was spent in training. I was an electronic technician in the Navy. I worked with engineers, and they encouraged me to go to college. One guy had been to Purdue. He spoke highly of it and sold me.

"But I didn't have the right credits because I had been to vocational school. So when I got out of the Navy, I went to an accelerated high school to get my necessary credits, and then I went to Purdue.

"I arrived on campus in the fall of 1947 and graduated in 1950. I accumulated some college credits while I was in the Navy, but I had to take a heavy load of classes to graduate in three years. I majored in electrical engineering.

"I lived in private homes. I went out and socialized with a group of veterans, and I belonged to the Chinese Student Association.

"There weren't many girls on campus, but that didn't bother me too much. I wasn't that crazy about dating at that time. I more or less just wanted to get done, get a degree, go out and work, and start a life.

"After graduation, because of my experience with the Navy, I was actively sought by industry. Even before I graduated, I had a job with Philco in Philadelphia. I worked in the defense industry in microwave research for about one year, then I moved to other activities.

"I helped to develop the anti-ICBM, which was the grandfather of the Patriot missile. I was with Grumman, and I participated in the lunar space program. We built the lunar module.

276

"It was a fantastic time"

"I was only one of thousands of engineers working on all this, but it was very exciting, very exciting. I would say we are the most fortunate ones. We had tremendous opportunities in engineering. We were able to participate in one of the most dynamic periods of engineering.

"We were very lucky."

From radar through space

chapter 10

" Like riding a "
roller coaster down

The night the bleachers collapsed

Two killed, hundreds injured
when stands at fieldhouse crash

Purdue University Tuesday was counting the toll taken in lives and injured when the east bleachers in the fieldhouse collapsed Monday evening during the Purdue and Wisconsin basketball game. The seats were filled with approximately 3,400 students and other spectators, all of whom were dropped to the ground when the stands buckled and fell.

Two students were killed and at least six others remained in a serious condition Tuesday noon from injuries as a result of the tragedy. The dead:

Roger R. Gelhausen, 22, a Navy veteran, freshman in physical education.

William J. Feldman, 20, a Merchant Marine veteran and sophomore student in aeronautical engineering.

Hundreds of students were injured, of whom an estimated 166 were taken to hospitals. . . .

Tuesday noon there were still 43 injured at St. Elizabeth and 42 at the Home Hospital while eight others remained in the university infirmary. . . .

Gelhausen, a veteran of nearly three years service in the Navy . . . had dropped down from his seat to get a Coke when he was caught under the bleachers suffering a fractured skull. Feldman was crushed and died of internal injuries.

The tragedy occurred shortly after 8 o'clock.

The fieldhouse was packed to its utmost capacity for the crucial game. The teams had fought through a torrid first half and Purdue was leading. . . .

An estimated 3,400 persons were seated in the east bleachers and many stood up and began to move when the rest period came. In a moment the giant bleachers began to collapse, cracking up like so many matches. Before anyone knew scarcely what had happened, the bleachers, which stood some 30 feet high, were flat. The collapse was marked by a crackling sound. Row after row of humanity dropped down. It was a terrifying and terrible sight. Cheers for the teams as they left the floor changed quickly to screams of fright and terror as the seats dropped. . . .

It was over in a moment. Those not injured were called upon over a loud speaker to leave the collapsed section. Soon only those were left who were unable to move and those who were starting to administer to them. . . .

In the east audience were many G.I.s to whom injury and tragedy were commonplace. They jumped into the breach and performed valiant service in many ways. . . .

The injured themselves were stoical and calm, permitting themselves to be attended without murmur or outcry even though many of them must have been in great pain. One physician said a pretty girl lying on the basketball floor had a compound fracture of one leg, yet she lay quiet smoking a cigarette. . . .

Many suffered cuts and other injuries which caused them to bleed profusely. Many had blood streaming down their faces. Others with lesser injuries were hobbling around on one foot or nursing bruised arms. Some were seated around the fieldhouse attended by friends. Many girls and women were crying.

279

An empty Greyhound bus came along and the driver
volunteered its use in hauling those able to walk to a
hospital. They were driven to Home Hospital, his load
numbering 45 persons.

Due to lack of sufficient ambulances and with so
many injured, there was considerable delay before all
could receive attention. . . . G.I.s formed a human chain
around the bleachers and groups of injured. . . .

The most prevalent injury appeared to be broken
limbs. Many temporary splints were fashioned from
pieces of the broken boards by young men who were
apparently G.I.s and expert in such things.

Journal and Courier, February 25, 1947

Bill Creson, student

"I was in the bleachers in the field house when they collapsed
during a basketball game. This was in early 1947. Those bleachers must have been fifty-five or sixty rows high. They must have
held five or six thousand people.

"I was in the fiftieth row—near the top. Purdue was playing
Wisconsin, and it was an exciting game. The first half had ended.
Everyone stood up all at once and gave a cheer. Then everyone
started to sit down . . ."

John DeCamp, radio broadcaster

"We were talking about the game, and Ward Carlson, the young
man who helped me, said, 'Oh, God, John.' Then he couldn't talk."

Creson

". . . and at that instant the bleachers collapsed and started to fall
forward. The frame tottered forward toward the floor. All the seats
got pushed forward, and it was like riding a roller coaster down."

"Like riding a roller coaster down"

DeCamp

"The basketball floor ran north and south in those days. We were broadcasting from the west side in the balcony. The whole east stand fell. They just surged forward and fell. I kept on broadcasting. I said there had been an accident at the field house and we needed doctors and ambulances. I think some responded because of my alerting them."

Mary Lou Kull Hopkins, student

"Fred and I were in the section that crashed. We were sitting about ten rows from the top. Normally, Fred dropped down between the seats and went underneath the bleachers right before the half to get some Cokes or candy. I remember that night—right before halftime—I said, 'Why don't you drop down and get some candy bars?'"

Fred Hopkins, student

"But this time we were sitting too high, so I didn't. I'd have been a goner if I had tried.

"The bleachers started moving forward. You went back on your butt and picked up your feet to keep the boards from cutting them off. I was stunned for awhile. It was quite a disaster. I walked out the door and a state trooper put me in his car with some other hurt people and took us to Saint Elizabeth Hospital."

Mary Lou Kull Hopkins

"I felt a surge forward, and all of sudden the bleachers started going forward. Fred told me to pick my legs up, which I did to keep them from getting crushed. I went into shock. I don't remember much about the crash after that."

Creson

"By the time I landed, I was halfway across the floor. Everyone's feet and legs were pinched. There were people who were killed. 281

They had dropped through the bleachers right at half time to get out fast, and they were trapped underneath and crushed."

DeCamp

"The game was called off but we stayed on the air for a long time, I think for an hour or so. I just kept reporting what I was seeing. There was a young man named Jim Ertel on the team. His wife was pregnant and she had been sitting in those stands. I remember him walking around looking for her."

COLLAPSED BLEACHERS. *"It was like riding a roller coaster down," one student said, when the bleachers collapsed during a Purdue basketball game in 1946.*

Mary Lou Kull Hopkins

"Some fellow who had been in one of my classes found me and took me to the hospital on the city bus. The buses were called in to take students to the hospital. I went to Home Hospital. I had a gouge in my foot, but it was not too serious. I didn't know where Fred was."

"Like riding a roller coaster down"

Fred Hopkins

"My shoulder was dislocated. I had no idea where Mary Lou was. I found out about midnight she had been taken back to her hall. I think she was in shock."

Mary Lou Kull Hopkins

"The same guy who took me to Home Hospital took me back to the dorm on a city bus. When I got there, my father was sitting in front of Cary Hall. He had been listening to the game on the radio, and he came right over. I went home to the farm for a few days.

"Fred called me there. When I got back to campus a few days later, it looked like a war zone.

"If Fred had gone under the bleachers to get that candy, he probably would have been trapped there and been killed.

"The one positive thing was that there were so many GIs on campus. Because they had been through the war, they didn't panic. They immediately began helping everyone. They knew what to do. This was a direct result of having been in the war."

DeCamp

"What still amazes me is that because of the presence of all the ex-GIs and their wives there was no panic. Nobody got loud and ran around. The ones who were hurt lay on the floor until the medics came in and cared for them. It was quite under control.

"Gradually the team left the floor. Of course they couldn't continue to play the game. Subsequently they played the second half at Evanston Township High School. I think the score at the end of the first half at Purdue was 33–31 and we were ahead. When they finally played the second half, we lost."

Creson

"The irony of it was that one of the guys who was killed was a B-25 pilot who had flown twenty-five missions from North Africa, bombing Rumanian oil fields—an extremely hazardous duty.

283

The night the bleachers collapsed

"He survived all that and then was killed at a basketball game."

Third student succumbs to crash injuries; probe begun

A third fatality was added Tuesday night to the toll of the Purdue University fieldhouse bleacher collapse. . . .

The latest victim is Theodore E. Nordquist, 25, a senior and wounded veteran of World War II in which he served as an Army flyer. . . .

Meanwhile, an official investigating committee named at Indianapolis by Gov. Ralph Gates and here by President Fred Hovde began its work at a joint meeting. . . .

JOURNAL AND COURIER, FEBRUARY 26, 1947

"Like riding a roller coaster down"

chapter 11

" We had a great "
wrestling team

Hoosier hysteria goes to the mat

Arnold Plaza

A retired school teacher, he lives in a "little, dusty town" in south-central New Mexico with his second wife, a woman he married in 1977. They have fourteen children between them.

"I love them all," Arnold Plaza says. "But it's a little harried around Christmastime."

He taught elementary physical education and junior high school science before he retired. These days he rarely thinks back to the years when he was a national champion.

Plaza wrestled at 121 pounds on a team that won three Big Nine championships during his four years at Purdue. He won the NCAA championship in his weight class in 1948 and 1949. He was second in 1950. He won the Big Nine championship in his weight class all four years he wrestled.

This was one of Purdue's greatest athletic teams. In 1950, five members of the wrestling team were champions in their weight class. That year the Purdue team more than doubled the score of the runner-up, Ohio State. It was the biggest margin of victory in the history of the conference's wrestling.

Some of his teammates say Plaza was the greatest of them all, but he just laughs when he is told this. He just waves it off.

He grew up in Chicago.

285

"I was born in 1925, and I was a product of the depression," he says. "I don't remember much about the twenties, but I remember a lot about the thirties. Those were lean years. Everyone worked. Little kids sold newspapers or polished cars. I did that kind of stuff, and I worked as an apprentice butcher, cleaning up and dressing chickens.

"When I went to high school at Tilden Tech, I liked auto mechanics, and I took mostly auto mechanic courses. I had a job at a garage after school when I was a junior and senior.

"I graduated in 1944. I was 4-F. I didn't pass the eye test. I had terrible eyes. So I worked as an auto mechanic.

"I really had never planned on going to college. But I had wrestled in high school, and after I graduated, I kept it up in gyms around the south side. I stayed in shape.

"There was an Amateur Athletic Association wrestling tournament in Chicago every year. Two years after I graduated from Tilden I was in the tournament. A scout from Purdue had come to see Joe Patacsil, who also attended Tilden and was two years younger than I was. Our high school coach introduced me to the scout, Casey Fredericks, the Purdue assistant wrestling coach. Fredericks invited Joe, me, and another guy to go to Purdue.

"I got a scholarship for books and tuition, but I worked for my room and board, first at the student union and then in various fraternity kitchens, washing pots and pans and dishes.

"Wrestling in college was a lot different from high school. High school was fun. I guess it was fun at Purdue, too, but there was a lot more pressure. Before each meet, anyone on the team in your weight class was eligible to challenge you. It wasn't so bad, I guess. It kept me in shape. But it was interesting to see how some of those guys would really tear into each other to try and make first string.

"I didn't date much on campus. I had a little girlfriend back home, and Chicago wasn't that far away.

"We had a great wrestling team"

"I graduated in June of 1950. I was a substitute teacher for a day or two before I was drafted on September 29. I got my notice and went for the physical, and this time I passed. I guess they were hard up. I served all my time in the United States.

"It was wrestling that got me my college education. I don't know what would have happened to me otherwise. I'm satisfied with my life. I look back and I think it was pretty good. But I don't think back much about wrestling or the NCAA championships.

"In this little town, they wouldn't mean much."

Joe Patacsil

A retired school teacher living in Logansport, Indiana, Joe Patacsil taught social studies, physical education, and driver's education.

He also coached, including being head wrestling coach at Logansport High School. It was a job well suited to Patacsil, who came from one of Purdue University's greatest wrestling teams.

"I grew up in Chicago and went to Tilden Tech," he says. "It was an all-boys school of about thirty-five hundred. I weighed 120 to 125 pounds, and when I looked at the boys on the football team, they were a lot bigger than I was. Many of the guys in my neighborhood were already on the wrestling team, so I went out for wrestling.

"World War II was going on when I was in high school. Many of us students thought we were going to be drafted after graduation, so we were all biding our time. Then the war ended during my junior year and the drafting ceased.

"While I was in high school, I was undecided about college. One reason was I didn't know if my parents could afford to send me.

"I was state champion my senior year at Tilden, and at that time, Purdue recruited and offered me a scholarship. That meant they would pay my tuition, fees, and books and give me a job to pay for room and board.

"I had a keen interest in going to college and went to Purdue because it was flattering that they had come and enticed me. At first, I went to Purdue to see what it was all about, but in my sophomore year, the feeling and commitment came that I really wanted to get an education. I realized that an education was what I was going to need.

"It seemed very few students who entered Purdue in the fall of '46 were right out of high school. Many of the students were vets. Those of us from Tilden were eighteen, while the other guys were twenty-two, twenty-three, and twenty-four. Most of my wrestling opponents were older than I was.

"Many of the vets did things we eighteen-year-olds could not do. They frequently went out drinking, but my friends and I were too young. At that time, the tavern owners in Lafayette were pretty sticky about underage drinking. You had to be twenty-one and have an ID.

"I started out living in Cary Hall and later moved to a private home. I ended up living in the home of the head of the physical education department, Wellman France. This proved to be good for me because he would get on me if I had any trouble in class.

"Wrestling went well. I was the Big Nine champ in 1949 and 1950 and NCAA champ in 1950. I was voted outstanding wrestler in the Big Nine in 1950.

"After graduation, I started teaching in Chicago, and I planned a career in teaching and coaching. But the Korean War started, and I went into the Air Force. I was sent to Germany for three years where I served in the weather service at Heidelberg. It was easy duty.

"When I got out of the service, I went back to Purdue on the GI Bill and studied for a master's degree in education. Upon completing my degree, I came to Logansport where I taught and coached for thirty-five years."

"We had a great wrestling team"

Waldemar VanCott

Born in 1924, Waldemar VanCott was a semester short of finishing high school in 1943 when he left and enlisted in the Navy.

"My brother had been killed," he says. "I felt a calling to go into the service. I can say my grades weren't good or it was just time to go to war.

"I was on the USS *Burke*, a destroyer escort, and made thirteen convoys to Europe. Then I went to the USS *Shea*, a destroyer mine-layer in the Pacific. We were hit at Okinawa. We lost one-third of the crew, but the ship didn't go down. We limped back to port.

"After the Navy, I went back and finished high school on the GI Bill at a prep school, Williston Academy, in East Hampton, Massachusetts. I graduated in 1946 and was wondering what college to attend.

"My choices were Williams, Springfield College, or the University of Illinois. I couldn't get into Springfield. Williams was too small. I went out to Illinois and they wanted me to enter, but they didn't have any place for me to stay. My mother knew the president of the Purdue Alumni Association. He got me a room, so I went to Purdue on the GI Bill.

"P" IS FOR PHENOMENAL. One of Purdue's greatest athletic teams was the wrestling squad between 1946 and 1950. Grabbing conference championships and NCAA titles, the best of the best were (left to right) Jack Moreno, Waldemar VanCott, Joe Patacsil, Chuck Farina, and Arnold Plaza.

"I went out for football, but I had been away in the Navy for awhile, and I didn't know what a T-formation or pulling guards were. And Abe Gibron just creamed me. I ended up on the slaughter squad. We ran the other team's plays.

289

Hoosier hysteria goes to the mat

"For four years, I followed the football teams wherever they played. What a wonderful experience—sneaking food in late at night, scalping tickets, moving the sideline chains, and more. There were so many wonderful guys—Bob Heck, Abe Gibron, Lou Karras, Pete Barbolak, Hank Stram, Bob DeMoss, John McKay, and so many more.

"One night, Pete Barbolak and I passed through the Cary West kitchen. We 'found' a box of steaks. Another patrol 'found' real good experimental corn in the ag school fields. So in an apartment house behind Harry's 'C' Shop, half of the football team feasted.

"I finally decided I didn't want to play football anymore. The coach of our group was Claude Reeck. I handed him my 'uniform.' After he had called me a couple names and said a few other things, I asked what else he coached. He said, 'Wrestling.' I had never wrestled in my life. I said, 'Okay. I'll go out for wrestling and make you eat those words.'

"Four years later in a bar in Lafayette, Claude and I sat and talked. He wrote those words down on a piece of paper, and he ate them. We were great friends.

"I wrestled at 175 pounds. During my freshman, sophomore, and junior years, I was either second or fourth in the NCAA. In the Big Nine, I was champ my fourth year, second a couple times, and one time I was fourth.

"We had a great wrestling team. Before us, maybe a hundred people would come to a wrestling match. We had five thousand people attend our matches. I was lucky. The rest of the guys were the best. On that team were Plaza, Patacsil, Moreno, Farina, Dasso, and VanCott.

"We were together for four years. Our first year we were second in the Big Nine, then champions for three years in a row, ending our last year with five individual champions. I know there was no comparable record before 1950, and I don't think any Purdue team since has matched that record.

"We had a great wrestling team"

"One time when our team traveled to a match, we slept in a hotel in Lehigh, Pennsylvania, where George Washington once slept. We know because they hadn't changed the sheets since he was there.

"The fraternities rushed us and talked to us. They talked about pledges crawling up and down the stairs on their bellies. I remembered the verse from the Bible that says, 'When I was child, I spoke as a child, . . . : but when I became a man, I put away childish things.' I never joined a fraternity.

"Most of the wrestling team became Reamers. We hazed each other and the bond became more solid.

"After I graduated, I went into the motion picture business. I was a contract actor for MGM. I was in twenty-two movies. If you had blinked during those movies, you would have missed me. I'd been in plays at Purdue and won the best-acting award there one time.

"In one movie, I think it was called *Above and Beyond*, I was the bombardier. I was in another one—*Midnight to Morning* or something like that—with Ray Milland. My parts were all very small ones.

"When I went to the interview for the first movie I was in, the casting person asked, 'Do you think you could play a college athlete?' I said I would try.

"After two and a half years of that, I went to McDonnell Douglas as a draftsman. I had failed a course in drafting at Purdue. Next, I got into labor relations—the only other course I failed at Purdue was the history of labor relations. I eventually became director of training.

"The things I ended up being good at were not the things I had studied at Purdue. But college taught me how to think.

"My experience at Navy boot camp had changed me. When I first went in the service, I said I was never going back to school. But my time in the Navy convinced me to go back to college. In the Navy, I saw a lot of people who didn't have an opportunity to get an education.

"I'm retired now—thankful and happy. My wife, Louise, and I have two wonderful children, Ann and Waldemar III, plus our grandson, Cole.

"Purdue gave me some of the most wonderful memories of my life. I say, 'Thanks! Hail Purdue!'"

"We had a great wrestling team"

chapter 12

" I never did go home "

Students from faraway places

Tsung Wei Sze

Tsung Wei Sze lives in Pittsburgh, a long way from his beginnings. Sometimes life takes you far from where you start to places you never thought you would see.

And if life takes you to one place, it takes you away from another—away from a home and parents and brothers and sisters and friends, away from a world you understood to one that is quite different.

Before retiring in 1993, Sze had returned to teaching at the University of Pittsburgh where he did research and was a professor of electrical engineering.

Teaching and research were his first and last loves. In between, he served at Pittsburgh as associate dean and dean of the school of engineering and dean of graduate studies.

"I'm from Shanghai, China," Sze says. "I was born in 1922. My father was a teacher. We had a depression in China, too. It was pretty bad. I will give you one example. Whenever there was a cold spell, a freeze, there would be corpses on the street.

"In 1939, I went to Chiaotung University to study electrical engineering. I had a scholarship, and Chiaotung had the best engineering school in the Far East at that time. With the fall of Shanghai, the school was moved to a wartime campus near Chunking. It had no electricity, no lab—nothing. However, the school did have dedicated professors.

"After my junior year, I volunteered for the Chinese Army. Because of my college education, I was assigned to work with the American Army. In the beginning, I worked with them in China, and then one hundred of us were sent to the United States. I was an interpreter attached to the Air Force. It was our understanding we would go in with the invasion of either Japan or southeast China. I felt very relieved about the bomb being dropped.

"I was discharged from the service in 1946 while I was in the United States. I went to the University of Missouri to finish my undergraduate work and graduated in 1948. I applied to Purdue and was admitted for my master's. Purdue has an engineering program known all over the world.

"I lived in Cary Hall at Purdue and belonged to the Chinese Student Association. There were about a hundred of us at Purdue at the time. We didn't intermingle very much with the other students. It was still pretty hard for Chinese students to get housing in West Lafayette. When a Chinese student was successful in finding a house that would take him, he helped others get a room also—usually in the same house.

"The Chinese Student Association met monthly. We had potluck dinners, and we went to Urbana, Illinois, to the University of Illinois to be with Chinese students there. We had volleyball matches and played bridge, and we returned the courtesy—the Illinois students came to Purdue.

"I felt the United States was a very good place to stay, but I always considered myself a guest. I always thought after I finished I would be going home to China.

"No matter how well we did in our studies at Purdue, it was very hard for us to get an assistantship. The chairman of the de-

"I never did go home"

partment told me there were no assistantships for foreign students. That's why I went to Northwestern for my Ph.D. I got married in 1952. My wife was also a student at Northwestern.

PURDUE CHINESE STUDENT CLUB. In the spring of 1950, the club numbered about one hundred. Class of 1950 grads who are in A Force for Change *are (front row, second from the right) Joseph W. Eng and (third row, fourth from the right) Tsung Wei Sze.*

"I never did go home. The Communists took over China in 1950, and that settled that. My parents were still in China along with my two brothers and one sister. Although I had left China in 1945, because of the war I had last seen my family in 1941.

"For a long time, we were able to write, although letters were watched. Anything that came from the United States, even alumni office materials, my family had to pick up from the police. The mail from the United States caused them a lot of trouble. Finally, my wife's mother wrote, 'Please, don't write anymore.'

"We stopped. There was a period of about twelve years when we didn't really know whether they were alive or dead. It was very hard, indeed.

"I became a United States citizen in 1962.

295

Students from faraway places

"I was not able to return to China to see my family until after President Nixon opened it up. I returned in 1979, and I was able to see my family. It was very emotional. The meeting was still very much under the control of the Chinese government. They decided whom you could see and where you could see them. My family came to see me at my hotel—not all at once, but I was able to see them all. I had been invited to come by the Chinese to establish a research center in image processing, which was my field. I was treated very well.

"I have been able to go back to China five different times, and each time I worked with various universities and visited with my family. My parents have passed away now.

"I consider myself very lucky because some of my classmates who remained under the Communists had a very tough time. Some of them were driven to suicide. If I had not been sent to the United States by the Chinese Army, my life would be entirely different.

"These things make you appreciate life much more."

Pedro Castillo

"At Purdue it was beautiful," he says. "There were a lot of good exchange students and not just Latinos like me. I had a friend from India, who became a well-known scientist. I had a friend from Iraq, who was a graduate student.

"People told my friend from Iraq if he wanted to be Americanized he had to learn the game of football. So one Saturday he asked me to go to a game with him, but he had a lab first and he asked me to save him a seat. When he got there, the game had already started, and he came running up the stands. The run wore him out, he was breathing hard.

"'Puff, puff,' he said. 'What's the score?'

"'Nothing to nothing,' I said.

"'Oh,' he said, still puffing. 'Who scored the first nothing?'"

296

"I never did go home"

Pedro Castillo is an easygoing, friendly man. He has been married since 1953 to Patricia, a woman he met in Lafayette. The Castillos have three children and three granddaughters. He works for a Lafayette furniture company.

Castillo was born in November of 1925 to a well-to-do family in the leather-goods industry in Arequipa, Peru, the country's second largest city, eight hundred miles south of Lima, between the mountains and the coastline.

"We had a depression in Peru, too, but I don't remember a lot about it," he says, sitting on his living-room couch, a dog lying nearby on the floor. His wife is in the kitchen at a table. He checks with her about certain dates.

"During the depression, I had an uncle who lost a fortune in the wool business," he says. "And I remember there was a person running the country whose policies caused a lot of discontent. The military came along and overthrew him in a big revolution. Everyone was very happy with the new leader. A few years later, he got killed. That's my first recollection of politics in Peru.

"Peruvians did a lot of business with the German chemical companies. We bought a lot from them. And I went to school with a lot of Italians. We used to sing Mussolini's national song in school. Before the war, all my intentions were to go to college in Germany. But the war came along, and it changed everything.

"Before the United States entered the war, feelings were mixed in Peru. There was a lot of sympathy for the Germans. Many of the Americans who came to Peru were the 'ugly American' type. The Germans were more friendly. After Pearl Harbor, however, everyone sympathized with the Americans. Peru was on the side of the Allies. But there was no draft of young men.

"I graduated from high school in 1947. I went to prep schools in the state of New Jersey. When I was ready for college, I decided the East Coast was too cold for me. My counselor told me to apply to UCLA and Stanford because the weather was more what I was used to. I did and I was accepted. But their semesters had already started, and I would have had to wait. So, I applied to Notre Dame, Rose Poly, and Purdue. I picked Purdue.

"I came to Purdue by bus in February of 1949, and we passed through miles and miles of snow. It was a good thing we went through at night when I couldn't see it. I had no idea it would be as cold here as on the East Coast.

"I arrived on a Saturday, and on Sunday, I needed to go to church. I got directions to Saint Mary's Cathedral in Lafayette. Afterwards, I was walking home and I heard a group of guys talking in Spanish. I thought, Oh man! That was my salvation. I made friends quickly.

"I never felt out of place at Purdue, but quite a few little things were difficult. There was a certain animosity against foreigners in Lafayette. I never really experienced it firsthand, but some of my friends did.

"I had Panamanian friends who were very dark, really black. They would go to the Lafayette Theater, and they couldn't sit downstairs. They had to climb up to the balcony. It's a good thing I didn't see that because as revolutionary as I was I don't know what I would have done.

"I remember once a friend and I were standing in a line somewhere and talking in Spanish. A man turned around and said, 'Why don't you talk English so we can understand you?'

"I never really had trouble on the Purdue campus. There was a lot of acceptance there. Many of the guys had come back on the GI Bill. They had been outside the country and came back with a much wider concept of life in other countries. But some guys who had never been anywhere but the next county were a problem.

"I was studying mechanical engineering, but the money dried up and my grades were not so good. My family in Peru had been

"I never did go home"

paying for everything, and economic inflation there was terrible. When I first came to the United States, it was 6.5 of our money for a dollar American. When I came to Purdue, it was 36 to a dollar. By 1950, it was worse. My family said, 'Come back home and finish school here.' I said, 'No. I have a job.' I thought I'd save some money and go back to Purdue. But I never did.

"In those days, I was just trying to have a good time, to have a good life. I'm older now, but still—if I had known then what I know now, I wouldn't have changed anything. If I had gone back to Purdue and finished my degree, I might have been in a better job now.

"But I wouldn't be any happier."

Students from faraway places

chapter 13

"Now it's your turn"

From college to Korea

Herbert Spoelstra

"Not all of us fought a war and then went to Purdue," says Herbert Spoelstra. No—some, like Spoelstra of Greenwood, Indiana, went to college and then went to war. The same month that the Purdue University Class of 1950 graduated, war broke out in Korea, and it changed the lives and plans of many young men and women.

A retired actuary with Farm Bureau Insurance in Indianapolis, Spoelstra was the son of a Lafayette accountant. He was born in 1929 and graduated from Jefferson High School in 1946.

"It was an interesting time," he says. "During the war, so many young men were gone it was easy to get a pretty respectable job. I worked part-time during high school at the Lafayette Life Insurance Company. I worked Saturday mornings and on weekday afternoons. You could work and get some high school credit for it.

"To be honest, I was never anxious to get into the war. It was over while I was still in high school anyway, and when I graduated, I went to Purdue. It was kind of a natural thing for me to do. I lived at home. There was a bus system that went back and forth between Lafayette and West Lafayette without any trouble. The buses were overloaded, but they were cheap.

"I continued to work at Lafayette Life while I went to Purdue. I probably worked fifteen to twenty hours a week, so between that and classes and study, I was pretty busy. I really didn't get involved too much with activities.

"At that time, ROTC at Purdue was compulsory the first two years for male students. By taking advanced ROTC, I was deferred from the draft until after graduation. I remember the military parades we took. We would leave the campus and march to Lafayette in the downtown area and then back to West Lafayette.

"I felt I would be called up if there was a war, which is exactly what happened. I graduated in 1950, but I wasn't called up until the spring of 1951. It seems kind

NAVY ON PARADE. *All young men entering Purdue who had not previously served in the military were required to take ROTC or play in the "All-American" Marching Band.*

of strange that I wasn't called until then. But I knew I was going to be called, so I spent that year in limbo. I continued to work at Lafayette Life.

"I was sent to Korea and stayed there until 1953. I was an ordnance officer and was always stationed at an ordnance base depot.

"It was my first time in a foreign land, and being in the service, I didn't know what to expect. I still have vivid memories of getting to the replacement depot in Pusan. Most of the guys who got there were sent farther north. But I was stationed there in Pusan, which was some distance from the fighting.

"I remember that first day in Korea and having the feeling I didn't know where my next meal was going to come from. At the replacement depot, they told me to relax. So I went to the shower,

301

From college to Korea

took off my clothes, and was showering when the lights all went out. I walked out of the shower room and the first thing I saw was a Korean man. I thought I was going to be captured. I thought, Here I am, my first day in Korea, I don't have any clothes on, and I'm going to be captured. The man turned out to be the janitor.

"He asked me if the water was warm enough."

Bill Creson

In the 1950 Purdue University yearbook, the *Debris,* he wears a light-colored coat, a light mustache, and glasses. He looks very young compared to some of the ex-GIs pictured around him. By comparison, he was young.

Bill Creson is the retired chairman and chief executive officer of a forest products company in San Francisco and a 1984 recipient of an honorary doctorate from Purdue. He is soft spoken.

He was seventeen years old when he entered Purdue and twenty-one when he graduated, the normal college age for normal times. But the years 1946 to 1950 were not normal times. In the fall of 1946, the average age of his pledge class at Sigma Alpha Epsilon was twenty-six years old.

In the 1950 yearbook, Creson is listed as president of Sigma Alpha Epsilon, a member of the Gimlet Club, a member of the Fraternity Presidents Council, and vice president of the Student Union Board. If his fellow students had picked someone to succeed, many would have named Creson. More than forty years later, a good number still speak of him.

Born in 1929 in Lafayette, Creson is the son of an executive with Ross Gear, a company founded by Purdue benefactor David Ross. Creson's family moved across the Wabash River into West Lafayette in 1936.

His father had an experience somewhat similar to the post-World-War-II era. In 1914, he had entered Purdue but went off to

"Now it's your turn"

fight in World War I before he could finish. After the war, he worked in Chicago before going back to Purdue, finishing in 1924.

In 1946, Creson graduated from high school in a class most of whom did what they had been raised to do in the university community of West Lafayette—go to college. Therefore, he went to college.

"What's interesting to me is the change Purdue University went through between 1939 when my sister started there and 1946 when I went," Creson says.

"When I was a kid growing up in West Lafayette, Purdue had an enrollment of something like thirty-five hundred students. It was what we think of as a classic college town. State universities were not the massive institutions they are today, and they weren't all that different from places like Wabash College down the road or DePauw University a little farther down, where the enrollment was maybe six to eight hundred.

"In 1941, West Lafayette was a sleepy little town. It was self contained, compact. Students didn't have automobiles. It was a campus and culture geared to pedestrians.

"As kids growing up, we learned our way around the university. We knew all the steam tunnels. We knew how to sneak into every one of them and travel for blocks without coming above ground.

"We knew how to sneak into every venue—the Hall of Music for performances, the field house for basketball games, and Ross-Ade Stadium for football games. The ticket prices for all these events were moderate, but we prided ourselves on being able to sneak in.

"For basketball games, this is what we would do. On the afternoon before the evening game, one of the guys would go in and open a window in a physical education classroom in the field house. That night, we'd go to that window, climb into the classroom, walk

303

From college to Korea

down the hall, climb down the stands of the varsity swimming pool, go back into the showers, enter a locker room, walk down the hall, and go into a men's room that was opened up for the basketball crowd, walk out into the field house, and watch the game.

"We all knew the guy who controlled admissions to the field house, and he would have let any of us in who wanted to come. But there was a mystique to proving we could sneak in without his catching us.

"Another interesting thing—in the field house in the men's locker room near the checkout counter was a candy stand. It was on an honor system. One of the athletes put it there, and he put out candy and fruit with a basket for money. Men who used the locker room would pick up an item, pay for it, and take their change from the basket. Hundreds of men walked by this stand every day, and no one cheated. It was an honor system, and it was respected. It was part of our background of values and behavior. We came to accept this as the natural way.

"Our curriculum in West Lafayette High School was college prep, and the expectation was that almost everyone was going to college. West Lafayette was a college town.

"In West Lafayette, we were very aware that the war was on because of all the military people on campus. One of the programs, the Navy V-12, brought a lot of guys from other schools to Purdue. Because of these guys, Purdue had a terrific football team—players like Bump Elliott and Alex Agase. In addition to the V-12 program, Purdue had ROTC. Everywhere you went there was a military presence.

"I was seventeen years old when I started at Purdue. It was an interesting, very healthy, and positive experience for me. It exposed me to the thinking of older people who had life experiences that I couldn't even begin to imagine. The older guys were very tolerant and very friendly. They didn't dump on the younger kids. By and large, there was mutual respect.

"Now it's your turn"

"I think the younger kids, right out of high school, tended to deal with the academic challenges better early on. A number of the older guys had to get cranked up again to get into a study routine.

"There was a subtle interaction among the vets—an occasional slight tension between the enlisted men and the officers. In our fraternity, this was never a serious issue. But I can remember one or two or three occasions when some tweaking went on between the former enlisted men and the former officers. It never was a really big problem, however. In fact, when I look back on this period, it was overall one of great goodwill. There was an absence of really bad feelings.

"The veterans brought energy and good humor with them. A lot of funny stuff went on that seventeen- or eighteen-year-olds would never have worked out on their own. The haircut boycott was an example of this.

"In the fall of 1946, there were three or four small barbershops in the West Lafayette village and a big one in the student union. At the beginning of the semester, the price for haircuts was seventy-five cents, but two or three weeks later, the barbers all raised the price to a dollar. Gradually, dislike of this increase grew. Some editorials appeared in the student newspaper. Then, some genius came up with the rally cry 'At a buck a throw, let it grow.' Literally, overnight there was a university-wide boycott of the barbershops. This was pretty unusual. In those days, we had short hair and got it cut every two or three weeks. The boycott died a gradual death. By the end of the year, we were paying a dollar.

"This was an upbeat time, and it wasn't just at Purdue. The whole country

The Whoopurdoo   By Sandy

"*This is WBAA, the voice of Purdue, West Lafayette . . .*" (*From the October 1946* Exponent)

305

From college to Korea

was upbeat through the 1950s and part of the 1960s—from 1946 through the Eisenhower era into the Kennedy presidency. We believed that this country could do almost anything. Probably the symbol of this feeling was when John Kennedy said we'd put a man on the moon—and we went and did it! And it was Purdue graduate Neil Armstrong who was first.

"I look at my kids now and at the grandchildren of some of the people I went to school with. These young people have serious doubts about what the future will hold and whether their quality of life will be as good as their parents'. That was not the way we thought. We knew our life was going to be better than our parents'. American industry was there, and the expectation was that we were going to make a better life for ourselves.

"I majored in mechanical engineering and graduated in June of 1950. I was planning to go to grad school to get an M.B.A. at the University of Pennsylvania in February of 1951, so I was taking a few courses at Purdue in the fall of 1950. However, the Korean War had started, and I was drafted.

"I ended up with a number of Purdue guys in a special program. I was assigned to a group working on the guidance and fusing for the original Nike missile. I served two years, then went back and got my M.B.A.

"We believed we could do anything. I'm sure the GI Bill and that postwar college group had a lot to do with that feeling. They had won the war, and hundreds of thousands of young men and some women were going to college who previously had no expectations of going to school. The war opened this door to them.

"Really, the unique contribution made by the GI Bill was not just that the veterans went to college. It was that it created a value system where it was appropriate for their kids to go to college. In the 1960s, we had a huge population explosion in our colleges in this country. These were the kids of the GIs, and their going to college was the payoff of the GI Bill.

"Now it's your turn"

"The bill imbued the GIs and their families with the value of a college education. That was very unlike their own experience. Now the grandchildren of GIs are going to college. These too are people to whom a college education is an expectation.

"And it has never been that way before."

Saul Meyer

Saul Meyer grew up in New London, Connecticut, a city that is home to the U.S. Coast Guard Academy, a port city where people are accustomed to the sight of military personnel, men in crisp white uniforms.

Born in 1928, he was one of the younger members of the class of 1950. He had to compete against returning veterans who were given priority at the time he was ready for college and later for medical school.

An ophthalmologist in Northridge, California, Meyer is a man who picks and pronounces his words carefully. He is married and has two sons.

He remembers going to high school during the war. He remembers rationing. He remembers Pearl Harbor.

"It happened on a Sunday morning," he says. "But on the East Coast where I lived, that was the middle of the day. I had been outside playing with some friends—football or something. I remember around lunchtime coming home, turning on the radio, and hearing the announcement. That set everything in motion.

"I was in the eighth grade, and I don't know . . . we kids looked at the war a little differently than our parents did. Kids looked at the romantic side of it. Our parents were saying it would be over before we were old enough to go.

"The next year, 1942, I entered high school. I remember we would save silver foil from Hershey bars. But sugar was rationed, so candy, too, became scarce, and we didn't get much foil. Meat

307

was rationed. Gasoline was rationed. We would listen to the radio and read newspapers to find out what was going on.

"Some of the guys who turned eighteen during their senior year were drafted or entered the military. The school gave them their diplomas if they were close.

"I got out of high school in 1946, and the war was over. A lot of GIs were coming back and going to college. It was a tough year to get into college.

"After the war, a branch of the University of Connecticut was started in New London, so I went there for a semester. Then, I decided I wanted to go away. I used to follow sports quite avidly, and I think during that time Purdue had a good football team. Also, a professor at the University of Connecticut had gone to Purdue. So, I put in an application for Purdue and was accepted for the second semester.

"I was sort of a chemistry major. I was interested in premed, but I knew it was going to be tough getting into med school because a lot GIs had that interest too. So I majored mostly in chemistry, in case I didn't make it to medical school.

"Many veterans wore their leather jackets and Navy jackets. Guys wore white bucks. In your senior year, you had the tradition of wearing yellow corduroy pants—cords. They had a pocket on the side where you could put your slide rule. You would paint different things on them. You put them on the first day of your senior year and wore them every day, never cleaned.

"I recall taking the Monon train to Chicago for weekends and holidays. The Monon had diesel engines and very nice cars. A lot of kids at Purdue were from Chicago, and a lot of other students went to Chicago from Friday to Sunday. The passengers on the train were mostly all students. There wouldn't be enough seats, so you'd sit on your suitcase.

"I remember taking a bus trip for the Notre Dame football game in my senior year. They were on an unbeaten streak and led

"Now it's your turn"

by eight points. Purdue scored on the last play of the game and the extra point left us one shy.

"A number of former football players came back to Purdue to finish their degrees. In my senior year physiology class, I sat behind Abe Gibron wearing his Buffalo Bills jacket.

"I graduated from the School of Science in June of 1950 and soon after had to sign up for the draft because the Korean War had started. I would have been drafted, but I was deferred when I got into medical school. I did my intern year in 1955. At that time, because of a doctor draft, I had to go into the Air Force for two years.

"I was at a base in Glasgow, Scotland. A good number of former college football players were there, and they had an exhibition game. I was doctor for the day. The players came back with bruises, and I talked to a few of them. Some of those guys had been football players at Purdue after I had graduated, and they had beaten Notre Dame in the early 1950s. Purdue had finally knocked off Notre Dame.

"It was a unique experience going to school during that time. After the war, the feeling was there wouldn't be any more wars. That was the feeling.

"But it didn't work out that way."

Bob Stauber

In 1946, he went right out of high school in Decatur, Illinois, to Purdue University—a kid from the "Soybean Capital of the World" to a place filled with men who had been all over the world.

"Purdue was full of all these older, returning veterans," he says. "I didn't know whether to call them 'Mister' or by their first names.

"I remember my first class at Purdue was surveying. My partner was a fellow named George Smith, who happened to be twenty-five years old. He seemed like an adult to me. He was just

309

out of the Seabees. I was very shy. I called him 'Mister' until he told me to call him 'George.'

"The funny thing was he had been surveying for a couple years in the Seabees. I never got to touch the instrument. All he wanted to do was get done in the field and get back in. He could do all that stuff with his eyes closed."

A metallurgical engineer, Stauber is retired from Modern Builder Supply Company in Oceanside, California. Typically for members of his class, he has worked for many companies over the years.

"The thing is engineering degrees gave us freedom to change jobs and not lose income," he says. "We could go and live where we wanted. If we found ourselves in a job we weren't satisfied with, we didn't have to stay. We could go on and find another job. We were able to move around until we found something that suited us."

During high school, he grew up looking forward to getting into the war.

"We—our age group—were all very patriotic," Stauber says. "We were in a patriotic fever. I worked summers in a defense plant. Since the older guys were gone, we had opportunities that otherwise wouldn't have come along. We would have gone off to the war, too, if our parents had let us. But we had to finish high school. The war ended in 1945, and I still had a year of high school to go.

"At the defense plant, I worked in the metallurgical department. All of my co-workers told me that metallurgy was the best future. I was all fired up about being an engineer, and since I had relatives in West Lafayette, I knew all about Purdue.

"Purdue was extremely crowded. I was lucky. I lived in a residence hall, but some of my friends had to live in those old military barracks the university brought in.

"There weren't very many girls. Really, it wasn't a matter of the older guys having all the girls. It was a matter of who had money to go out with them. Most of us were pretty broke. We couldn't afford much of a date.

"Now it's your turn"

"Everybody was pretty serious about studies. We all believed that if we got our degree, we would get a job, get married, have kids, have a house, and live the American dream.

"I graduated in June of 1950 and I couldn't get a job. The Korean War had started. Employers told me when I got my draft status cleared up to let them know and then they would hire me. I was 1-A. I went for my physical and flunked. I was classified 4-F.

"Living through that whole period made us feel very satisfied and made us feel lucky with what we had in this country. It made us patriotic.

"All of us came out of the depression and World War II feeling that this was a great country and we were lucky to live in it. We had great opportunities, and for most of us, that was the way our lives went.

"We went from being in poverty to being middle or upper-middle class because of our education and our ability to move from job to job."

Thomas J. Hahn

Thomas Hahn graduated from Purdue University with a degree in chemical engineering. He is a Cadillac-Pontiac-Oldsmobile dealer in West Caldwell, New Jersey.

"Most people change," he says. "They don't end up doing what they went to school for. If you trace guys with their degrees, you'll find many of them are doing something different. You have to stay flexible in life, and take offers as they come."

Hahn is a busy man. He talks like a person who knows what he is going to do next. He used the GI Bill to get an M.B.A. from Wharton.

"I got to Purdue in 1946, right out of high school," he says. "The draft stopped just two weeks before I would have been taken. I was kind of—well, I was a minority at Purdue. I was wet behind the ears compared to the other guys who had come back from the war.

311

"I probably wanted to get into it while I was in high school. The mentality was entirely different from what it is today. Going through high school during World War II, you knew you were going to be drafted into the Army and be shot at. It didn't happen that way for me. But that's what you expected.

"At Purdue, with all those ex-GIs there, you hustled. You studied. You kept your nose to the grindstone. One advantage of going to school then was you didn't have to put up with the usual nonsense on college campuses.

"There's no question about it, being around those older guys, being forced to work hard at studies, was good for me. The vets considered the younger guys to be kids. They related mostly to people their own age who had been through similar experiences, but they were tolerant of the younger kids.

WHEN IT RAINED, THEY CLANGED. *Metal Quonset huts served as auxiliary classrooms for the late forties' deluge of students. But when it rained, the din on the metal made hearing lectures difficult.*

"Girls? What girls? The ratio of guys to girls on campus was something like five or six to one. The competition was tough.

"Housing was tight. We lived in attics with double-decker bunks all around. We had maybe a small study room with desks for two or three people. It was crowded.

"A lot of the vets lived in temporary housing and in Quonset huts. Some married vets lived in Quonset huts, and some classes were held in them. If it rained when you were inside those metal huts, it sounded like someone was beating drums in your head.

"I graduated in June of 1950, the same month Korea broke out. The older guys kind of looked at us younger ones and laughed. They said, 'Now it's your turn.'

"Now it's your turn"

"In November of 1950, I was drafted for Korea. I felt the same way everyone felt. It was our turn. Those vets had been right.

"I was never sent to Korea. My degree was in chemical engineering, but I liked to fiddle with electronics. I was drafted into a chemical warfare outfit, which made sense. But they had a program called Scientific and Professional Personnel, so kids who were engineers and college graduates were tested and shipped to different places. My electronics came out strong in the test, so I was sent to Fort Monmouth, New Jersey.

I was sent on detached duty to the National Bureau of Standards in Washington, D.C. We did instrumentation work for atomic bomb testing.

"In 1951, we went out to Camp Desert Rock, Nevada, for the tests. I don't know how many tests I was around for. They were doing all kinds of shots—some from a tower, some underground. This may sound funny, but after awhile, you got so you just stayed in camp. You didn't even get out of bed to see the shots.

"We went back to Washington and were assigned to another group on Enewetak, a Pacific atoll. That's where they did the first thermonuclear shot. That scared the hell out of me! The pictures you've seen of this don't give you the proportion. When you're out there looking at the explosion and you realize you're thirty miles from ground zero, yet you're looking up at that mushroom cloud—that's when you get an idea of the power.

"I hadn't been to a church in a long time. I was at mass the next day."

For a scheming, industrious lad, dates at Purdue are to be had

By Dick Williams

When asked by the Sweet Shop roving reporters, "Do you think dates are hard to get on campus?" Bob Williams answered, "No! No! D'you want some?"

313

From college to Korea

Reeling with surprise at this apparent thwarting of the Ratio, I confusedly said "yes," and stumbled up to the counter. While ordering a chocolate shake, Ray Schwomeyer, EE 8, said that you can get campus dates if you think it's worth the effort. After some thought he added, "I haven't had a date in a year." Joe Baughman leaned over to say that he, too, could get dates if he tried.

Defeatist policy

Mary Lou Kull, Home Ec. 6, stated, "That's the trouble with Purdue men! They never honestly try to get a date—they're too defeatist. Too often they think they're God's gift to women and refuse to give the lucky girls a break. Not that my steady fellow is like that," she finished hastily.

One male student sneered cynically but simply, "Yeah, it's hard," and was staring bitterly into space when I last saw him. But more seemed to think that a little ingenuity and a lot of patience were a surefire combination. "Pick out a queen and call her up just a few hours before the big dance," advised Bob Schmal, Science 8, from the depths of a log-table. He went on, "Since everybody will think the gal is busy, she'll be sitting there with nothing to do."

Persistence always wins

Ernie Prow, Chem. E. 6, pooh-poohed this advice, saying that you should "just ask ahead of time, way ahead of time. Persistence helps, of course." His companion, Bill Creson, agreed, stating, "You said it. My motto is, 'If at first you don't succeed . . .'"

Looking up from the selling of the new issue of the Rivet, Joan Kreuser, Science 4, said, "Any fellow who's pretty easy to get along with can get a date on campus. What they need to do is stop griping and start asking." It seems that though two-thirds of Joan's sorority house

314

"Now it's your turn"

is either pinned, engaged or going steady, the other third are available if properly called upon.

Requirements

Phyl Wilson, Liberal Science 4, disengaged her hand from that of George Clark, to whom she is pinned, and said dreamily, "If he's tall and broad shouldered, with curly hair and a light green Futuramic Oldsmobile, and his name is Ed Sweeney, he's set!" George looked ready to snatch Phyl's Coke out from under her hand.

R. W. Ellington, AE 8, cried in his root beer that the BTU content of University coeds is too low.

The polls of Sweet Shop opinion were expressed at the last corner booth. There Tor Kolflat, ME 6, thought dates easy to get provided you had either long-range planning (if you want a date next fall ask now) or ingenuity (money, car and beer capacity). But Bob Koegler, Chem E 8, advised cheerily, "Save your money and spend it on whiskey."

The last victim was a small blonde thing alone at a table, to wit, I thought, a queen. I asked her name, explaining that I was the roving reporter. Quick as lightening she shot back, "Betty. What's your name?" I— well, that's all folks. It's not so hard to get a date, men. Your reporter is really ro-o-o-oving tonight.

PURDUE EXPONENT, APRIL 23, 1949

Lew Wood

Lew Wood is director of national public relations for the American Legion. He believes the GI Bill that sent millions of young men to college after World War II changed the country forever.

"I was not a veteran of World War II myself," he says. "I was a seventeen-year-old kid who went to college with these guys who were four or five years older than I was, who had flown fifty missions in Europe, or who had fought hand-to-hand in the Pacific. They wore bits and pieces of their uniforms because those were the only clothes they owned. It was an eye-opener for me.

"These guys were serious. But that didn't mean they didn't party. I remember the night I joined my fraternity. After they ushered me into a room, a member told me they would like me to join and they had a pledge pin for me to wear. The guy who said this had a bottle of whiskey on his desk. My eyes bugged out. I'd never seen anything like that. But after these guys got back from flying bombing missions, when they got back to their base in England or wherever it was, they knocked a few back. They continued some of those customs in college.

"I was born in Indianapolis. I didn't graduate from high school until 1946 and, oh, was I disappointed I wasn't getting in on the war! One of my buddies, a few years older than I, had gone to the Pacific. Another had gone into the Air Force.

"We grew up in a patriotic time. You couldn't wait to do your duty and service.

"After high school, I went into the Navy and went to Purdue on the Holloway Plan. Admiral Holloway was the superintendent of the U.S. Naval Academy. He felt the Navy would need more regular officers. He decided a way to insure this was to supplement the Naval Academy graduates by sending young men to schools all over the country on Navy ROTC scholarships. I received tuition, books, fees, uniforms, and fifty dollars a month for room and board.

"Even though I was in the military, I could decide where I would live on campus. I first lodged in a rooming house on Waldron Street. I lived there with one guy who fought at Iwo Jima and another guy who spent two years in a German stalag. Here's this kid in with combat veterans. I couldn't believe all the stories they told.

"I opted for the Marine Corps in my junior year, and I graduated as a second lieutenant, USMC. After I graduated in 1950, I headed immediately for Quantico. The training there for all new

"Now it's your turn"

officers was supposed to last nine months. But on June 25, 1950, the North Koreans invaded the south. It hit the fan and they shortened the training to six months. I spent 1951 in Korea.

"I was lucky. I was assigned to a support unit. I never did get shot at. When I found out I wasn't going to be up front, I was very disappointed—for twenty-four hours. Then I saw those guys coming down off the hill to be rotated. When I looked at their faces, they resembled Bill Mauldin's 'Willie and Joe.' I thought, Is that what combat does to you? I got over my disappointment in a hurry.

"When I came back from Korea, I decided to resign my commission and get back into civilian life. I became a news broadcaster. I wound up having a pretty good career in broadcast journalism as a CBS News correspondent, an NBC News correspondent, and news anchor on the 'Today Show.'

"You know, when we came through that period of 1946 to 1950, we were imbued with the spirit and values and dedication of those who had just come back from fighting World War II. Those of us who served in Korea wanted to be as good as, if not better than, those veterans had been in their service to our country.

"I think we were."

Virgil Grissom

As told by Norman Grissom and Bill Head

Purdue man becomes nation's second successful astronaut

CAPE CANAVERAL, Fla. (AP)—Astronaut Virgil (Gus) Grissom took a 5,280 mile-an-hour ride in space Friday, then had to swim for his life as his capsule-craft sank in 2,800 fathoms of water. . . .

Grissom, a Purdue University graduate from Mitchell, Ind., rose 118 miles high on the nose of a Redstone rocket and 303 miles down the Atlantic missile range. And he looked down on a view so fascinating he forgot momentarily that he had chores to perform during the 15-minute journey.

President Kennedy watched on television with millions of other Americans as Grissom followed the space trail blazed May 5 by astronaut Alan B. Shepard Jr. Then he expressed "great pleasure and satisfaction" in a telephone call to Grissom. . . .

The 35-year-old Air Force captain had flown higher (two miles), farther (one mile) and faster (by 180 miles) than Shepard.

His petite wife Betty sat glued to a TV screen at Newport News, Va. . . .

JOURNAL AND COURIER, JULY 21, 1961

Gus's folks happy but worried, too

MITCHELL (UPI)—Virgil (Gus) Grissom's father said Friday he had just spent "the most nervous hour of my life."

Railroader Dennis Grissom emerged beaming from his white frame home after watching the telecast of his astonaut son rocketing into space. . . .

One of the dozen newsmen assembled on the Mitchell lawn asked, "Would you like to see Gus make a trip to the moon?"

"No!" the astronaut's mother replied. . . .

Inside the small, white frame house were the elder Grissoms, their younger son, Norman, an employee of the Mitchell Tribune, and their daughter Mrs. Wilma Beavers. . . .

JOURNAL AND COURIER, JULY 21, 1961

Norman Grissom

He is the brother of Virgil Grissom, and he owns the weekly newspaper in their hometown of Mitchell in southern Indiana. His father

"Now it's your turn"

has just died in late 1994 at the age of ninety-one. His mother, at ninety-three, is still living.

Norman Grissom remembers living in a small home on Main Street in Mitchell when Virgil and he were growing up.

"We grew up during the depression," he says. "We got along okay. I don't think anyone really did well, but we didn't starve.

"Virgil was four years older than I was. He was a good brother, a pretty regular guy. He was into Scouts. We all played ball, fished, and hunted—that kind of thing.

"All the boys wanted to be pilots. This was before World War II. Japan had invaded China, and they showed airplanes on the newsreels. Everyone wanted to fly. Virgil was one of the few who made it.

"He was not outgoing, but he got along very well with people. He was well liked. He was intelligent, which I think is a given for what he went through. And he had his sights set on what he wanted to do with his life. I don't think he had any doubts about wanting to fly. That was back in the time when Buck Rogers was in the the comic books.

"Of course, we were proud of his being an astronaut. But I don't think we realized the impact the space program would have. I didn't realize how it would affect the world.

"There was always a nagging worry about Virgil because we knew that while they were probing space they didn't know precisely what they were doing. But we had a lot of confidence."

Grissom happy with Gemini pilot assignment

MITCHELL (AP)—A quiet man, satisfied and proud of his job, for whom the sky is the limit. . . .

This is the way the family of Maj. Virgil (Gus) Grissom pictures the man who is scheduled to become the United State's first astronaut to make a second venture into space.

319

From college to Korea

The 38-year-old crew-cut flying veteran was named Monday to help guide the 2-man Gemini team effort in space exploration later this year. . . .

The astronaut was born and raised in this small city of 3,500 in southern Indiana's limestone and persimmon country. . . .

His father . . . and mother . . . live in a white frame home on a lazy-looking side street.

When the short, quiet-spoken Gus was still in grade school he was already building dozens of model airplanes and expressing an avid interest in a flying future. . . .

After the war Gus married his high school sweetheart, Betty Moore, and enrolled at Purdue University, working 30 hours a week as a hamburger grill man to finance his schooling. . . .

He . . . (won) the Distinguished Flying Cross in the Korean Conflict.

Gus became a military test pilot in 1956 and was named one of the original seven astronauts in 1959.

JOURNAL AND COURIER, APRIL 14, 1961

Bill Head

A native of Mitchell in southern Indiana, Bill Head worked for the Purdue University Extension Service before retiring in 1981. Retirement took him home to Mitchell where he lives not far from his birthplace in the farm country outside the small town.

He is a happy man, quick to laugh, who likes to talk. He puts off the interview until a televised Purdue basketball game is ended.

Born in 1926, he graduated from Purdue in 1952, but was in the same high school class as Virgil Grissom. When Head married, Grissom served as his best man.

"I grew up out west of Mitchell on a farm," he says. "My dad worked at the Lehigh Portland Cement Company. My mother

"Now it's your turn"

was the farmer. We had a dairy business. My dad had a flock of laying hens that he took care of, but my mother tilled the soil—she was the farmer. Yes, that was unusual in those days. That's why I'm telling you about it.

"I met Virgil in the fall of 1940 when I started at Mitchell High School. We were both freshmen. My wife attended grade school with him. I guess what really tied us together right away was that in physical education class we were the two smallest boys. In those days, you had to take phys ed for one year, but after Pearl Harbor the president said all males in high school must take physical education for four years. So we were always paired off. I suppose we were about five feet, two inches, and he weighed a hundred pounds and I weighed ninety-eight. Or maybe it was the other way around. I don't remember. We were always the same size. I'm about five feet eight now.

VIRGIL "GUS" GRISSOM (Photo from the 1950 Debris)

"Virgil lived in town and I lived out in the country, so most of our activities together were in school. He was interested in flying and so was I. He made model airplanes and I did too. And there was a third connection that solidified our friendship. His future wife, Betty, and I lived near the same road where we caught the school bus. She rode the same bus as I. He started dating her when she was a freshman. He walked out from town to see her.

"He was just like the rest of us in Mitchell. In those years after Pearl Harbor, the streetlights were not on after dark. Gas was rationed, but neither of us had an automobile anyway. There were very few places open. All we did was get up and go to school. Virgil belonged to the Boy Scouts in town, and I always had something to do on the farm when I got home.

"We didn't have electricity or running water on the farm. We pumped the well by hand, milked by hand, and used kerosene lanterns for light. There was a path to the outhouse, and sometimes that was a long path. I didn't know any different. I didn't think conditions were too bad. But I'd hate to go back. I hear people talk about those 'good old days.' They may have been good, but these are better.

"Over the years, many reporters have called Virgil's brother, Norman, and he tells them to call me. They're all looking for the same thing. 'Was he a daredevil?' they ask. I tell them to come and live in Mitchell. If you've been here, you know what I'm talking about. This is small town. There isn't any night life. It's pretty calm, pretty simple. Our parents were worried mainly about how to keep the family going and keep a roof over our heads—the whole family was pretty much involved in that. There just wasn't too much excitement.

"When the war started, we were all red-blooded Americans, and we figured we were all going to go in the service. The air cadet program was appealing. Virgil and I graduated in May of 1944. He had turned eighteen in April, so he went right into the cadet corps. I wasn't eighteen until July. That little span of time made a considerable difference in when you would enter the service.

"I eventually went into the Army Medical Corps. It turned out the Air Corps had more pilots than it knew what to do with at that time, and Virgil ended up a clerk-typist. He married Betty, and when he got out of the military, he came back to Mitchell and worked at the Carpenter School Bus Factory.

"In the summer of 1946, we both went to the Purdue campus and were admitted. Virgil entered Purdue as a freshman in the fall of 1946. I was still in the Army. I didn't start until the fall of 1948.

"When I arrived on campus in '48, Virgil was being called "Gus." I'd never heard that name for him. Later, when we were walking back to where he lived, he said, 'Well, they all call me Gus.' He said a boy in one of his classes thought his name was

"Now it's your turn"

Gus and started calling him that. Then his friends and his wife started calling him Gus, too. It stuck. But I have a hard time calling him Gus to this day. To me his name was Virgil.

"I got home from the military in December of 1947 and farmed through the fall of 1948. One day Virgil hitched from West Lafayette to Mitchell, and he said, 'I know where you can get a room at Purdue, but you will have to go with me tonight.' So we hitched back together and I enrolled. A boy Virgil knew was moving out of a basement and into a fraternity. He left an empty bed, so I took it.

"I majored in ag education. Virgil majored in mechanical engineering.

"In the spring of 1949, I was finishing my freshman year and Virgil was finishing his junior year. One day we were walking together through the Purdue Memorial Union, and there was a big sign that said the Air Force was recruiting pilots. All you had to do was walk up to the table and say you were interested. They sent you upstairs where you took a test. If you passed it, they signed you up for pilot training.

"Virgil's intention was to become a pilot, so he said, 'Come on, let's take the test.' By this time I had had all the college I wanted anyway, so we went up, took the test, and passed.

"You could pick when you wanted your training. I picked August. I can't remember when Virgil picked, but it was after his graduation. Lo and behold, I received a telegram telling me to report for induction the same day I was having finals at the end of my freshman year. I knew if I went to be inducted that day I'd lose credit for the whole semester at Purdue. And what if I didn't make the grade as a pilot? You had to reply if you were accepting or refusing. I called and refused. The man I talked to said, 'Fine, but you'll never have another opportunity for pilot training.' I said, 'Fine with me. I was in the military once and I wasn't too thrilled about it. We'll part friends.'

323

"I didn't become a pilot. But Virgil made it. He made it good—he sure did! He became an F-86 jet fighter pilot. They shipped him around the U.S. and then to Korea where he flew one hundred missions. They were flying eight or ten missions a day. He wanted to fly another one hundred, but the commanding officer said, 'No, my boy, you're young. There'll be other wars. You're going home.'

"Being a jet pilot, he looked at most of Korea from a pretty high altitude. He never said much about it. He saw a lot of enemy planes, but it was the flying he talked about, not the war. He liked flying.

"When we were still in high school, we used to go to the Bedford Airport, and go up one at a time with an instructor who would take us for fifteen-minute rides in a Piper Cub.

"One day I was leaning against the hangar when Virgil was coming in for a landing with the instructor. The runway was on a hill, and there were utility wires at the end of the runway. If you came in long, you had to do something or you would land in those wires. The plane came in and it kept diving. The pilot gunned the plane and yanked it to the left. The wing tip wasn't a half inch off the ground, and it skimmed over an apple tree.

"I looked up and Virgil was waving at me. When he was out of the plane, I told him I would have done something other than wave if I was in his situation. But he said what could he do? That's the way he was. What will be will be.

"I was married in 1949. After I graduated from Purdue, we lived in Shelbyville, Indiana. One weekend we went to Mitchell. I was driving to the family farm, and I saw Virgil opening a gate at his wife's grandfather's house. I stopped to talk with him and told him that one day I was going to come to Wright-Patterson in Ohio, where he was stationed, to see him. He said, 'I might not be there long. I might be leaving soon.' I said, just joking around, 'What

"Now it's your turn"

are you going to do—go to the moon?' He said, 'Pretty close.' It wasn't long before he went to Edwards Air Force Base in California and became involved in the space program.

"When our family heard NASA was going to introduce the first astronauts on TV, we all said we were certain we would know one of them. And, sure enough, there was Virgil.

"Virgil was sent to Virginia and our family went to see him. We saw the capsules and the space suits, and we met Alan Shepard and Deke Slayton.

"Once when he was home on leave, he heard my daughter say she didn't have an uncle. He told her he'd be her uncle and she should call him Uncle Gus.

"We all followed the space program quite closely. When you knew someone in it, you paid close attention. I remember one day I said to him, 'Why don't you come back to Mitchell, and you and I will whittle and spit and live to be old men.' But he said this space project was something new.

"He was always interested in engineering, both as a pilot and an astronaut. It wasn't the thrill of being an astronaut that kept him going. It was the engineering.

"When we were growing up, we were told we couldn't get into space, there was no way of getting there. When he got into the space program, it was an engineering program for him. It was a new frontier. He was a graduate engineer and here was a chance to ply his trade. That's the way he approached it.

"I remember one day Virgil showed me a training capsule for the *Mercury* program. He said, 'See that gauge down there? Do you know what that does? When I'm in space, that gauge tells me if I'm perspiring. Do you know why the Russians beat us? Weight. Weight is a critical thing. We don't have a big enough rocket to load extra weight on the capsule. If I'm in space and that gauge says I'm perspiring, what are the people on the ground going to

325

From college to Korea

do? Come up and fan me? I know when I'm perspiring. We could reduce some weight if we took that gauge out.'

"He said it was easy to get things put on those capsules but hard to get them taken off. He talked pretty straight, and I think sometimes that didn't sit too well with people. He was a regular guy. He wasn't a bragger. He didn't waste words. I think that's why he was not involved more in public relations. When he was on a mission, he never liked to talk to the people on the ground. He said when he was in space he had better things to do than to chitchat with the people on the ground.

"People keep asking me to tell stories about what he was like. They want him to be 'Peck's Bad Boy,' and he wasn't. They want him to have been a daredevil, and he wasn't. He was just a boy from Mitchell, but that didn't make very good headlines. Reporters would ask me what he did after school. He worked in a filling station. They said, 'What else did he do.' There wasn't anything else to do.

"Once he got caught driving too fast in Florida. Reporters called me and asked about it. I said, 'In Mitchell, the only auto he ever owned was a 1937 Chevy with mud grips on the front. If that's all you'd driven and you got a chance to drive a Stingray, I suspect you'd try it out too.' I suppose most of those reporters didn't even know what a 1937 Chevy looked like.

"That *Mercury* capsule he was in sank in the ocean. He told me it was getting hot in there. He was lying on his back, and the next thing he knew the ocean was pouring in on top of him. The thought went through his mind, I made it back from space and now I'm going to drown.

"He got out of the *Mercury* capsule, but he didn't get one of the vents on his suit completely closed and the suit filled with water, so he was struggling to stay above the water. The pilot flying the helicopter came overhead, and the downdraft almost forced

326

"Now it's your turn"

Virgil under the water. He waved at the pilot to move the helicopter aside. The helicopter crew just waved back at him.

"We always realized what he did was dangerous. One time I talked to him about flying a jet, and I said, 'Don't you ever worry about crashing?' He said, 'No. What I worry about is the cooling system going out, because at the speed at which I'm flying if the cooling system goes out, I'll fry.' Having talked with him all those years about the dangers involved in what he did, I know he realized the risks.

"One day when I came in the house, the voice on the TV stated there had been an accident at the Cape. I knew Virgil was down there. It wasn't long before they announced what happened.

"He would have made the first trip to the moon. Of course, no one from NASA has ever said. But *I* think he was the one who was going to be the first to go to the moon."

Two Purdue alumni in Apollo

The National Aeronautics and Space Administration late Monday announced the names of two veteran astronauts and a spaceflight rookie to fly the nation's first three-man mission—and two of the three are Purdue University graduates.

The Space Center at Houston, Texas, said the three would constitute the crew for the maiden manned voyage of the Apollo spaceship which is being designed for the moontrip program.

Veteran astronaut Virgil (Gus) Grissom . . . and Roger B. Chaffee, a 1957 aeronautical engineering graduate, are the two from Purdue.

Edward White, first U.S. astronaut to take a walk in space, is the third. . . .

JOURNAL AND COURIER, MARCH 22, 1966

From college to Korea

GREAT MEN, GREAT DREAMS. *In January of 1967, (left to right) Virgil "Gus" Grissom, Edward White II, and Roger Chaffee pose for a photo during training for the first manned* Apollo *space flight. On January 27, 1967, during testing at the launch pad at Cape Kennedy, Florida, their command module caught fire. All three died. Grissom and Chaffee were Purdue graduates, Grissom in the Class of 1950. During the* Apollo 11 *flight in 1969, Neil Armstrong, another Purdue graduate, realized their dream by walking on the moon. (Photo courtesy of NASA)*

Apollo tragedy shocks Hoosiers
Purdue mourns loss of 'own' spaceman

Virgil (Gus) Grissom, the daring little Hoosier whose space exploits captured the hearts of a nation, was dead Saturday and all of Indiana as well as the nation was plunged into a state of deep mourning.

The tragic fire that snuffed out Grissom's life along with that of Roger Chaffee hit hard at the Purdue University community.

The deaths cut in half the number of Purdue graduates who were members of the America's space team,

"Now it's your turn"

a point of deep pride with the university and its graduates. . . . No other American college or university had
as many as four men in the space program. . . .

Left to carry the university's banner in the space
program are Neil A. Armstrong and Eugene Cernan.

Lt. Col. Grissom and Navy Lt. Chaffee and Lt. Col.
Edward White died instantly when a mysterious fire
swept the interior of their Saturn Apollo Mooncraft
during stationary testing.

Grissom, the old veteran of the space program . . .
and his wife had two sons, Scott, 17, and Mark, 12. . . .

The astronauts were in their space suits in a pure
oxygen environment when the blaze flared up. . . .

Gordon Harris, chief of public affairs for NASA's
Kennedy Space Center, said the men probably died
without any knowledge that there was serious trouble
aboard. . . .

"If we die," Grissom once said, "we want people to
accept it. We are in a risky business and we hope that
if anything happens to us it will not delay the program.
The conquest of space is worth the risk of life. . . ."

JOURNAL AND COURIER, JANUARY 8, 1967

Bill Keefe

You can no longer see the streak of white that once ran through
Bill Keefe's hair. It is all white now. His hair may have changed,
but his memories have not. They are as clear as ever.

He lives in Glen Elyn, near Chicago, and works as a
manufacturer's representative. Born in an area south in Chicago
called Beverly Hills, he went directly from high school to college—
no depression, no war experience.

"I didn't know there was a depression," he says with a laugh.
"My dad was with the Pullman Company for a long time. He had

a degree in engineering from Notre Dame and played football for Knute Rockne. My mother was a graduate of Saint Mary-of-the-Woods in Terre Haute.

"I went to Saint Ignatius High School. I was too young to enter the Army for World War II. I didn't really want to get away from the war, but I didn't want to get into it, either.

"One of the things I had tried to do in high school was enter the Navy programs for electronics. I took some special programs at Morgan Park High School so that if I were drafted I could go into the Navy, rather than walk through the mud with the Army.

"As it turned out, the military gave me an eye test for colors. When they were finished, the doctor said I was perfect red and green color-blind. He'd never seen anyone like that before. That kept me out of electronics.

"I graduated from high school in 1946 and wanted to be an engineer. Before graduation, my father had taken me to various schools, including Notre Dame and Illinois. He said he thought Purdue was the best he had seen. I had an uncle who graduated from Purdue in 1922. So I went there.

"In my freshman year, I joined Phi Kappa Psi fraternity and moved in because I didn't like the house where I had been living. There was hazing in the fraternity. Mostly it involved making a fool of yourself every Monday after a meeting. They made you sing the fraternity songs and answer silly questions. That was about the extent of it until hell week, when they got you up and yelled at you. But you could take it for a week.

"There were only four people in my pledge class because of the space problem in the fraternity. All these people from years earlier had come back, and they only had room for four pledges. Two of us were high school graduates and two were Naval fliers. One other pledge had quit earlier. He said he'd been in Iwo Jima with the Marines and didn't need that stuff.

330

"Now it's your turn"

"During the week, most of our time was spent in the dining room of the fraternity doing homework, supervised by brothers who helped us if we were having a problem.

"In my junior year, I was in charge of the junior prom, and I was chosen 'king.' One of my responsibilities for the prom was to choose a band. So the committee went to Chicago and listened to musicians. I always said the last band I'd choose would be Sammy Kaye. But when it came time to choose, he was the only one left. He turned out to be excellent. He played a variety of good music.

"I was involved with the Student Union Board, and we planned all kinds of activities, including dances every Saturday night. We used a lot of local musical groups. Some of them were very good. One really good band was from the ATO house. Dancing was a big thing in those days. People would come in groups or they would come with dates. With a five or six to one woman to man ratio, a lot of us had to come in groups and just look around.

"I majored in mechanical engineering. A big problem was that so many people were trying to get into the same courses that occasionally you missed a course and had to take it some other time. Things were good, but crowded.

"I graduated in mid-June of 1950 and went to work for Johnson Controls—air-conditioning, heating, and ventilation controls. That lasted until the twenty-eighth of June at which time I received a letter from the government saying they would like to give me a chance for an all-expense-paid tour of the Far East.

"My group was assembled in Chicago and sent to Fort Knox where they kept us for two months. We were graduate engineers, and they didn't know what to do with us. So we hung around for a month doing very little—just walking around, carrying a rifle, that sort of thing.

"Next, they shipped us off to the Pentagon—Fort Myers— and we were kept there in storage until after Christmas. We lived

331

in barracks, and they would line us up every morning to make sure everyone was there—then we took the rest of the day off. This lasted for a long time. One of the people I met there was Bill Creson, who was from my class at Purdue.

"After awhile, they sent some of us to Fort Belvoir, Virginia, and we spent time teaching various subjects to lieutenants. We worked as soldiers five days a week, eight hours a day, and for the rest of the time, we were on our own. We drove to Washington, which was only fifteen or twenty miles away.

"That ended. I was allowed to go home for Thanksgiving for two weeks in 1951. After the holiday, they put me on a train for San Francisco, then on a troop ship. I finally got that all-expense-paid tour that I had been promised.

"I ended up with the Second Engineering Battalion in Korea. We were back in the safe areas where we taught. I had a nine-month tour there and spent it in the back with the majors, instead of up front with the lieutenants.

"In the back areas, sometimes we slept in bunkers because they were warm. Winter got very cold in Korea. I remember one night someone kicked my bed and woke me up. The other guys said they had been outside. Someone had been strafing the field, and they had gone out to see what was going on. It had turned out to be an American pilot off course.

"That was my only combat experience. And I slept through it."

Richard Freeman

Richard Freeman grew up in West Lafayette where his father was a professor at Purdue University and later associate dean of agriculture and director of resident instruction.

Freeman has a gentle speaking voice. During a recent visit to West Lafayette from his California home, he drove past all the old places he knew and loved, and he recalled their importance in his life.

"Now it's your turn"

"I was born in 1928. Growing up in West Lafayette was absolutely marvelous," he says.

"Driving around today, I pointed out to my wife that a church now stands where the old high school used to be. When you grew up in West Lafayette in the 1930s, you knew all the streets and all the people who lived there. Walking through Grandview Cemetery today, I saw the names of many people I had known. The university at that time was quite small—maybe three or four thousand students.

"I don't remember much about the depression. As children, we didn't know what the depression was, but I do remember people talking about it. Looking back on it, we were lucky. We didn't have to chase rabbits down with a car in order to eat. We didn't eat all that well, but we weren't hungry.

"During the war, I remember the food rationing. We'd have paper drives and scrap iron drives. I'm sure they didn't help the war effort much, but they were good for morale.

"Our high school was quite small and we knew everyone, so every time someone went into the service, we knew about it. We saw a lot of seniors go off to World War II, and I remember feeling very jealous when they came back in their swell uniforms. They always looked so sharp. Everyone would point them out. I thought, Why can't I do that?

"We all looked forward to joining the service. We thought that was the right thing to do. The feeling then was so much different from what it is today. The armed service at that time was a high calling—an aspiration for all of us.

"I graduated from high school in 1946. I wanted to be an architect, and I thought my life would be ruined if I didn't go to the University of Wisconsin. But all my friends were going to Purdue, and it made sense for me to go to Purdue—dollarwise. Even though college fees weren't that high at the time, salaries weren't high either.

333

From college to Korea

"I was fortunate. I got in at the tail end of the Navy V-12 program. This was essentially an officers' candidate program. I remember registering for classes at the field house and being sworn into the Navy on the same day. It was a wonderful deal. The Navy paid for all my fees, tuition, and my books—and I got fifty dollars a month.

"I liked being around all the older guys at Purdue. It was interesting to get to know them and learn what was going on in the world. A lot of those guys had war stories to tell, and I thought it was great to find out about their experiences.

"It bugged me that the veterans were so dedicated to getting an education. Their dedication came from seeing what happens if you aren't educated. Most of the vets were very good students. The younger students called them 'curve-raisers.' They got good grades and raised the curves. A lot of the older guys were married, and they went home at night and studied. If we younger guys didn't work extra hard, we found ourselves at the tail end of the curve.

"We had a lot of fun, too. We would go to the 'C Shop'— that's what we called Harry's Chocolate Shop, which of course was a bar and still is. The Kappa Sig house was a block from Harry's, and we finally pledged Harry's son to make sure we always had a good seat in the bar.

"There was a great song we sang. It went, 'Oh, Purdue, oh, Purdue, how you make me shiver / With your old C Shop and the Wabash River / Oh, I love you with my heart and I love you with my liver / Oh, Purdue, by the river.'

"I was pinned to a Pi Phi, and I started a group called 'Iota Chi Rho' made up of guys pinned to Pi Phi's. We were from all different fraternities, and we'd get together and have 'bridge parties,' which amounted to nothing more than getting a keg of beer and going under a bridge. I remember going under a bridge over the Wildcat Creek, building a fire, roasting chicken, and drinking beer.

"Now it's your turn"

"On dates, we occasionally went to a drive-in movie. At that time, there were also five regular movie theaters in Lafayette, and you could take the bus over the Wabash to downtown Lafayette. The movie houses were the Lafayette, the Mars, the Luna, and the New Main. On Fifth Street, there was a dark, dank place everyone called 'The Arc' and said it was full of rats. We stayed away from that place.

"I met the girl who would become my wife in 1946, not long after we arrived on campus. She was from Lakewood, Ohio, near Cleveland. Her name was Jane Barkman. We were Dick and Jane. I was introduced to her by a friend of a friend.

A GOLDEN AGE OF MOVIES. After the war, Hollywood cranked out upbeat movies to fit the upbeat times. A movie date meant a walk or a bus ride from campus to Lafayette, where all the theaters were located.

"I remember one night I was driving my dad's car, a brand new blue 1946 Packard. What a gorgeous machine it was. I was driving it on the sidewalk in front of Cary Hall East. I don't know why. I just felt like it. The sidewalk was wide, and I wasn't going fast. Well, Jane saw me, and she asked the person she was with who that nut driving on the sidewalk was. Her friend said it was Dick Freeman. She said, 'Oh, my gosh, I've got a date coming up with him.'

"I didn't drive on the sidewalk a lot.

"On our first date, we went to the Hall of Music and sat in the first row. We saw Spike Jones and the City Slickers. Boy, could he put on a show!

"I graduated and was commissioned a second lieutenant, United States Marine Corps, in the summer of 1950. Jane and I were married the next day, August 21. I was due to report to the

335

From college to Korea

Quantico Marine School, near Washington, D.C., on the twenty-second. We drove there, so it was a short honeymoon.

"There was no place on the base for a brand new second lieutenant to live, so we set up housekeeping in an attic in Fredricksburg, Virginia. We still communicate with the family that owned that home.

"The Korean War had started. From Quantico, I went to Camp Pendleton in Oceanside, California. 'Tan your hide in Oceanside' the sign read as you drove to the base.

"From there, I went to Korea. I was in Korea from the end of 1951 through all of 1952, and I got home at the start of 1953. I ended up a battery commander of a ninety millimeter gun battalion. For a short time, I was a forward observer for the artillery, and I saw some action. We were north of Seoul.

"I remember when I came home and people saw me in my uniform, they would ask where I'd been. I'd say, 'Korea.' They'd say, 'What were you doing in Korea?' There was a great deal of apathy toward that war.

"War is bad. I can't see anything about it that makes sense. You never know what's going on. You mostly remember the fun things and don't think about the horrible things. Many people were killed in Korea. It was a very harsh country. The temperature got very cold—down to thirty degrees below zero. War is basically stupid.

"As a Marine, I thought I was just doing my job and I felt we were doing the right thing in Korea. Even now I believe we did the right thing. I don't know if Korea was a good place to draw the line, but at the time, someone thought it was. When the Chinese intervened, we were lucky to hold them at the thirty-eighth parallel.

"It was good to get home. I hadn't seen my wife the whole year that I was in Korea. I was able to call her only once from Japan. While I was gone, our first child, our daughter Debra, was born. I didn't see

336

her until she was six months old. The first thing she did when she saw me was cry. We eventually had four children.

"When I returned from Korea and left the Marines, I went back to Purdue to work on a master's in labor economics on the GI Bill. I graduated in 1954. My undergraduate degree was in aeronautical engineering.

"I went to work for a division of General Motors in Warren, Ohio, where I stayed five years. Then, I took a job with a little company called Ramo Wooldridge, started by Simon Ramo and Dean Wooldridge. They later became the *R* and the *W* of TRW.

"TRW was just beginning as a company, and the United States was just getting started with ballistic missiles. No one in the military understood the electronics and space mechanics of launching a missile from one place and getting it to another, so we became the company that helped do that. It was extremely interesting. We worked hard and played hard. I became production manager.

"After three years with TRW, I worked one year at Curtiss-Wright in Albuquerque, New Mexico. We supported a company called Sandia, which built all the nuclear warheads.

"Next, I went to Hughes Aircraft in Culver City, California, where I stayed for six years. It was an outstanding place to work. I conceptualized two missiles while I was there, one of which is still in use. It's called the Maverick, the AGM-65. The other was the Spirit, the AGM-76. It was an anti-radar missile that rode the beam of enemy radar and followed it right to the source. Hughes kept improving on those missiles and eventually built thousands.

"After that, I went to LTV in Dallas, where I became a vice president. Then, I went to North American Rockwell in Los Angeles. Today it's called Rockwell International. I became a vice president there as well.

"After two years, I'd had enough and went out on my own as a consultant, which I'm still doing. For example, I'm working now

337

with an inventor who has a new design for hard disc drives for computers.

"The technology I've seen in my lifetime is incredible. I just kind of wallow in it. I really love it. I can't take my hands off the technology. I can't let go until I find a way to put something to use.

"I've seen incredible change. When I was with General Motors, I worked with the first IBM computer. It had vacuum tubes. I go back even further than that. I started with mechanical computers, the first analogues used for fire control solutions.

"Back then so much about technology was unknown to us. I look at developments today, like the computer games sold on every street corner, and I remember the difficulty we had in the transition from vacuum tubes to transistors and from transistors to chips. Today people talk readily about chips—people who don't really know what a chip is and how it works. Watching all this happen has been wonderful.

"I couldn't have lived in a better or more fun time."

"Now it's your turn"

chapter 14

" They could do anything " they wanted to

College, careers, children, and careers

> Wabash College and DePauw University are trading
> foreign students for three days this weekend. The trade
> is part of the festivities arranged for the traditional
> Wabash-DePauw football game.
>
> Purdue eds have been trying to trade off the coeds
> here for a couple of years, but so far still no takers.
>
> Purdue Exponent, November 12, 1949

Eleanor Scheidler McNamara

Her picture appears six different times in the 1950 Purdue University yearbook. The biography beside her senior class picture looks like a listing of all the extracurricular activities available to women.

Eleanor Scheidler McNamara came to Purdue in 1946, barely seventeen years old, from Hartford City, Indiana. She never slowed down.

"Hartford City had a population of about seven thousand when I lived there," she says. "And it has pretty much stayed that way.

"My father owned the ice plant. He was always successful. He worked very hard. He had left school after the eighth grade, and he left home at fifteen. There were ten children in his family—two girls and eight boys, two were priests. His father, a blacksmith and the son of a German immigrant, gave a five-thousand-dollar loan

339

to the oldest of the other six sons. As that son repaid the loan, the next son in line took the loan and started his business, and so on.

"There were six in my family. I had two sisters, and the second oldest went to Purdue. As far as my parents were concerned, whatever I wanted to do was fine. I think my dad would have loved it if we all just came home and stayed there. However, I never considered not going to college. There were ninety-five students in my high school and only eleven went on to college.

"I wanted to go to Rosary College in Illinois. But I had taken only one year of Latin. At that time, it was hard to get into college, and I would have had to take another year of Latin to get into Rosary. I didn't want to do that. Happily Purdue accepted me. My second oldest sister was already studying there.

"I was just seventeen when I arrived on campus—pretty young. I lived in Cary Hall my freshman year, and we had very small rooms. I was very homesick. A lot of people were.

"I didn't think much about the fact that so many of the guys on campus were older. I started dating men who were twenty-four and twenty-five years old, and that was kind of strange. Before that, I'd been going out with young high school kids. It was a big change from a little town to a big campus.

"I had been in a lot of activities in high school. I thought that was the way to meet people. I think I would do it differently today. Back then, activities were the main thing for me. I didn't know what I wanted to do.

"I was very involved with the yearbook. In my senior year, I wanted very much for this one girl to be named editor for the next year. She didn't make it. Maybe it was because they didn't want a girl being editor, I don't know. But I never felt left out of things because I was a female.

"I majored in home ec. We had a program in which you lived in a house and took care of it for six weeks. I had dreaded having

"They could do anything they wanted to"

to do that because my sister hated it. But a WAC (Women's Army Corps), who was sort of our adviser, lived there with us. She was wonderful. We had so much fun. One night, someone made hot rolls for the next day. They smelled so good that we all sat down and ate them right away, which was unheard of.

"I was in Chi Omega sorority. I remember eating those huge ice cream cones from Smith Hall. Living in Cary Hall when all the other wings of the dorm were for guys and having fire drills in the middle of the night were also interesting experiences!

"I remember Mortar Board, which was an honorary for women. During my senior year, I was in charge of 'tapping' girls into it. You would surprise them and present them with a Mortar Board hat. I had a car on campus to do this. In those days having a car was very rare, and this was my one week a year to have the family car. I had all the Mortar Boards locked in the car, then I went shopping and lost the keys. I had a frantic time getting into that car in time for the 'tapping.'

"Christmas was the best time on campus. There were lots of teas and music. The sororities went caroling to hospitals or in the neighborhood. The fraternities came over to our sorority house and serenaded. It was a special time.

"I met my husband, Bob, at Purdue. We both were active in the Newman Club. Mass

ELEANOR SCHEIDLER. (Photo from 1950 Debris)

was held in an old house before Saint Thomas Aquinas Catholic Church was built. Five of us, including my future husband, formed a choir called the 'Hoot Owls.' We sang at mass twice a week.

"Bob and I were good friends, but we weren't serious. After graduation, he went off to the Army. I went to Europe for the summer, and that's when I decided what kind of a job I wanted. I

341

wanted to do something where I could be off in the summer so I could go back to Europe. I decided to become a teacher. I earned my teacher's license from Ball State in a year and a half and taught English and journalism at Mishawaka High School.

"When my future husband got back from the Army, we hadn't written much. He stopped by Hartford City to see my mother to find out what had happened to me. She told him what I was doing, and he wrote.

"I taught just one year, and then we got married. I really regret that I stopped teaching. I liked it and I had gone to school for an extra year and a half to do it.

"We moved to Indianapolis where my husband had flower shops. I helped in them, as did all of our seven children. They really kept me busy at home, however.

"I did a lot of volunteer work—and still do. I guess I've spent most of my life volunteering in many different organizations.

"I know women today keep right on working after they have children. That would have been extremely difficult for me. I would've had to give up something. However, I say more power to young women today.

"But I really liked being home with my kids."

Katie Dittrich McMillin

It is all in a yearbook Katie McMillin still keeps—dance cards, photographs, letters, pressed flowers. It was a wonderful time to be alive in the years just after the war, she says. It was a wonderful time to be young and in college and looking to the future.

She works in Lafayette on a project to relocate railroads that intersect the town, placing them in a corridor that allows traffic to flow without being stopped by trains. She sits in an old railroad depot that serves as the project office. In the background, trains rumble nearby on a cold, winter afternoon.

"They could do anything they wanted to"

Inside the depot, her dark hair combed very similarly to the style she wore in 1950, McMillin points to items in her scrapbook and explains them. The memories are preserved in her thoughts as carefully as the mementos pressed in her book.

Raised in Highland, Indiana, she was the only girl in her high school class who went to college.

"I wanted to go," she says. "My mother and father had both been to Purdue, and I had an uncle who graduated from Purdue. All my mother's family had been to college.

"I was the oldest of five children. I had two younger brothers and two younger sisters. My father told me he would send me to school for one year and after that he needed to save money to send my brothers, so I would have to leave. I understood that. Today, young women wouldn't stand for that, but that's the way it was when I was growing up.

"Fortunately, at Christmas time of my freshman year, my father got a promotion, and he told me I could finish. Things have a way of working out.

"My father was superintendent of Plant 2 Mills, Inland Steel, in East Chicago. Personally, I never did without, even during the depression. I always had food and shoes. My father was a good provider and we didn't talk about money.

"We did without during the war. We didn't go to restaurants. We didn't do a lot of things. We had gas because my father was involved with the war effort at the steel plant. We had a victory garden and grew food. And we had an Olson rug. There wasn't any wool available during the war, but you could turn in your old wool coats and blankets to Olson, and they would make a wool rug for your floor. It curled on the edges.

"My father didn't want me to work while I was in high school. He said when I got married I'd have plenty of work to do. But I did get a job at a department store in Hammond. I thought it was

343

wonderful. I spent all my earnings on clothes and had a good time. We all rode buses. We didn't have cars.

"I graduated from high school in 1946 and went to Purdue. I was a real 'green bean.' I had grown up very protected. I was terribly naïve and I didn't even know it. I don't think I'd say I was prudish, but I was certainly a 'straight arrow.' I was kind of a social misfit in high school because I was a girl who was planning to go to college. I didn't date very much and I had only a few friends.

"But when I got to Purdue, I found out I was popular and interesting. It was really fun! And there were lots of men.

"Before classes started, I went to sign up to be in the choir. While I was standing in line, one of the guys in the Glee Club came over and talked to me. He came back later, asked for my phone number, and asked if he could call me. He did, and he invited me to go to a picnic, a hayride.

The Whoopurdoo   **By Sandy**

"She finally took his pin." (From a 1946 Purdue Exponent)

"The freshman women had been to a convocation at Elliott Hall. The woman who was president of the Association of Women Students spoke to us. I was so impressed with her. She spoke to us about what to expect in college and what a great place Purdue was. I thought, What must it take to be a leader like that?

"When I got to the hayride, who was drinking beer—and right out of the bottle—but that same girl. I thought it was shocking. Like I said, I was a 'green bean.'

"I pledged Kappa Alpha Theta and moved into the house my sophomore year. Moral standards in our sorority were very high. We had a formal dinner every night,

"They could do anything they wanted to"

and we didn't sit down until the housemother sat. We had waiters from the fraternities.

"It was a time when there was a lot of serenading. Men's groups came and serenaded us—and I thought it was the neatest thing. Our house was between the Sigma Chi and Beta fraternity houses, and we were the only sorority over there. We liked that.

"When I was applying to Purdue, I had received a letter that said I was eligible for the new School of Liberal Science. The school admitted forty women. There were also a couple of men. This was a pilot program for the School of Liberal Arts at Purdue today. We had theory of mathematics and theory of chemistry.

"It was all an eye-opener for me. I was a good student in high school. I was third in a class of something like a hundred and twenty. But when I got to Purdue in this program of forty students, I was in the middle. They were all so smart.

"Dances were held every weekend at the Memorial Union building—mixers we called them. There were Varsity Variety and Victory Variety shows. When you came to school, you paid for convocation tickets, which was a wonderful way to experience different kinds of culture. You'd already paid for it, so you went to see Shakespeare and Burl Ives and Bob Hope.

"It was a happy time but serious in the classroom. With all the mature students on campus, there wasn't so much goofy stuff.

"When you look at the yearbook from 1950, you can see that the attention was put on the men. But I didn't mind that. I've told you what role my father thought women played. I admired my mother, who took care of the children and saw that we did everything. She and my father went to dances. They had a happy life. I could see myself getting my 'Mrs.' degree.

"I realized, however, when I was a junior that I'd better be able to do something when I graduated. I chose to be a teacher and got my certificate.

College, careers, children, and careers

"But I did do everything my father told me to do. I think the last virgins to march down the aisle were in my generation.

"When I graduated from Purdue, I got a good job with the Speedway School Corporation in Indianapolis. I taught junior high English and received the amazing salary of twenty-nine hundred dollars for nine months. That was wonderful. I lived in a rooming house so I could save money and buy clothes at Peck and Peck on the Circle in Indianapolis.

"The first television I saw was at the Theta house. It was just snow on the screen. I didn't think too much of it. The first time I was really impressed by television was that fall after I graduated, when I was working in Speedway. On the day of the Purdue-Notre Dame football game, I went by a furniture store and saw the game on a TV. Oh, it was wonderful! I couldn't believe it.

"Those college years were joyful years. There was a great deal of relief that the war was over. There weren't so many worries. We heard early on that we were going to have problems with the Russians, but we weren't worried about it. I didn't know what was going on. You know, when you're going to college, you don't read the newspapers.

"As I look back on it now, I see that I grew up as a girl during the depression, followed by a war, followed by a wonderful time in college—followed by another war.

"I think that set the tone for me for the rest of my life."

Patricia Bagley Ross

Patricia Ross got her degree in electrical engineering from Purdue University in 1950. She started using it in 1975.

Like all young people, she had plans upon completion of her studies. She was married, and she planned to spend some time working in her career.

"They could do anything they wanted to"

"But I found out I was pregnant," she says. "That kind of stopped that. We eventually had four children, and with all that, I didn't have much chance to work. In those days, women didn't work much outside their home when they had children.

"I raised children for twenty years and didn't have time for my engineering. So ever since I've gotten back into it, I've been like a kid in a candy store. I love it.

"I grew up in a Chicago suburb, Park Ridge. I graduated high school in 1946, and I applied to Purdue to study engineering. But the war had just ended and all the veterans were coming back. The university wasn't taking women in engineering unless they had pull, which I did not have.

"So I went to the University of Illinois at Navy Pier in Chicago. I was there for a year and a half. While there, I met another woman engineer who also was turned down when she applied to Purdue. However, her father was able to get us both in. We had very good grades. We both started at Purdue in the middle of our sophomore year. We're still friends.

"It was February of 1948 when we started at Purdue. We lived mostly in barracks built for men stationed on campus during the war—Bunker Hill, it was called. The only time I lived in a residence hall was my first semester and one semester when I went to summer school. The rest of the time I was in the barracks. I guess I was too independent to join a sorority.

"While I was at Purdue, I don't think there were twenty-five women in all the engineering branches at all levels—only twenty-five among all the thousands of men. We were in all different levels and different areas. There was never another woman in any of the engineering classes I was in. I was always the only woman. And I'm sure the other women were the only ones in their classes, too.

"We were treated beautifully. Everyone thought we might be discriminated against, but we weren't. There was absolutely

347

no discrimination against women in engineering. I was very grateful. Actually, the only time I came across discrimination at Purdue was in a psychology class, and it was because of my religion. That surprised me.

"I'm a Christian Scientist. The professor said some things, but it only lasted a few minutes because a young man in the class spoke up and said he admired Christian Scientists because they don't have to wait to get into heaven. They're there now. I don't remember that professor. I don't remember that class. But I still remember that boy.

"In college in West Lafayette, I felt secluded from the world. We didn't have television. Unless we listened to the radio or read the newspapers, we were secluded. Really, it was all I could do to keep up with my studies. I had roommates who were studying home ec, and they had all kinds of spare time. I never did.

"I met my husband at Purdue in the fall when I was a junior and he was a senior. We got married a month after I graduated, and we moved to Cincinnati where my husband had a job with the Trane Company. He was a mechanical engineer.

"My husband was in the Navy during World War II for a year and a half, mostly going to school in this country. After his service, he went to Purdue on the GI Bill. He always felt bad that he had taken so much from the government, so he stayed in the reserves for years. He felt he owed it to his country.

"With four children to raise, I was very busy. And I did a lot of volunteer work. I had expected to work after college, but with the family, it was not possible. There wasn't any financial reason for me to work, but I always wanted to.

"In 1968, we moved to Bethesda, Maryland, and my husband started his own company. He designed and manufactured special purpose air-conditioning equipment. I started out volunteering to help my husband. I was office manager. My youngest

"They could do anything they wanted to"

child was in the fifth grade. I worked there a little over six years, and then during a recession, the business went under.

"That was in 1975. A month later I was hired by Comsat—Communication Satellite Corporation. When I started working for Comsat, I was in charge of the technical library. However, when they found out what I could do, they sent me to school to get my master's degree. I had to drop out to care for my husband for several years before he passed on.

"It was hard to pick it all up again. The hardest thing was relearning my calculus. When I graduated from Purdue, I was using a slide rule. When I started working in engineering, they were using computers and calculators.

"With Comsat, I began my first engineering job. I worked in their lab in the Washington, D.C., area doing research and development. It was great.

"From there, I went to Arbitron, which did television ratings. I developed equipment for monitoring television and commercials, but they stopped doing that and laid us off.

"Next I went to work for Information Systems and Networks. That's where I am now. I'm working on a Federal Aviation Administration contract to modernize the air traffic control system.

"I really never considered myself a trailblazer at Purdue or in later years. I just loved being an engineer. I think of it as being a problem-solver.

"My father had stopped his schooling in the eighth grade because his father had died and he had to help support his mother and sister. But he went to night school for years and studied electricity. He decided electricity would be too dirty a field for me, but it's what I liked.

"It turns out that my sister, who is four years older than I am, was going to Northwestern University during the war, and there was a program for Curtiss-Wright. The company promised

349

to pay students' way if they would go to school eight hours a day, seven days a week, and then go to work at the factory. My sister took the offer. She became an aeronautical engineer.

"Life has been wonderful. I just wish my husband were here to enjoy this with me. He died in 1986.

"I think it's great the opportunities women have today. If a woman really wants to do something, I don't see any reason why she shouldn't. I would have been very happy to work right away, but I had a family. Now, I have two daughters-in-law who have worked. Women are capable. There's no reason why women can't do what they're comfortable doing. I don't think it's a threat to anyone.

"I hope that I helped pave the way for other women, but I don't know if I did. I guess I'd like to think that I did. But I've never thought of myself as a 'women's libber,' and I've never felt hemmed in by being a woman. I never had any bonds on me. Here I am, sixty-six years old and still working, and they're still happy with my work.

"I am very pleased."

Barbara Sutton Thoennes

Barbara Thoennes was born in Muncie, Indiana, in 1928, the daughter of a salesman for Ball Brothers. She graduated from high school in 1946 and headed for Purdue because she wanted to major in home economics.

"Purdue offered the best," she says. "I wanted to go into dietetics at the time. My parents were very supportive. They thought a college education was a necessity. I was the first person in my family to go to college.

"I first lived on campus in Cary Hall East. Conditions were very crowded. Three people were assigned to dorm rooms where there should have been only one. There were classes of three

350

hundred and four hundred people. Having come from a large high school, I was ready for this, but there were so many older returning GIs. At first, this was a little frightening. But after awhile, I got used to them.

"I worked on the student staff in the women's residence halls while I went to school for the grand sum of thirty-five cents an hour. It provided me with some spending money and helped to buy some books.

"My last year I lived in a Quonset hut. That was a lot of fun. The university was going to tear down the huts very soon, so we could put things on the walls. Ten of us lived in that room, five bunk beds. I don't remember its being cold in the winter in the Quonset huts. Of course, we were younger then.

"We could do a variety of things around campus that didn't cost much money. We went to the movies, and we had exchange dinners with other living units. Around the holidays, there were formal dances. We didn't spend a lot of money because we didn't have a lot of money.

"Back then, women could not wear jeans or slacks on campus. We could wear them in the dorms but not to class. We wore skirts—sometimes cord skirts—and sweaters and blouses.

"I went into teaching my junior year. My father said teaching offered security, and he was paying the bills. I graduated in June of 1950 and taught school in Michigan.

"In the summer of 1951, I came back to Purdue and started graduate work in guidance. That's when I met my husband. He was a returning GI. We got married in May of 1952.

"My husband was on the faculty of Jefferson High School in Lafayette, and I taught primary school for a few years. Then, I took time off to have our children.

"I was one of those who wanted to stay home with their children. I did go back and teach when my children were past the

351

toddler stage. I did substitute teaching, so I was home at lunch-time and when they came home from school.

"If I wanted to work, I worked. If I didn't, I didn't."

Only women may try to de-skirt senior women

"No men allowed" may well be the motto concerning rules to be followed in regard to senior women's cord skirts. Although rules in general are the same as those pertaining to men's cords, there is one essential differ-ence. Any hiding, decorating and removing of cord skirts must be done by freshmen women—no men al-lowed. . . .

Rules for cord skirts:

1. Open season on senior cord skirts worn in resi-dence units begins at noon today and ends at 6 p.m. Friday, September 30.

2. Any senior coed caught wearing a senior cord skirt in residence units my be de-skirted on the spot by any freshman woman.

3. The hunt for cord skirts, whether hidden or worn, will begin Wednesday noon, Sept. 28, and will end Friday, Sept. 30 at 6 p.m. Cord skirts must be kept on the grounds of the residence units between those two dates. Freshmen women cannot enter other residence units to hunt for cord skirts, but must confine their ac-tivities to their own living units.

A senior cord skirt worn on campus may be marked with chalk, crayon, lead pencil or lipstick by any fresh-man woman, but ink may not be used. Nothing ob-scene may be written on the cord skirts and they may not be mutilated.

PURDUE EXPONENT, SEPTEMBER 24, 1949

"They could do anything they wanted to"

Mary Titus Houston

She was the third generation in her family to receive a college education, and the tradition continues.

"My husband and I have three children," says Mary Titus Houston, of Woodland, California. "I have a daughter who's a teacher of the deaf, I have a son who's a urologist like my husband, and I have another daughter who's a lawyer. I have two grandchildren who are in accelerated programs in school, so we should go on for a fifth generation."

Houston graduated from high school in Anderson, Indiana, in June of 1944.

"In some respects, it was hard going to high school during the war," she says. "There were members of our class who left to go into the service. It was kind of scary because people were getting killed.

"We couldn't get a lot of things. We couldn't get leather shoes, so manufacturers came out with high-heel dress shoes covered with fabric. Things like nylon stockings, chocolate, and chewing gum were hard to get.

"Cigarettes were impossible to get. People would stand in lines for cigarettes. I worked in a drugstore as a cashier at the soda fountain. The store sold cigarettes, and employees would save them for their favorite customers. A lot of people smoked in those days.

"After I graduated from high school, I worked for a year to save some money for college. I went to Purdue in the fall of 1945.

"I spent five years at Purdue. At the end of my freshman year, a bone cyst developed in my right hand, fracturing a bone and requiring a lower-arm cast. This prevented me from completing some lab classes and writing exams.

"It was an exciting time. A lot of the GIs were coming back from the war. You felt a little sorry for them because many of them

353

were used to a different kind of life—living on the edge, excitement, and glamor. Then they were in college and were nobodies. Some fellows weren't nearly as glamorous looking in their civilian clothes as they were in their uniforms.

"Some of the veterans were a little wild. The transition must have been hard for them. I knew a couple guys who would scrape together every dime they could, then they'd rent a plane—one of those little planes—and they'd fly it. You could tell they missed flying.

"Most of the veterans that I knew didn't talk much about the war. But they wore parts of their uniforms—especially the ones who had been pilots. They wore their pants and shirts and jackets.

"I majored in science—microbiology. I thought maybe I'd go to work in a lab for Lilly in Indianapolis. Instead, after I graduated, I went to the University of Utah Medical School and interned a year in laboratory sciences under a pathologist. That's where I met my husband. He was a medical student. We moved to California in 1953.

"I haven't been back to Purdue since I graduated. I'm sure I wouldn't recognize the campus now. In those days, the big things were football games and basketball games, and you could use the swimming pool on Friday night. They let the boys and girls swim together, that was kind of fun. And there was a bar called the Chocolate Shop. I'm sure it's still there.

"When the war ended, it seemed like everyone was in a hurry to get on with their life, to get back to normal. It wasn't easy for everyone. I guess I felt fortunate because I had been too young to marry during the war. There were girls in my co-op whose husbands were away in the military while they were going to school.

"After the war, it was a time when there were a lot of fellows to date and a lot of adventurous types of people.

"It was a happy time."

"They could do anything they wanted to"

Marilyn Garrett Zack

Her mother would have liked seeing the way her name is written here—Marilyn Garrett Zack. She was born Marilyn Garrett, an only child to a couple in Canton, Ohio, in 1928, only eight years after women had won the right to vote.

"My mother never gave me a middle name," Zack says. "She explained that the reason was, when I got married, my maiden name could be my middle name. You'll notice how many women use their maiden name for a middle name now."

Zack was always ahead of her time.

"My father graduated from Wooster College in Wooster, Ohio, and my mother was a registered nurse," Zack says.

"From the day I was born, I was going to college. My mother always said that every woman needed a profession in order to support herself. Mother was way ahead of her time.

"I wanted to major in chemistry when I went to college, and our high school guidance counselor suggested Purdue. I never did major in chemistry, but that's how I got to Purdue.

"Maybe I was naïve, but when I got to campus, I didn't think it was so crowded. They housed all the freshman women in Cary Hall East. That was marvelous because we got to know all the women in our class except those from town who lived at home. Those friendships we made the first year lasted all four years.

"I joined Kappa Alpha Theta sorority and moved into their house my sophomore year.

"I started out in the pharmacy school for one semester. I got a 6-point average and decided that was not what college was all about. It was just too much memorizing. I wanted to learn things that would help me have a broadening experience. Everyone was shocked, but I transferred into liberal science. It was wonderful.

"I joined a lot of activities. My senior year I was president of the Women's Athletic Association. The university didn't have a

355

College, careers, children, and careers

women's sports program like they have today. I would have loved it if they had. You either participated in Women's Athletic Association activities or you did nothing. I guess Purdue did have a swimming program for women, but that was it. You made up your own teams and entered them in the sports that were offered. We had volleyball, basketball, and softball. I can't remember what else.

"There were all kinds of university teams for the males, but none for the females. It never occurred to us that this wasn't fair.

GOOD SPORTS. *The Women's Athletic Association offered sports opportunities for female students—but little intercollegiate competition.*

"Going to Purdue was a wonderful experience. I loved every minute of it. Oh, the dances! I'll never forget them. Our freshman year we had Eddie Howard and bands of that quality playing at the Memorial Union.

"I would often turn down the older guys who asked me out because I didn't feel comfortable with them. I was seventeen when I came to Purdue. I was absolutely astounded when a twenty-four-year-old man asked me for a date.

"A fellow who worked next to me in pharmacy lab asked me out. As it happened, he was a wonderful dancer. We got to the dance as soon as it started and for the first hour had the dance floor to ourselves.

"Since I was in liberal science, I had to prepare to do something when I graduated. I decided upon teaching, but I really didn't care for that. So, I went to the University of Michigan where I got

356

"They could do anything they wanted to"

my master's in business administration. I was one of the very few women enrolled there in that program.

"I met my husband, Frank, at Michigan. He's a dentist. My husband was in the Navy when we got married.

"At one point, I worked in marketing for the Deep Freeze Appliance Corporation, the original manufacturers of home freezers. I did some market research, which is what I had been trained to do. Really, I was just hired as a secretary, even with my M.B.A., but my boss was enlightened enough to let me participate in substantive things. He realized I was willing to take on intellectual challenges.

"Frank and I settled in a suburb of Cleveland. I probably worked less than a year before our first child was born, and I didn't work after that. We had two children.

"I guess I was about thirty-nine years old when my older child was out of high school and my younger one was in high school. That's when I started law school. I had been very active in the League of Women Voters. Over and over again I would say to my husband, 'I wish I were a lawyer.' Finally after hearing that a hundred times, he said, 'Then go to law school.' So I did, at Cleveland State.

"This was in the late 1960s, and there were very few women students in law. It was rare. I completed my degree in 1972 and took a job in the law department with the City of Cleveland. I worked there during the terms of three mayors. At one point, I was the city's top lawyer. I had that title a little over three years. Now I'm retired.

"When I went to work in the 1970s, none of the women my age that I knew were in the workforce. Of course, it's much different today. I don't know what caused everything to change so much. I guess more and more women were brought up to think that they could do anything they wanted to.

357

College, careers, children, and careers

"It's wonderful that women now have all these opportunities. But I would have been very hesitant to work full time when I had young children. No, I would never have done that."

"They could do anything they wanted to"

chapter 15

" Back home again "
in Indiana

Memories of more Purdue athletes

William Darley

He has visited more than a hundred countries, which easily qualifies him for his membership in the Adventurers Club in Chicago.

After he graduated from Purdue, William Darley took over a family business, W. S. Darley and Company. Founded in 1908, the firm manufactures fire pumps and fire apparatus and equipment, in addition to selling law enforcement equipment and municipal supplies worldwide.

Darley was just seven years old when his father died in 1935. His high school years in Chicago came during the war.

"It was an interesting time," he says. "We dated older women because all the older guys were in the service. It was an exciting time.

"I was an All-American swimmer in high school. It was kind of interesting competing with older guys. Our high school had meets with the Great Lakes Naval Station.

"My event was the freestyle. Swimming was really my springboard to Purdue. I had good grades in high school, but it was difficult to get into a good college in those days when the GIs were returning. The Purdue swimming coach helped me to get in. He interviewed me, noted what my achievements were, and encouraged me to come to Purdue. I wanted to study mechanical engineering, so it worked great. I didn't have a scholarship. They didn't have any scholarships for swimming in those days.

"During my first year at Purdue, I lived in Cary Hall. Then I pledged Phi Delta Theta. I was seventeen years old when I arrived on campus. I grew up very quickly around all those older guys.

"In swimming, we had great trips to Fort Lauderdale every Christmas. They had a tremendous swimming program, and all the colleges went there for meets during the holiday season. I remember there would be bed checks to make sure we were in. All the older guys would sneak out at night. I'd be the only guy left with all the dummy-beds made up.

"Swimming was great. I've always felt everyone has to excel in one area as an entry into social and other aspects of life. Swimming was wonderful for me at Purdue.

"I kept pretty busy with swimming and studies, and I worked for awhile in the kitchen at the fraternity house. I was in a number of organizations. I was president of the Letterman's Club. Here I was a 155-pound swimmer in this club where most of the guys were 220-pound football players. But I was elected.

"I remember the Dolphin swimming fraternity. As an initiation, you had to carry a goldfish around in a mason jar for six weeks. At the end of that time, you had to swallow the goldfish. And if you ate an extra one, you got kissed by Jeanne Wilson, one of the prettiest coeds.

"It was rather hard to swallow that goldfish. While you were carrying it around, you didn't know you were going to have to eat it.

"And after you had carried it around for six weeks, you became kind of attached to it."

Lou Karras

He is sitting on the top of the world in a Clearwater, Florida, condominium that is beautifully decorated in delicate yellows and white.

"Back home again in Indiana"

From his eighth-floor windows on a warm Saturday afternoon, the view over his shoulder is of the inland waterway and the gulf. Sailboats and yachts glide back and forth on tranquil water. As he leans back in his chair, he can look down on pelicans flying by.

An ice bag rests on his right shoulder, which is sore from a morning of handball. Lou Karras has a goal of being a world-champion handball player for his age group. He almost made it once but tore a rotator cuff. Now, he is again trying to achieve his goal.

"Lou Karras, he was a nice young man from Gary. He was tall— a big kid. Kids weren't as big then as they are now. He was hardworking. He had a couple of younger brothers who were tremendous, too."

—John DeCamp

Competition has always been his calling—from his days as a football star at Purdue University, through his days in the National Football League, into his days of owning tire stores in Gary, to these days of retirement and handball.

His hair is salt-and-pepper and his carriage remains erect. Karras has the look of a proud man from a proud Greek family.

"You know the family tree?" he asks early in the conversation.

Three sons in the family played in the NFL. He was first, the oldest son, who went from Purdue to the Washington Redskins. Next in line, Ted, started at Purdue, transferred to Indiana University, and played nine years in the pros—seven of those with the Chicago Bears, including the 1963 championship team. Finally, Alex went from the University of Iowa to fourteen years with the Detroit Lions and then to Hollywood.

"Ted ruined everything for Alex at Purdue," Karras says. "Alex planned to go to Purdue. It was all set. Then, when I was at training camp with the Redskins, Ted pulled out of Purdue and transferred to Indiana without my knowing it. Our father had died. I was the oldest and the head of the family, but Ted didn't tell me he was going to do this.

361

Memories of more Purdue athletes

"Ted wanted Alex to go to Indiana, and I was vehemently opposed to that. It would, however, have been a personal insult to Ted to send Alex to Purdue. So we sent him to Iowa, which had a progressive program."

Football is Karras's life. He wears a large ring with a replica of a football on it, the gift of teammates when he left the Redskins. In his senior year at Purdue, Karras was voted most valuable player by his teammates. He can recall scores and game situations from forty-five years ago as if they had happened yesterday.

He was born in 1927 in Gary, Indiana. Eventually, there were six children in the family—five boys and one girl. Their father, who came to the United States from Greece when he was eleven years old, was a physician. Their mother was a nurse.

Their father's profession did not provide the family with an escape from the hardships of the times.

"The depression—" Karras says. "We were hit so hard by it we still haven't recovered. When the steel industry shut down, everyone went on relief. My poor dad—his patients were those working-class people.

"During those hard times, the township trustee chose the doctors the sick people could see, and he showed favoritism in his choices. My dad didn't have any patients.

"We suffered in the depression, but we just hung in there, and somehow we survived. There never were any big bucks like you would expect in the medical profession.

"I went to Emerson High School in Gary and played football. We had a very good coach. It was a different time.

"You've got to remember, I went to school during the war. There wasn't any gas. Whenever we had an away game, it was a big deal because generally we didn't get to go anywhere.

"Normally on Friday nights, we played on Gleason Field near the steel mills in Gary. The pollution was so bad that often it

"Back home again in Indiana"

was difficult for someone sitting in the grandstand to get a good view of the game.

"Our school was very football minded. Every time one of our players got drafted, we felt bad about losing someone the team was counting on. Between my freshman and senior years, we must have lost twenty guys to the draft. In those days, if you were over eighteen, you were gone.

"We had other problems, too. Not only was gas in short supply, but also we had trouble with material for the athletic supporters. Our coach was an innovator. He introduced to the team some rubber-type athletic supporters that he thought would be much easier to maintain. Then, all of a sudden, there was a shortage of rubber, and we couldn't get that kind of athletic supporter.

"Many times we had to walk to the stadium, which was a mile and a half from the school. But that was okay. When it was over, we felt like we'd accomplished something.

"I graduated from high school in January of 1946 and went right to Purdue.

Lou Karras. One of Purdue's great football players, Karras came from one of the great football families. Voted the team's most valuable player in 1949, Karras went on to play in the East-West Shrine game, was chosen for an all-star team, and played in the pros until an injury cut short his career.

I had been solicited by Purdue when I was a junior, and I had a feeling of closeness to the university. First, it was just a hundred miles from home. Second, when I went there to visit, the staff made me feel comfortable. They put me up in a fraternity, and someone took me out to dinner.

"A lot of universities tried to get hold of me in the spring, not knowing I was a midyear graduate. Paul 'Bear' Bryant, who

363

was then coach at the University of Kentucky, tried to reach me in May. I was already at Purdue.

"In January of 1946, I went to Purdue. You've got to know this. I was an eighteen-year-old boy trying to make it on the varsity football team where the average age of the players was twenty-six. It was almost unreal. Some of the returning vets were eight years older than I was.

"Those of us just out of high school were playing with guys who had experienced much more in terms of war and life than we had. Some had played at Purdue before they entered the service. It was really an unusual time.

"It was particularly hard for the coaches. When I started at Purdue, Cecil Isbell was our head coach, and Joe Dienhart was our line coach. You have to remember, those guys couldn't very well criticize and reprimand war veterans who had been through so much. A lot of those players had made bombing runs into Germany or were involved in the D-Day landing. It was hard for a coach to chastise them for mistakes they made or for being lazy. They simply were not playing on the same field.

"So you know what happened? The coaches picked on the eighteen-year-old kids. They had to have fall guys to use as the butt of it all. And we were the guys who took it.

"The Purdue athletic department had a great relationship with the fraternity houses. Since I was on a scholarship, I was selected to go the Acacia house. My scholarship entitled me to books and tuition and the opportunity to work in the kitchen of the Acacia house for room and board. Also, I had a small job at the field house that paid me five dollars a week. That was my spending money.

"Eventually, I didn't have to work in the kitchen anymore. Work and practice just got to be too much. There were no rules to set the length of spring practice. If I remember correctly, spring practice started in January and went to the end of May. Then, we had to begin practice again in August.

"Back home again in Indiana"

"In August of 1946, we had preseason practice at Ross Camp off campus. Oh, man, what a place! We had a vet on the team who had seen concentration camps in Europe, and he talked as though the similarities were great. Ross Camp was infamous in the eyes of the players. We were under very strict surveillance. It was unbelievable how much practice they demanded from a Big Ten team from 1946 to 1950.

"We had one guy on the team who had a brand new 1946 Studebaker. He was from South Bend where Studebakers were prevalent. To have any car in those days was something, but to have a brand new car was unbelievable. Somehow he got permission to bring that car to camp, but he still wasn't allowed to leave.

"Now, there was a guy named Abe Gibron on the team—you know who he is. He went on to coach the Chicago Bears. It was so hot that August! Indiana summer days and practices were really exhausting. So Gibron, the fellow with the Studebaker, another guy, and I decided we'd go to a watermelon patch not too far from camp and bring back some watermelons for the all guys. We went in that new Studebaker to pilfer the watermelons.

"We got to the poor farmer's field, parked the car, and quietly went into the watermelon patch. Now, you've got to picture this. One of the guys must have weighed 240 pounds, Gibron weighed even more, and I was big. Naturally, the farmer could see us out in the field. He got out his gun and fired a shot. We started running to the car as fast as we could with the watermelons in our arms. In our haste, we dropped the melons as we got in the car, and they exploded all over the trunk and the back seat of the car. That brand new Studebaker was loaded with crushed watermelons!

"Purdue opened that season against Miami of Ohio, which at that time was a small unknown school. We thought we wouldn't have any trouble with them. We won, 13–7. That wasn't much of a victory. However, when you look back at that Miami of Ohio

Memories of more Purdue athletes

team, they had some great players. Ara Parseghian, who became a great coach at Notre Dame, was one of them.

"The second game we played was against Iowa. We spent the night before the game in Cedar Rapids. A Quaker Oats factory located there gave off a smell that permeated the city. It made half the team sick. We couldn't sleep. We ended up losing the game. The whole season went down from there. We had a disastrous season.

"Poor Cecil Isbell would try to give us pep talks—you need pep talks in football. But the vets didn't like them and made faces behind his back. It was a terrible time to coach. The veterans would tell him, 'Oh, sit down! We don't want to hear that.' Many times they would threaten to leave and go to another school. Or they would threaten to leave, go to the pros, and come back to college to finish their studies when their playing years were over.

"We younger guys had good rapport with the vets. One of those older guys on our team was Johnny McKay. He was seven years older than I was. He became coach at the University of Southern California, national coach of the year, and the first coach of the professional Tampa Bay Bucs. He played for Purdue two years, then he transferred to Oregon.

"We had a classic game in 1949. We got to travel to Miami to play the University of Miami in the Orange Bowl. It was the first time a Big Ten team had come in Florida. You wouldn't believe how many people showed up to look at a Big Ten team! You'd think we were warriors of ancient Rome returning after a victorious campaign.

"We played on a Friday night, and we won. They had a great party for us at a hotel in Miami on Saturday. I'll never forget that night. I took Bill 'Moose' Skowron, who became a New York Yankee after he left Purdue, to his first nightclub. I was a senior and he was a sophomore.

"Back home again in Indiana"

"I played four years and got four letters at Purdue. I played tackle. At that time, team members played both defense and offense. It was Michigan that started the platoon system after the war. They had the heavy hitters and they had the personnel. But our guys played both ways. My senior year I played more than any other lineman.

"In 1948, I experienced one of my greatest disappointments. I played left tackle against Notre Dame, and they were the number one team in the nation. We played them in South Bend. I played fifty-eight minutes. We lost 28–27. We should have won that game.

"Our captain was a guy who played in front of me that year. He was hurt and couldn't play. I was his replacement, and Notre Dame ran everything at me at the beginning of the game. I stopped them. After that, there was no more running on me.

"I made their all-opponent team that year. Although I was only a junior, I was lineman-of-the-week. But Purdue lost. It was a big disappointment. I think my dad listened to the game on the radio. The following Thursday he died.

"Our biggest victory of all was my senior year—I always get excited when I tell this. Those years from '46 to '49 weren't winning years at Purdue. But we had a team that never really quit.

"In 1949, Minnesota was picked to win it all and go the Rose Bowl. They had a team that was as big and as tough as any team in the NFL. Bud Grant, an NFL Hall of Fame coach played on that team. They were a twenty-seven-point favorite.

"We went up there at the tail end of the season, and it was cold and snowy. I was a senior and the captain that game. Minnesota had just been beaten by Michigan. But all they had to do was beat us and Iowa, and they were going to the Rose Bowl. We won 13–7. The next week they beat Iowa 55–0—and Iowa had beaten us earlier in the season. Ohio State went to the Rose Bowl.

Memories of more Purdue athletes

Purdue Engineers Victory. The Purdue football team was a 21-point underdog in 1949 when it played Minnesota's Golden Gophers, favored to go to the Rose Bowl. It was homecoming in Minneapolis, but the victorious homecoming was in Lafayette when the Purdue team rolled back into town with a crowd of four thousand waiting to help celebrate. The final score was 13-7.

"After that season, I played in the East-West game, and then I went over to Hawaii for the 1950 Hula Bowl. I played in the college all-star game in Chicago. Next, I went to the Redskins training camp in California. We had an exposition game against Los Angeles in the Coliseum, and I was amazed to see 102,000 people show up.

"I'll tell you how I got drafted into the pros. During my senior year, Abe Gibron—I've told you about him—signed a contract with the Buffalo Bills. He had a great year. On my way to the East-West game, I stopped over in Chicago at the Palmer House. In the evening, a friend from Purdue and I went to the Blue Note nightclub, and who should walk in but Abe Gibron.

"I hadn't seen him in a year. Gosh, he had on this beautiful suit—you could see there were dollars in it. We looked him over closely, and when we got to his shoes, he was wearing his Purdue athletic socks. That broke us up! He refused to let anyone pay the rest of the night. He picked up the tab and said how great professional football was.

"After that, he made a point of telling the coach for the Bills to draft me. The Detroit Lions wanted me, too. They both drafted me with their second pick. I wanted to see who came up with the best contract. They were both talking ten grand with a one-grand signing bonus. That was good in those days.

"At the time, there were two leagues—the American and the National. All of a sudden the leagues merged. They dropped

"Back home again in Indiana"

the Bills and brought in the Forty-niners and the Browns. The Buffalo players went to the Browns, and they had a re-draft.

"I ended up with the Redskins. I thought the Redskins might be in the state of Washington. That's how far out of it I was. Isn't that terrible? But that's what happens when you're so preoccupied with your own game.

"In June of 1950, the war in Korea got going, and I thought that's where I was heading. There was a guy from Ohio State playing basketball with the Washington Caps, and he and I went to take our Army physicals together. I felt it was all over. I wouldn't be playing with the Redskins.

"After the physical, they told me I was healthy and was going to be part of the military. But lo and behold! I got a letter that stated I was 4-F. When I got that information, I didn't pursue as to why. I just figured that's the way it was.

"In the pros, I was six-foot three-inches and weighed about 240 pounds, which was pretty good. I stayed with the Redskins for two good years. In Washington, the treatment you get as a Redskin is better than you get as a senator.

"The third year was going really well when all of a sudden I developed a detached retina. I couldn't see clearly. It came from being hit. The doctor said, 'If you want to save the eye, you've got to quit playing football.' I was devastated. It was the end of my football career. I wanted to be an NFL coach, but there wasn't big money in coaching like there is now.

"I was advised to go into sales because that's where the money was. So I went back to Gary and worked for Firestone Tire for two years before I opened my own business. I ended up with three tire stores, and I brought my youngest brother in.

"When I was twenty-five, I married a woman who was a teacher. We met on a blind date. We were married fourteen years and had two daughters. Then, she died. Two years later I married Dorothy, who was from Gary, too. She had been a homecoming queen.

369

Memories of more Purdue athletes

"At Purdue, getting a date was always a problem for the average guy because there were so few girls. As a football player, however, I was always able to get a date. I don't know why, but it always works out that way for football players.

"With all those vets around, the average guy coming out of high school in 1946 didn't stand a chance with the girls. So a lot of the younger guys went down to DePauw University, about an hour's drive south. The pastures were green there. Pretty girls, too.

"In those days, life was very competitive. That spirit stayed with us all our lives. In those days, you had to hold your own and be productive. You couldn't wait for someone to do something for you.

"You know, when I think back on those years—the depression, World War II, and the Korean War, as well as the good times we had and the way we were taught—it was like the book *Tale of Two Cities*.

"It really was the worst of times, and yet it was the best of times, too."

Dan Wawrzyniak

Dan Wawrzyniak lives in Lebanon, Indiana. He is in sales and is part owner of a company in Sheridan, Indiana—United Feeds.

Born in South Bend, Indiana, in 1929, Wawrzyniak graduated from high school in 1946.

"I was too young to get into the Army," he says. "I was at Purdue for a semester before I even turned eighteen. My brother, who graduated from high school a year before me, was in the Army, and we all knew our time was coming. Everyone generally wanted to do his part. My brother served twenty months in the service and then came to Purdue. I had gotten a semester ahead of him. Eventually our younger brother came, too, and we were all on campus at the same time.

"I came to Purdue in the fall of 1946, and the university was so short of housing that they sent me to live in the third floor of

"Back home again in Indiana"

the ag engineering building. It was just like an Army barracks with bunk beds. Twenty-six guys lived in one room. Down the hall, twenty-four were in another room. In the attic were 148 guys.

"There were no showers in that building. We had to take our showers in the field house, which was over a mile away. We would take our clean clothes and towel and stuff to class. In between classes, we'd go take our shower and go back to class the next hour.

"That was just the way it was. I don't remember many guys complaining about it. Everyone wanted to go to school. The university was short of housing, so you just accepted it. I lived in ag engineering for a year and half. Then my two brothers and I rented a place together.

"There were a lot of vets in that ag engineering building. They were nice fellows. They were older than we were, but I think they helped us younger guys mature quickly. They had their minds on their studies, and that rubbed off on us.

"I played on the Purdue baseball team, but I played very little. There were a great many servicemen just back from the Army who played. In my first year, I think the average age of the guys on the team was twenty-three, and I had just turned eighteen. I was a left-handed pitcher, and I pitched a lot in intersquad games.

"I'd had a good record in high school, and I was a pretty decent hitter, too. In high school, I batted clean-up all the time. I often think, I wish I could have played with guys my own age when I went to Purdue. I think I would have had more opportunities.

"Purdue only gave maybe two baseball scholarships in those days. If I remember correctly, the university gave twin brothers half of their tuition in the spring for playing baseball.

"It was hard to get a date on campus with so many guys and so few women. Because there wasn't any money either, I didn't worry much about dating.

"I graduated in the spring of 1950. I had taken ROTC at Purdue and was in the reserves. After about two years, I received

Memories of more Purdue athletes

a letter from the draft board saying if the reserves didn't call me up I was going to be drafted. In the summer of 1952, I volunteered so I could go in as a commissioned officer. It seemed as if most of our class got called in right away, but some, like me, didn't.

"The Korean War was unexpected, but the way I looked at it, it was my turn to do my part and I was willing to do it. I got to Korea right at the end of the conflict. A full tour there was sixteen months, but after fourteen months, it was almost time for me to get out of the service, so I was sent home. I was there from July of 1953 to August of 1954.

"When I came home, I flew in and my wife met me at the airport. We had gotten married in 1953 just before I left. I hadn't seen her for thirteen months. We had been able to talk only one time on the phone—at Christmas. I used to write her letters at night after dinner.

"I don't know how popular that war was back home. I know one of the guys who came home before us wrote that we weren't that popular. After the war was over, people didn't pay a lot of attention to Korea.

"We didn't get any parades. There weren't parades for a lot of the World War II veterans, either. And I don't think any of us cared.

"We all just wanted to get on with our lives as quickly as possible."

Abe Gibron

"When you talk to him, ask him about singing 'Back Home Again in Indiana,'" says Lou Karras. "Tell him I told you he could sing it like an opera star."

Abe Gibron is touched when he hears that.

"Karras, God bless him," he says.

"Back home again in Indiana"

Karras and Gibron—former great Purdue football players, former professional greats, still friends—live on the west coast of Florida in retirement.

Gibron is the older. He is sixty-nine, almost seventy, at the time of the interview, and his health is not the best. He has had two brain tumors. He mentions a stroke.

"I walk around. I can do everything," he says. "But . . ."

He does not finish.

The night before, Gibron had been out watching Monday Night Football, and just a couple days earlier he was involved watching Purdue suffer through a big football loss to Ohio State on national television.

"Terrible, just terrible," he moaned.

Football is his life. Always has been. Still is. Always will be.

You have to listen carefully to understand what Gibron is saying these days. But you do not have to understand every word to sense the deep feelings he has.

When he is asked how he

"Abe Gibron—as I recall, he was from Michigan City, a good player, short and stocky, and muscular. And he was very opinionated. The coaches had to jump on him. They had to kick him in the pants sometimes. He was a great player. He was just independent."

—John DeCamp

feels about the State of Indiana and if he misses it, he tells you the best way he knows how. He sings the song. He sings it perfectly, as if there had never been brain tumors, never been a stroke. His diction is clear. His pitch his perfect. He sounds like an opera star.

"I was born in Michigan City," Gibron says, speaking slowly, often pausing to gather his thoughts. "I graduated high school in 1943 and I went into the Marine Corps. I got acute sinusitis in the Marine Corps and I still have it all the time. I got out in 1945 and went to Valparaiso University that fall and played football there. I was all-conference.

373

"In 1946, I came to Purdue on the GI Bill. I was six feet tall and weighed 230 to 235 pounds. I played guard. I was an all-Big-Ten player."

In his last game at Purdue in the fall of 1948, he recovered an onside kick in a 39–0 win over Indiana University. Then Gibron left without a degree to go to the professional ranks.

"I went to the Buffalo Bills when they were in the All-American Conference," he says. "I got a thousand-dollar bonus and a thirty-five-hundred-dollar salary. I came back to Purdue in the off-season in 1950 and finished my degree.

"Then, Paul Brown brought me to Cleveland. I played eleven years in the pros. I was in the championship six times. I won three times and I lost three times. I played in the Pro Bowl. I was an All-Pro.

"I coached thirteen years with the Chicago Bears, three of them as head coach in the 1970s.

"I have these brain tumors, but I'm all right. I got on with the Seattle Seahawks and was their special assistant and, boom, I got a tumor. I still help at the Seahawks training camp. They take care of me.

"I miss Indiana. I miss Indiana all the time. [He begins to sing, slowly.] 'Back home again in Indiana.' You see—I can sing, but I can't talk. 'And it seems that I can see the gleaming candle-light, still shining bright . . .'"

He stops. "I don't know," he says. "Let me tell you, the Purdue guys mean a lot to me. I love football. I love the life . . ."

And he longs for his Indiana home.

Senior class will be graduated Sunday
Engineering schools, others will have separate exercises

On Sunday, June 18, the university will graduate the largest class in the history of the school. The class of

1950 will be the 75th to go through commencement and a total of 2,297 persons will receive degrees. Of this number, 1,978 will receive bachelor's degrees, 253 will receive master's degrees and 66 will receive Ph.D.s.

Due to the large number of graduates there will be two commencement exercises. . . . Be on time. . . .

There are a few requests to seniors during the procession.

Act dignified and try to keep from smoking and waving the commencement program around. If possible wear dark clothing and avoid wearing white "buck" shoes. . . .

Purdue Exponent, June 14, 1950

Last issue of the year brings best wishes

The lucky students have only one barrier between them and a summer of joy—the grade report due next week. . . .

This week should be one filled with celebration and apprehension for most of us. . . . The seniors who have found jobs are apprehensive concerning graduation and the seniors who know they will graduate wonder if they will be able to secure positions. But, for the most part, when this week ends we will all leave behind us a portion of our lives which has been lived to the hilt. . . .

We will always remember the year of '49–'50 at Purdue.

We will remember the Purdue Relays of this year, the biggest and best since their inauguration. We will remember the Vagabond King with its hit song "Only a Rose."

We will never forget the football games, the basketball games and especially the conference champion wrestling team. Purdue sports were not at the top of the ledger in all respects this year, but the contests certainly provided thrills for all of us.

We will try to forget the tests and quizzes without rhyme or reason while we try to retain the knowledge gleaned from our various courses. We will try to overlook the lop-sided ratio and try to remember that date we had "sometime in September." But most of all we will remember this year as one which was filled with good and bad times, a miniature life-time lived by us, with the ups and downs and the tedious as well as the tremendous times.

To those of you who are leaving the campus for the outside world of industry, we can only wish luck and send with you the feeling that you are among a group of men and women which is leaving a university that is tops in the country. We were glad to have had you here and we know that you will do justice to yourselves and your education when the final count is taken.

Purdue Exponent, page 1 editorial, June 14, 1950

"Back home again in Indiana"

A GRADUATE DAD. *Jim Blakesley, a member of the Purdue Class of 1950, shows his new degree to his two oldest daughters, (left) Roseanne and (right) Susan while wife, Rosemary, looks on. Like many members of the class, by the time Blakesley received his bachelor's degree from the university, he had already passed an advanced course in life. He had seen a depression and a war and been pilot of a plane—all before starting college. Dreams of this generation were long delayed, but upon graduation in 1950, they all started coming true. And it goes on still. This is a class that has never stopped doing justice to itself and its education. And, it has never stopped dreaming.*

377

APPENDIX

Campus Maps

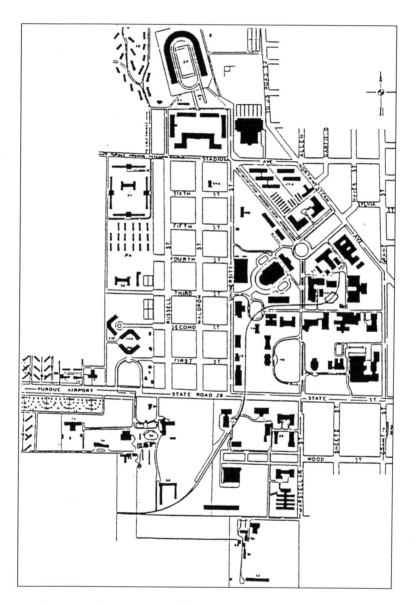

Purdue University, West Lafayette Campus 1949

APPENDIX

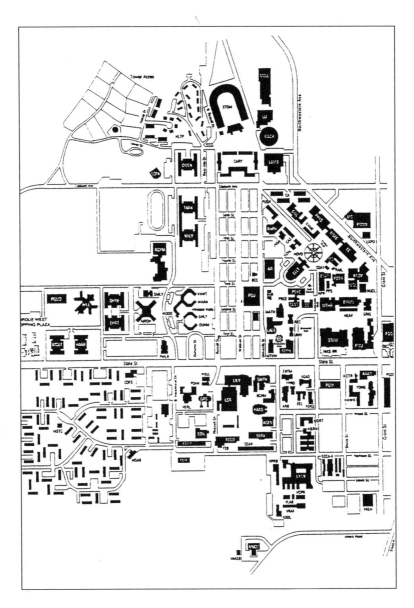

Purdue University, West Lafayette Campus 1995

INDEX

INDEX

INDEX

388

INDEX

INDEX

INDEX